Kovels'
Antiques
&
Collectibles
Fix-It
Source Book

BOOKS BY
RALPH AND TERRY KOVEL

American Country Furniture 1780-1875

Dictionary of Marks — Pottery & Porcelain

Kovels' Advertising Collectibles Price List

Kovels' American Silver Marks

Kovels' Antiques & Collectibles Fix-It
    Source Book

Kovels' Antiques & Collectibles Price List

Kovels' Book of Antique Labels

Kovels' Bottles Price List

Kovels' Collector's Guide to American Art Pottery

Kovels' Collectors' Source Book

Kovels' Depression Glass & American Dinnerware Price List

Kovels' Guide to Selling Your Antiques & Collectibles, Updated Edition

Kovels' Illustrated Price Guide to Royal Doulton

Kovels' Know Your Antiques

Kovels' Know Your Collectibles

Kovels' New Dictionary of Marks — Pottery & Porcelain

Kovels' Organizer for Collectors

Kovels' Price Guide for Collector Plates, Figurines, Paperweights,
    and Other Limited Editions

Kovels' Antiques & Collectibles Fix-It Source Book

by Ralph and Terry Kovel

CROWN PUBLISHERS, INC., NEW YORK

Published by Crown Publishers, Inc., 201 East 50th Street,
New York, New York, 10022
CROWN is a trademark of Crown Publishers, Inc.
Manufactured in the United States of America

Library of Congress Cataloging-in-Publication Data
Kovel, Ralph M.
  Kovels' antiques & collectibles fix-it source book/by Ralph and Terry Kovel.
  —1st ed.
    p. cm.
1. Antiques—Collectors and collecting. I. Kovel, Terry H. II. Title. III. Title:
Antiques & collectibles fix-it source book. IV. Title: Kovels' antiques and
collectibles fix-it source book.
NK1125.K659   745.1'028'8—dc20   90–1681
ISBN 0-517-57333-4
10 9 8 7 6 5 4 3 2 1
First Edition

Contents

How to Use This Book

It's beautiful. It's valuable. But it's broken. If you want to preserve the value of your antiques by keeping them in top condition or if you want to restore them properly, this is the book for you. It will help you learn about that hard-to-find repair shop or replacement part no matter where it is located in the country. It will also guide you in do-it-yourself restoration. This book is a directory to the services you might need for the care and repair of the antiques and collectibles you own.

There are three main sections in this book. Part I lists more than 60 different types of collections. A short paragraph tells what flaws should be repaired, how repairs affect value, and other tips. Craftsmen, supply sources, informative books, and other material related to restoring antiques are listed. If you are missing the wheel on a toy truck, need a glass liner for your silver mustard pot, or a restorer for your Tiffany lamp, look in Part I.

Part II lists those who repair and refinish many different types of antiques, gives sources of supply for conservation materials, and suggests ways to display collections. This is where you will find places to buy acid-free paper, special waxes, products for wood graining, gold leafing, and the like.

Part III, Loving Care for Your Collection, gives simple instructions for the care and repair of china, glass, furniture, paper, and textiles. If you're looking for advice on the best way to wash your antique quilt, polish your Chippendale chair, or display your treasured Audubon print, read Part III.

We have tried to make this book easy to use, but we realize that many subjects overlap. If you are restoring a piece of furniture, start with the Furniture section, but also look under Wicker, Rattan & Basketry, Hardware, Metals, Textiles, and other headings. You will find helpful comments like "See also Metals" in the Fireplace Equipment section. There is also an index at the end of the book.

Many useful books, leaflets, videotapes, or computer programs are included. We have also listed available reprints of original instruction books. Although most of the books are in print and can be found at a bookstore or library, a few are harder to locate. These can be ordered at your library through an interlibrary loan. Ask the librarian to help you. Specialized publications listed in *Kovels' Guide to Selling Your Antiques & Collectibles,* the companion to this book, have articles and advertisements that list additional restorers and suppliers.

To assemble the names in *Kovels' Antiques & Collectibles Fix-It Source Book,* we wrote to the thousands of suppliers, restorers, and repair services we heard about. Only those who replied are included. We felt that if we could not get an answer to an offer to give a free listing, you would have trouble getting a mail-order repair. There are many other reliable repair services and conservators we have not yet heard about and we welcome any suggestions for additions or corrections in future editions. We have not used the services of everyone listed in this book, and inclusion here should not be considered an endorsement of any kind. You will find local restorers' names in the Yellow Pages of the phone book.

Each listing in this book includes the address and phone number. If you write, send an SASE (self-addressed stamped envelope) or an LSASE (a long self-addressed stamped envelope). If you telephone, don't forget that the time listed is the time in the area where the restorer lives, not necessarily the time where you live.

Always contact the company by phone or letter before sending anything. The firm will tell you the best way to ship: postal service, delivery service company like UPS or Federal Express, or motor freight. Insure your piece when sending it. If using the post office, send it registered, with a return receipt requested. Other delivery services can track the package from your receipt number.

When we list a company as doing repairs by "mail order," that does not necessarily mean that it is *only* by mail. If you live nearby, you may be able to take the piece into the shop. Many places that do a primarily walk-in business will send you a part by mail if you pay in advance. We have found that a good craftsman will try to fix out-of-the-ordinary items if the challenge and pay are appropriate. It doesn't hurt to inquire about difficult repairs.

The lists for this book were correct as of March 1, 1990. Some firms may have had a change of location or phone number since then.

Part I

The Who
&
What of
Fixing
Your Collection

The country store and its contents have delighted collectors for years. Around 1950 the first big group of serious collectors of advertising materials began searching for signs, containers, bottles, store bins, and other objects that would have been found in an old country store. It became the vogue to decorate restaurants, homes, and shops with the nostalgic collectibles from these old stores, and prices rose as supplies dwindled.

There are many facets to advertising collecting. Cola-Cola, Planters Peanuts, Campbell's Soup, fast food memorabilia, and other trademarked names have created collector interest and have spawned books and clubs for the collector. Some collectors want only nationally known brands; some want tobacco ads, advertising dolls, and the like. The specialized clubs and publications are listed in *Kovels' Guide to Selling Your Antiques & Collectibles.* Many current companies publish books or pamphlets on their history that will serve as visual guides to help with restoration of old materials; these are available from the companies. Some repair information is found under other headings, such as Paper, Metals, Glass, Dolls, or Clocks. Reproductions of decals and other details of trademarked pieces are available. It is also possible to buy old parts through ads in collectors publications.

Beware of reproductions in this field of collecting. Many lithographed tin and paper items have been made for the gift shop trade and are now found at flea markets. New belt buckles and watch fobs with brand names have been made in old styles. One dealer boasts that he has sold over 130,000 new printed tin signs--some copies of old ones, some "concoctions" made with the help of art from old magazine ads or letterheads.

When restoring old advertising, remember, less is best. Don't repaint tin or paper unless the defect is glaring. Frame all paper items with appropriate museum-approved nonacid mounts.

The old brass cash register is now wanted by both collector and shopkeeper. Many are in use in stores that feature nostalgia. The machines made by National Cash Register or other companies still in business can often be restored by the company. Call the local sales representative to find if it is possible. Parts are available for some models. Remember that inflation has had a great impact; early machines register only to $10 or perhaps $100, not the high numbers seen today.

For other helpful information, see Coin-operated, Paper, Pottery & Porcelain, and other sections.

Sources

Play It Again Sam's Inc., 5310 West Devon, Chicago, IL 60646, 312-763-1771, 9:00 a.m.-5:00 p.m. Cash register restoration and supplies. Restoration of wooden barber chairs, saloon backbars, and floor standing barber poles.

Weber's Nostalgia Supermarket, 1121 South Main Street, Fort Worth, TX 76104, 800-433-PUMP outside of TX; 817-335-3833 in TX and for inquiries. Reproduction supplies for gasoline pump restoration, including decals, globes, porcelain signs, and books.

Joe Knight, 372 Bluff View Drive, Largo, FL 34640, 813-584-8566 or 813-595-1414. Florida citrus labels repaired.

Architectural Antiques

Every time a building is demolished a bit of history is destroyed. Collectors today search for parts of old architecture that can be saved and reused. Stone pillars, old oak doors, elaborate carvings, church pews, statues, tiles, and other parts have been rescued and included in new building projects. Most cities now have at least one antiques dealer or specialist who has architectural pieces and can help you restore any pieces you might find. Marble yards and tombstone makers can help restore stone and marble. Wrought-iron fence makers can often make the parts you need to reuse a radiator grille as a door or a gate as a wall ornament. Some cities are so concerned with saving the best of the past that they have established a government-run shop to recycle the architectural pieces found through urban renewal.

Sources

A. Ball Plumbing Supply, 1703 West Burnside Street, Portland, OR 97209, 503-228-0026, 9:00 a.m.-5:00 p.m. Plumbing fixtures and accessory items, including custom faucets for older pedestal basins, footed tubs. Showers for claw-foot tubs, Victorian-style oak high-tank toilets, floor grates, products for repair and maintenance. Specializing in restoration and historic renovation. Catalog and price list.

A.F. Schwerd Manufacturing Company, 3215 McClure Avenue, Pittsburgh, PA 15212, 412-766-6322, 8:30 a.m.-5:00 p.m. Wooden columns, ventilated aluminum plinths, turned bases, ornamental capitals. Custom wood columns. Mail order. Catalog.

Alexandria Wood Joinery, George & Judy Whittaker, Plumer Hill Road, P.O. Box 92, Alexandria, NH 03222, 603-744-8243, 10:00 a.m.-5:00 p.m. Custom woodworking, reproduction, stripping, refinishing. Serving New England.

Architectural Antiques, 110 Second Avenue North, Nashville, TN 37201, 615-254-8129, Tues.-Sat. 10:00 a.m.-4:00 p.m. Stained-glass windows: restoration and custom work; antique mantels, doors, hardware, woodwork. Serving Southeastern U.S.

Architectural Antiques Exchange, 709-15 North Second Street, Philadelphia, PA 19123, 215-922-3669, Mon.-Sat. 10:00 a.m.-5:00 p.m. Architectural antiques including bars, doors, fireplace mantels, stained glass, paneling, light fixtures. Custom reproductions.

Art Directions Inc., 6120 Delmar Boulevard, St. Louis, MO 63112, 314-863-1895, 7:30 a.m.-5:00 p.m.; fax: 314-863-3278. Stained and beveled glass windows and doors; refurbished lighting fixtures.

Bank Architectural Antiques, 1824 Felicity Street, New Orleans, LA 70113, 504-523-2702, Tues.-Sat. 8:00 a.m.-5:00 p.m.; fax: 504-523-6055. Shutters new and old, sales and repair; doors, architectural millwork.

The Brass Knob, 2311 18th Street NW, Washington, DC 20009, 202-332-3370, 10:30 a.m.-6:00 p.m. Architectural antiques, period hardware and lighting. Stairway parts, claw-foot tubs, pedestal sinks, fireplace mantels and equipment, stained and beveled glass. Brochure.

Brass Smith, Inc., 2625 Walnut Street, Denver, CO 80205, 800-662-9595, 8:00 a.m.-5:00 p.m.; fax: 303-296-2320. Architectural and decorative railings, brass fittings and tubing, bar fixtures, glass racks, custom fabrication. Brochure.

Carpenter and Smith Restorations, Box 504, Highland Park, IL 60035, 312-831-5047, 8:00 a.m.-5:00 p.m. Historic structure restoration, interior and exterior. Mill shop. Serving northern Illinois, southern Wisconsin, northwestern Indiana.

Chatham Glass Co., Jim Holmes and Deborah Doane, Box 522, North Chatham, MA 02650, 508-945-5547, Mon.-Sat. 10:00 a.m.-5:00 p.m. Handblown bull's-eyes for doors and windows.

Chelsea Decorative Metal Co., 9603 Moonlight Drive, Houston, TX

77096, 713-721-9200, 8:30 a.m.-5:00 p.m. Embossed metal for tin ceilings, ranging in style from Victorian to Art Deco styles in 2 x 4 ft. sheets. Cornices. Catalog.

Conant Custom Brass, P.O. Box 1523A, 270 Pine Street, Burlington, VT 05402, 802-658-4482 or 802-658-9978, 8:00 a.m.-5:00 p.m. Plumbing fixtures, hardware, complete metal restoration and repair, custom fabrication, plating, rewiring. Brochure.

D.E.A. Bathroom Machineries, 459 Main Street, P.O. Box 1020, Murphys, CA 95247, 209-728-2031. Victorian-style plumbing fixtures, shower parts, claw-foot tubs and accessories, pedestal sinks, hardware. Catalog.

18th Century Design Associates, 397 Massey Road, Springfield, VT 05156, 802-885-1122, 8:00 a.m.-6:00 p.m. Architectural historian; period-oriented design for new or old homes, documentation, restoration. Will procure antique or reproduction parts and supervise construction.

Fancy Front Brassiere Co., P.O. Box 2847, Roseville, CA 95746, 916-791-7733, Mon.-Fri. 8:00 a.m.-5:00 p.m. Victorian gingerbread, molding, ceiling medallions, door hardware. Custom duplicating and consultation. Catalog.

509 Studio, Inc., 1410 East Fourth Avenue, Tampa, FL 33605, 813-248-1380, 8:30 a.m.-5:00 p.m.; fax: 813-873-8886. Ornamental restoration; custom model and mold making; cast items in plaster, concrete, and resins. Serving Southwestern U.S., but will go where services needed. No mail order.

George Taylor Specialties Co., 187 Lafayette Street, 4th Floor, New York, NY 10013, 212-226-5369, Mon.-Thurs. 7:30 a.m.-6:00 p.m., Fri. 7:30 a.m.-4:00 p.m. Specializing in obsolete repair parts for sinks, showers, and toilets. Custom parts manufactured on premises. Solid brass reproduction plumbing fixtures, parts, tools, hardware. Some repairs done in shop. Mail order and shop. Catalog $6.

Grand Era Reproductions, P.O. Box 1026, Lapeer, MI 48446, 313-664-1756, 8:30 a.m.-5:00 p.m. Authentic period hardware and hardwood, Victorian and country bentwood screen and storm doors, custom doors and brackets, Victorian mailbox posts, teakwood outdoor furniture, Victorian wicker porch swings. Mail order.

J.M. Gray, Inc., 509 West Fayette Street, Syracuse, NY 13204, 315-476-1003, 9:00 a.m.-5:00 p.m., 315-475-9498, evenings. Wood and wrought iron repair and reproductions, including moldings, staircases, porch columns, windows. Repair or replacement of burned, missing, or rotted components. Serving Northeastern U.S. Call first.

Jerard Paul Jordan Gallery, P.O. Box 71, Slade Acres, Ashford, CT 06278, 203-429-7954, 9:00 a.m.-5:00 p.m. Architectural material through the Federal period.

Linoleum City, Fred Stifter, 5657 Santa Monica Boulevard, Hollywood, CA 90038, 213-469-0063, 9:00 a.m.-5:00 p.m.; fax: 213-465-5866. Marbleized battleship linoleum, solid-color linoleum, sheet vinyl, asphalt, cork, and vinyl tiles. Free brochures. Set of cork, marmoleum, and vinyl tiles $5.

Mad River Woodworks, 189 Taylor Way, P.O. Box 1067, Blue Lake, CA 95525, 707-668-5671, 8:00 a.m.-5:00 p.m. Custom millwork, specializing in class Victorian era design. Moldings, pickets, screen doors, porch parts, gable end treatments, corbels, fan brackets, dentil, wainscoting, and more. Mail order. Catalog $3.

Medusa, 236 Prospect Street, Cambridge, MA 02139, 617-776-6667, 9:00 a.m.-5:00 p.m. Faux marbre, faux bois, stencils, trompe l'oeil, custom-designed murals, glazes. Folding screens, floors, ceilings, and furniture painted with unique finishes. Faux marbre and faux bois painted to match real materials or older faux finishes.

Pagliacco Turning & Milling, P.O. Box 225, Woodacre, CA 94973, 415-488-4333, 8:00 a.m.-5:00 p.m.; fax: 415-488-9372. Standard and custom California redwood turnings. Other woods on request. Victorian turnings and millwork based on manufacturers' catalogs from 1870-1920: railings, newel posts, wooden columns, balusters, porch posts. Mail and phone orders worldwide. Catalog $6.

R.G. Brown & Associates, Ron Brown, 7530 East Hinsdale Place, Englewood, CO 80112, 303-721-6514, 9:00 a.m.-6:00 p.m. Embossed wood carvings, decorative ornaments, and moldings, designs from 1880s-1960s. Mail order. Catalog $4.

Renaissance Restorations, Ltd., Wilmington, VT 05363, 802-464-2343, 7:00 a.m.-6:00 p.m. Structural repair, woodwork consultants and engineers. Blacksmith originals and reproductions. No mail order.

Renovation Concepts, Inc., 213 Washington Avenue North, Minneapolis, MN 55401, 612-333-5766, Mon.-Fri. 8:30 a.m.-5:00 p.m., Sat. 10:00 a.m.-2:00 p.m.; fax: 612-333-5782. Tin ceilings, millwork, plumbing, hardware, and lighting products. Showroom and mail order. Brochure.

Renovator's Supply, 149 Northfield Road, Millers Falls, MD 01349, 413-659-3152. Plumbing supplies, architectural elements, wall coverings, tin ceilings, marbleizing kits, and accessories. Catalog.

Restoration Resources, 200 Webster Street, Route 123, Hanover, MA 02339, 627-878-3794, 10:00 a.m.-6:00 p.m. Reproduction moldings, mantels, woodwork, stained glass, decorative metal ceilings, antique plumbing fixtures, decorative and nostalgic items. Brochure.

Restoration Works Inc., P.O. Box 486, Buffalo, NY 14205, 716-856-8000, 9:00 a.m.-5:00 p.m. Decorative hardware and plumbing fixtures, bath accessories, architectural trims, and medallions. Brass products refurbished. Catalog $3.

Roy Electric Co., Inc., 1054 Coney Island Avenue, Brooklyn, NY 11230, 718-434-7002, 800-366-3347, 9:00 a.m.-9:00 p.m. Antique and reproduction plumbing fixtures. Mail order. Catalog $6.

Steptoe and Wife Antiques Limited, 322 Geary Avenue, Toronto, ON M6H 2C7, Canada, 416-530-4200, Mon.-Fri. 9:00 a.m.-5:00 p.m., Sat. 10:00 a.m.-4:00 p.m. Spiral staircases, tin ceilings, architectural enrichment, hardware, plumbing. Custom metal fabricating, reproduction of antique designs in cast iron, stamped metal, etc. Mail order. Brochure.

Tromploy Inc., 400 Lafayette Street, New York, NY 10003, 212-420-1639, 10:00 a.m.-5:00 p.m. All types of faux finishes and murals for walls, ceilings, and floors. Trompe l'oeil, faux marbre, faux bois, and stencils. Mail order. Murals done in studio and mailed anywhere.

Vintage Plumbing Specialties, 9645 Sylvia Avenue, Northridge, CA 91324, 818-772-6353, 8:00 a.m.-midnight. Restoration of old plumbing fixtures, manufacture of missing pieces, stems, valve parts, and drain parts. Obsolete parts, reproduction parts. Pull-chain toilets, claw-foot tubs, pedestal lavatories, brass accessories. Mail order.

Vintage Tub & Sink Restoration Service, 701 Center Street, Ludlow, MA 01056, 413-589-0769, 800-525-TUBS, 8:00 a.m.-5:00 p.m. Restoration of old tubs and sinks. Claw tubs, pedestal sinks, reproduction faucets, and accessories sold. Serving New England. Brochure.

Vintage Wood Works, 513 South Adams, Fredericksburg, TX 78624, 512-997-9513, 8:00 a.m.-5:00 p.m. Victorian gingerbread wood trim, including appliqués, balusters, corbels, finials, gazebos, rails, and parts. Mail order. Catalog.

William Hunrath Company, 153 East 57th Street, New York, NY 10022, 212-758-0780, Mon.-Fri. 9:00 a.m.-5:30 p.m., Sat. 9:00 a.m.-4:00 p.m. Bathroom fixtures, door hardware, pulls, knobs, brass tubing, fasteners, closet accessories, cabinet hardware, door knockers, and more. Mail and phone orders. Flyers on products available.

Wrecking Bar, 292 Moreland Avenue NE, Atlanta, GA 30307, 404-525-0468, Mon.-Sat. 9:00 a.m.-5:00 p.m. Architectural components for displaying art. Custom-designed pedestals. Antique architectural ornaments: wood carvings, mantels, capitals, lighting fixtures, doors, hardware, beveled glass, stained glass, and other items.

Mike Beschler, 644 Chaffeeville Road, Storrs, CT 06268, 203-487-1658, 7:00 a.m.-6:00 p.m. Restoration of stairs and staircase surrounds.

John Crosby Freeman, P.O. Box 430, Norristown, PA 19404, 215-539-3010, 9:00 a.m.-5:00 p.m. Color and design consultant on exterior residential, and commercial building decoration. By mail or on site.

Francis J. Purcell II, 88 North Main Street, New Hope, PA 18938, 215-862-9100, 9:00 a.m.-5:00 p.m. Restored antique fireplace mantelpieces, 1740-1830, shown by appointment.

Helen Williams, 12643 Hortense Street, Studio City, CA 91604, 818-761-2756 anytime. Firebacks, antique tiles, Delft and others. Suitable for fireplace facings, tables, countertops, bathrooms. Mail order.

Leaflet

Old House Journal (69A Seventh Avenue, Brooklyn, NY 11217). (Magazine that has been published since 1973; articles, reprints, and leaf-lets on everything concerning restoration of old houses.)

Videotape

Porcelain Bathtub & Ceramic Tile--Repair & Refinishing (Olde Virginia Restoration, Box 3305, Portsmouth, VA 23701). (Softspray spray equipment and GLAZ-COATE system.)

Autographs

It's not only the signature on the bottom of a check that is worth money. Autographs are enthusiastically collected by many and have a value all their own. The most valuable are those written as part of a historic personal letter. Be careful of fakes and the machine-written autographs used by many politicians. Autographs that have been cut off letters or documents have very little value. It is better to keep a complete but damaged piece of paper than to trim any of it for a better appearance. If the damage is too unsightly, try to frame the paper with acid-free mounts so only the perfect parts will show.

Most of the repair and conservation information you need can be found in the section on Paper.

Barbed Wire & Insulators

The first barbed wire was patented by Lucien Smith of Kent, Ohio, in 1867. More than 1,500 different varieties of barbed wire are known. Collectors prefer pieces that are 18 inches in length. Telephone and telegraph insulators have been collected since the 1960s by serious collectors who know the makers, use, and patent histories of the various insulators. Never attempt to remove an insulator from the top of a pole. There are often power lines on the poles and collectors have been electrocuted. You can sometimes find old insulators left by repairmen and buried at the base of the pole. Glass and ceramic insulators can be repaired by specialists and by those listed in other sections of this book who do other glass and ceramic work.

Barber Poles

The barber pole is said to have been made to represent the blood-soaked rags wrapped around the pole in earlier days. The red-and-white-striped pole has been a symbol of the pharmacist or barber since the 18th century. Old barber poles are now considered folk art.

Source

William Marvy Company, 1540 St. Clair Avenue, St. Paul, MN 55105, 612-698-0726, Mon.-Fri. 8:00 a.m.-5:00 p.m., Sat. 9:00 a.m.-1:00 p.m.; fax: 612-698-4048. Restoration of antique barber poles. Manufacturer of barber poles and replacement parts. Mail order. Brochure.

Baseball Cards & Other Sports Collectibles

Baseball cards and other sports cards have been collected since they were first distributed in the 1880s. The first cards were placed in packs of cigarettes or tobacco as free advertising promotion pieces. From 1910 to 1915 the cards were made by the millions; then only a few were made until the 1930s. The second period of baseball cards came with their use by candy and gum companies. The modern baseball card really started in 1933 with the Goudey Gum Company. World War II caused paper shortages and baseball cards were not made. In 1948 the Bowman and Leaf Companies made cards. Topps Gum Company cards were introduced in 1951.

Baseball cards are the favorites of collectors but there are cards for other sports figures. Value is determined by condition, rarity, and the popularity of the player pictured. Collectors also save gum wrappers, Dixie cup lids, and other paper items that picture sports stars.

There are special shows and publications for sports card collectors. *Kovels' Guide to Selling Your Antiques & Collectibles* explains how to find these. Most major cities have card shows on a regular basis. Ask anyone you see selling cards where the nearest shows will be held. They are often not announced in general publications.

Cards should be stored so that they will be dirt and insect free. Plastic holders made to hold the cards are sold through shows and publications. Little can be done to restore cards, except for dusting or a simple cleaning with an art gum eraser. Condition is very important in determining price. Bent corners might be ironed straight; use a cool iron and protect the card with a thin piece of fabric.

Old golf clubs, fishing tackle, tennis rackets, and other sports memorabilia are actively collected. If you want to fix a tennis racket, see a pro at a tennis shop. You may have trouble getting old materials such as gut for stringing, but it can be done.

See sources listed in the section on Paper.

Sources

Restorations, 563 North Pine Street, Nevada City, CA 95959, 916-477-5527, 8:00 a.m.-4:00 p.m. Mylar bags, restoration supplies and services for baseball card collectors. Mail order.

Ship's Treasures, P.O. Box 590-EM, Milton, MA 02186, 617-964-8010, anytime. Baseball card polyprotectors.

Beer Cans & Breweriana

The way collectors of beer cans and breweriana organize themselves into special-interest factions with shows, publications, and clubs can be confusing. There are collectors of early tin containers (like tobacco cans) who consider themselves tin collectors and attend advertising shows. There are collectors of beer bottles who are bottle collectors and go to bottle shows. Beer can collectors usually buy at beer can shows or flea markets. Books about beer often discuss the cans as well as the bottles and all of the brewery history that is available under the broad term "breweriana."

There is one clever restoration tip for crushed beer cans that you might want to try. Fill the dented can about one-third full with dry beans, then add water and seal the can. The pressure from the expanding beans will push outward and remove most of the dents. Cone-top cans can be repaired by experts who solder new tops on the old cans. Repairing beer cans is almost the same as repairing any commercial tin container. More information about this can be found in the section on Metals.

Source

Museum of Beverage Containers and Advertising, 192 Ridgecrest Drive, Goodlettsville, TN 37072, 615-859-5236, 9:00 a.m.-6:00 p.m.; fax: 615-859-5238. Cleans and derusts cans. Book list available.

Books & Bookplates

First editions, paperback books, pulps, and comics are all of interest to book collectors. Rebinding antique books reduces their value and should be avoided unless it is absolutely necessary. However, if you must, there are bookbinders in many cities. They are listed in the Yellow Pages under "Bookbinders" or you can learn about them from some of the better bookstores or decorating studios.

Bookplate collecting was a major hobby 50 years ago and many fine old books were mutilated by eager collectors who only wanted the bookplates. That is not recommended today. Unless the book is in very bad repair, it is worth more with the bookplate than a mutilated book and a cutout bookplate. Little can be done to restore a bookplate outside of simple cleaning and pressing with an iron. Nothing can be done if old glue has stained the plate. Keep bookplates, books, and all paper items in a controlled environment where they will not become too wet or dry or be attacked by insects, bookworms, or rodents. If you collect paper items, it would be wise to buy the necessary humidifier or dehumidifier for your home.

Sources

Cellar Stories Books, 190 Mathewson Street, Providence, RI 02903, 401-521-2665, Mon.-Sat. 10:00 a.m.-6:00 p.m. Restoration of books.

Harcourt Bindery, 51 Melcher Street, Boston, MA 02110, 617-542-5858, 8:00 a.m.-4:00 p.m. Bookbinding, repair, and restoration. Archival quality portfolios and slipcases, dropover boxes made in cloth or leather.

J. Franklin Mowery, 201 East Capitol Street SE, Washington, DC 20003, 202-544-4600, ext. 232, 9:30 a.m.-5:00 p.m. Restoration of rare books, manuscripts, prints, and bindings. International.

James Macdonald Company, Inc., Jacques Desmonts, 25 Van Zant Street, East Norwalk, CT 06855, 203-853-6076, 8:00 a.m.-5:00 p.m. Restoration of old and rare books, cloth or leather bindings, slipcases and other boxes. Bookplates and stamping on leather.

Northeast Document Conservation Center, Gary E. Albright, Abbott Hall, School Street, Andover, MA 01810, 508-470-1010, Mon.-Fri. 8:30 a.m.-4:30 p.m. Nonprofit regional conservation center specializing in treatment of paper-based materials including books. Preservation microfilming, consultation workshops, preservation planning surveys, disaster assistance.

Restorations, 563 North Pine Street, Nevada City, CA 95959, 916-477-5527, 8:00 a.m.-4:00 p.m. Mylar bags, restoration supplies, including ink touch-up kits, tape-removal kits, stain-removal kits, and adhesives. Restoration services for books and magazines. Mail order.

Sandlin's Books & Bindery, 70 West Lincolnway, Valparaiso, IN 46383, 219-462-9922, Mon.-Sat. 9:00 a.m.-6:00 p.m. Books rebound and repaired, deacidification of paper and documents, mylar encapsulation, handmade linen or leather slipcases and pamphlet folders. Out-of-print book search. Mail order.

Saturday's Book Arts Gallery, Jan Sobota, 235 South Broadway, Geneva, OH 44041, 216-466-9183, 9:00 a.m.-5:00 p.m. Restoration and conservation of rare and collector's books, prints, etc. Original design bookbindings and book boxes, hand-marbled paper. School, workshops, and lectures on bookbinding and restoration. International. Brochure.

Vogel Bindery, 150 West 26th Street, New York, NY 10001, 212-727-8180, 10:00 a.m.-7:00 p.m., after hours 201-863-7894. Conservation and restoration, presentation bindings, and desk accessories.

Wei T'o Associates, Inc., P.O. Drawer 40, 21750 Main Street, Unit 27, Matteson, IL 60443, 708-747-6660, Mon.-Fri. 8:30 a.m.-5:00 p.m. Deacidification sprays and solutions, application equipment, and related products. Wei T'o prevents yellowing and embrittlement and protects documents, books, and works of art. Consultant services. Available through distributors or mail order worldwide.

Linda A. Blaser, 9200 Hawkins Creamery Road, Gaithersburg, MD 20882, 301-774-2267. Restoration of books and book bindings. Flat paper restoration. Classes.

Kathleen Wick, 41 West Cedar, Boston, MA 02114, 617-523-4748, 9:00 a.m.-5:00 p.m. Bookbinding. No repairs. Mail order.

Books

Binding and Repairing Books by Hand, David Muir, 1987 (Arco Publishing Co., NY).

Care of Fine Books, Jane Greenfield, 1988 (Lyons & Burford Publishers, NY).

Cleaning and Caring for Books, Robert L. Shep, 1983 (Sheppard Press, London).

Cleaning and Preserving Bindings and Related Materials, Carolyn Horton, 1975 (American Library Association, 50 East Huron Street, Chicago, IL 60611).

An old privy or dump may not seem like the perfect vacation spot. To a bottle collector it is heaven. Bottle collecting is a family hobby. Some of the best bottles are dug from old dumps, construction sites, or privies or are pulled from river bottoms. Many are in need of repairs. Local bottle clubs always welcome members and bottle shows are filled with collectors who delight in talking about their hobby, the bottles they have found, and possible restoration services.

There are all types of old bottles, including inkwells, flasks, bitters, medicines, poisons, and whiskeys. Many collectors search for recent bottles such as milk bottles, fruit jars, and figural whiskeys made by Jim Beam, Ezra Brooks, or Ski Country. Some manufacturers now have their own publications and books, which are usually available at bottle shows. Check the clubs and publications lists in *Kovels' Guide to Selling Your Antiques & Collectibles*. Each group has special information about the correct appearance of the bottle, which could help with repairs. In the 1970s, collectors often soaked labels off bottles so the display would show only the glass. Today advertising collectors and some specialty bottle collectors pay a premium for bottles with original paper labels, even if the labels are damaged. When regluing a label, be sure to use an adhesive that will not eventually stain the paper.

"Go-withs" are the accessories that "go with" a bottle and interest bottle collectors: openers, corkscrews, advertising materials, and even rubber rings that were used on fruit jars. The restoration rules for metal go-withs, such as openers, are the same as for other iron collectibles, like toys or doorstops. Never repaint; it lowers the value.

Never display glass bottles in a sunny window. The sun may "color" the glass, or the combination of the glass and sun may cause a fire. Beware of "sick" bottles. The cloudy effect inside the bottle is etched in the glass. If the bottle is for display, you can swish some clear mineral oil in the bottle, then seal the bottle. This temporarily covers the cloudy look. It is possible to polish the inside of a bottle, but it is very expensive, requires talent, and is a risky repair. Only the most expensive historic flasks or early bottles are usually restored in this manner. Bottles can be repaired with the new plastics. Some of the repairs are invisible except under black light, but there is an even more expensive plastic that cannot be seen by black light. See the section on Writing Instruments, for inkwells, and the section on Glass.

Sources

Castle's Fair, Lawrence and Sara Castle, 885 Taylor Avenue, Ogden, UT 84404-5270, 801-393-8131. Antique glass restoration. Bottles polished inside and out. Mail order only.

Lid Lady, Virginia Bodiker, 7790 East Ross Road, New Carlisle, OH 45344. Glass, pottery, porcelain, metal, plastic, and zinc stoppers and salt and pepper lids. Mail order. Open by appointment.

McCurley Glass Repair, Don and Joyce McCurley, Route 1, Box 738, Big Pine Key, FL 33043, 305-872-2359, 9:00 a.m.-10:00 p.m. Glass and crystal replacement parts. Specializing in stoppers for all kinds of bottles. Glass and crystal repaired.

Michael Garrett, 6747 Grandville, Detroit, MI 48228, 313-593-4634, anytime. Bottle cleaning. Mail order.

Videotape

Bottle Digging Video, Mark Anderton (Route 257, P.O. Box 13732, Seneca, PA 16346).

BRONZE, see Metal

Carousels & Carousel Figures

The carousel has become an accepted part of American folk art. Museums and collectors are adding horses, carvings, cresting, chariots, and musical mechanisms to their collections.

It is best to keep most of these wood carvings in unrestored condition unless the finish has deteriorated or been badly damaged. Some restorers remove the old finish and repaint the animals, or restore damaged wood and finish. Do not restore one of these figures yourself unless you are talented and trained. A poor restoration can destroy the resale value. Most antiques are less valuable if restored. Oil paintings, automobiles, and carousel figures may be the major exceptions to this rule. Newly painted old carousel figures sell at auction for very high prices, often much higher than for similar figures with "park paint." Be very careful if you plan to strip and paint a carousel figure. The tastes of collectors may change and the aged original paint may become the preferred finish. This has already happened with painted Shaker furniture: Unpainted, refinished pieces brought the highest prices in the early 1980s; now any piece with the original paint demands a premium price.

Sources

Carousel Works, Inc. 44 West Fourth Street, Mansfield, OH 44902, 419-522-7558, 8:00 a.m.-4:30 p.m. Restoration of carousels and carousel figures, repainting, and replacement of missing figures. Replacement parts for mechanisms. Parts by mail order.

Flying Tails, John & June Reely, 1209 Indiana Avenue, South Pasadena, CA 91030, 213-256-8657, 8:00 a.m.-9:00 p.m. Carousel stands, glass eyes, jewels, horsehair tails, books, and related items. Custom restoration. Mail order sales and service.

Tony Orlando, 6661 Norborne, Dearborn Heights, MI 48127, 313-561-5072. Carousel restoration and conservation, repainting, gold and silver leafing, missing parts replaced. Figures repainted to original factory look. Horsehair tails, glass eyes, jewels, brass poles, and other supplies. Lectures on history or restoration of carousels. Mail order.

Catalog

Carousel Shopper, Box 47, Dept. K, Millwood, NY 10546. (Catalog of resources, including restorers, supplies, books, and more.)

Christmas & Holiday Collectibles

Christmas, Easter, and Halloween collectibles are extremely popular. Old Santa Claus figures and pressed cardboard pumpkins are collected. Early Christmas decorations are of special interest. Save the old metal caps from broken early glass ornaments. They are different from the new ones and can be used on other early glass ornaments that are missing them. It is possible to find new old-style tinsel, paper cutouts, and spun "clouds" when restoring old ornaments. Many old glass ornaments are now being sold again; with a little ingenuity, you could buy a new glass bird for your old glass and tinsel bird nest, or use other combinations of old and new to save treasured pieces. Look in gift shops that sell stickers and fancy wrapping paper. Many reprints of Victorian "scrap" figures are now available. Feather trees are being reproduced and there are a few craftsmen who can repair old trees. The old base is one of the clues to age, so don't repaint or remove it. If it is unsightly, cover it with a cloth.

Halloween pieces made of pressed cardboard or crepe paper will fade if kept in too sunny a spot. Never light a candle in the center of a cardboard pumpkin. It may be attractive, but it is a fire hazard. Many old jack-o'-lanterns had tissue paper inserts for eyes. You can easily make a reproduction if you can find an old one to use as a pattern. Easter eggs and candy containers should be carefully stored where the remains of food will not attract rodents and insects. Bits of paper lace used on some Easter pieces can be replaced by using parts of paper doilies found in stores that specialize in gourmet cooking supplies.

Specialized information can be found in the Glass, Paper, and Pottery & Porcelain sections.

Clocks & Watches

Clocks can range from an 18th-century tall case style to the 20th-century animated "electric." Repairing clockworks is a job for an expert. It is always best not to try to fix the inside of a broken clock unless you have the required talent. Clock face and dial repainting and reverse glass painting for clock doors require specialists. Refinishing a clock case can be done at home. The materials and information can be found in Part II. Clocks with pendulums need special adjustments to keep accurate time and often must be leveled on a shelf or floor. A local clock repair service will do this, or you may be able to correct the swing by following the directions available in various books.

If you acquire an electric clock that is more than 20 years old, always have the wiring checked and replaced. Old wiring is a fire hazard.

When you buy an old clock or watch, the first thing to do is to take it to an expert to see if it needs cleaning. This is usually the only restoration required. Old-style bands for wristwatches can be found at many jewelry stores.

Sources

Acme Clock Repair Service, 1737 Devon Avenue, Chicago, IL 60660, 312-973-5789. Antique clocks repaired, including fabrication of parts and movements.

Antiques Olde & Nue, 6960 North Interstate Avenue, Portland, OR 97217, 503-289-2922, noon-5:00 p.m. Clock repairs.

Armor Products, P.O. Box 445, East Northport, NY 11731, 516-462-6228, 9:00 a.m.-5:00 p.m. Clock components: quartz and mechanical movements; bezel, brass plate and plastic dials; hands, numerals. Catalog.

Barap Specialties, 835 Bellows, Frankfort, MI 49635, 616-352-9863, 8:30 a.m.-5:00 p.m. Clock dials, hands, numerals, movements; tools and supplies.

Burt Dial Company, P.O. Box 774, Route 107N, Raymond, NH 03077, 603-895-2879, 9:00 a.m.-5:00 p.m. weekdays. Refinishing and restoration of clock dials and reverse glass paintings. Specializing in refinishing of silver and silver and gilt dials, primarily by mail. Price lists available.

Clocks Etc., 3401 Mount Diablo Boulevard, Lafayette, CA 94549, 414-284-4720, 10:00 a.m.-5:00 p.m. Restoration of antique clocks; complete movement, case, and dial restoration. Ship anywhere. Brochure.

Dial House, Martha and Richard Smallwood, Buchanan Highway, Route 7, Box 532, Dallas, GA 30132, 404-445-2877, 7:00 a.m.-9:00. Restoration and/or replacement of antique clock dials. Custom hand-painted dials. Brochure.

Fendley's Antique Clocks, Gerald Fendley, 2535 Himes Street, Irving, TX 75060, 214-254-2834. Specializing in wheel and pinion cutting for antique clocks. Custom-made clock parts, repairs, restorations, and books. Brochure.

Gaston Wood Finishes, Inc., P.O. Box 1246, 2626 North Walnut Street, Bloomington, IN 47402, 812-339-9111, 8:30 a.m.-4:30 p.m. Clock movements, dials, and numerals; wood finishing products. Stripping and refinishing. Mail order, retail shop. Catalog $2.50.

Gordon S. Converse & Co., 1029 Lancaster Avenue, Berwyn, PA 19312, 215-296-4938, restoration dept.; 215-296-4932, sales dept., Mon.-Fri. 9:00 a.m.-5:00 p.m. Restoration of antique clocks.

Horton Brasses, Nooks Hill Road, P.O. Box 120-Q, Cromwell, CT 06416, 203-635-4400, 8:30 a.m.-4:00 p.m. Clock parts, reproduction brass and hand-forged black iron hardware. Mail and telephone orders. Showroom open 8:30 a.m.-3:45 p.m. Catalog $3.

Johnson Watch Repair, 2735 23rd Street, Greeley, CO 80631, 303-330-5228, 9:00 a.m.-6:00 p.m. Watch repair and restoration, specializing in pocket watches and 1930s-1950s wristwatches. Free estimates. Mail order.

Martines' Antiques, Margaret and Joseph Martines, 516 East Washington, Chagrin Falls, OH 44022, 216-247-6421. Antique clocks serviced and repaired. Tall case clock repair a specialty. Mail order service on most clocks.

Merritt's Antiques, R.D. 2, Douglassville, PA 19518, 215-689-9541, Mon.-Fri. 7:30 a.m.-5:00 p.m., Sat. 7:30 a.m.-12:30 p.m.; fax:

215-689-4538. Clock parts and supplies, books, and tools. Mail order worldwide.

Simonson, 240 East Washington Street, Medina, OH 44256, 216-725-7056, Mon.-Sat. 10:00 a.m.-5:00 p.m. Clock repair and restoration. Serving Medina, Akron, and Greater Cleveland area.

Tec Specialties, P.O. Box 909, Smyrna, GA 30081. Clock dials, decals, and backboard labels, calendar strips. Reproduction of originals. Second bits, Coca-Cola dials, decals. Mail order only. Free catalog.

Timesavers, Box 469, Algonquin, IL 60102, 312-658-2266, 8:30 a.m.-5:00 p.m. fax: 312-658-9033. Parts and supplies. Mail order. Catalog $2.

Yankee Drummer House of Time, Appletree Mall, P.O. Box 909, Londonderry, NH 03053, 603-437-2410, Mon.-Fri. 10:00 a.m.-8:00 p.m., Sat. 10:00 a.m.-5:00 p.m., Sun. noon-5:00 p.m. Restoration, refurbishing, and repair of antique clocks and watches, fabrication of parts. Mail order.

Daniel Bosworth, 27 Merrimack Street, Concord, NH 03301, 603-224-6150, 7:00 a.m.-4:00 p.m. Watch restoration, specializing in railroad watches and American pocket watches and wristwatches.

Dorothy Briggs, 410 Ethan Allen Avenue, Takoma Park, MD 20012, 301-270-4166. Clock dial restoration.

Fred Catterall, 54 Short Street, New Bedford, MA 02740, 508-997-8532, evenings. Banjo clock replacement pictures and paper dials. Spring banjos repaired. Mail order. Brochure.

Jandi Goggin, Box 175, Huntington, NY 11743-0175. Repair and restoration of antique clocks. Material, tools, and instructions for recovering cuckoo clock bellows.

M.D. King, 403 East Montgomery, Knoxville, IA 50138, 515-842-6394, 8:00 a.m.-10:00 p.m. Clock repair.

George Paladics, 414 Route 523 North, Whitehouse Station, NJ 08889, 201-534-2981, 9:00 a.m.-5:00 p.m. Complete restoration and repair of clocks. Mail order worldwide.

Sal Provenzano, P.O. Box 843, Bronx, NY 10469, 212-655-7021. Clock repair.

Stephen Sanborn, P.O. Box 810, Hillsboro, NH 03244, 603-464-5382, Mon.-Fri. 9:00 a.m.-5:00 p.m., closed Wed. Clock repair and restoration, clock movement parts.

Paul N. Smith, 408 East Leeland Heights Boulevard, Lehigh Acres, FL 33936, 813-369-4663, 9:00 a.m.-5:00 p.m. Clocks repaired.

Books

Black Forest Clocks, E. John Tyler, 1977 (NAG Press, London).

Black Forest Cuckoo Clock, Karl Kochmann, 1976 (Antique Clock Publishing, P.O. Box 21387, Concord, CA 94521).

Clock Repairer's Handbook, Laurie Penman, 1985 (Arco Publishing Co., NY).

Essence of Clock Repair, Sean C. Monk, 1983 (American Watchmakers Institute Press, 3700 Harrison Avenue, P.O. Box 11011, Cincinnati, OH 45211).

Grandfather Clock Maintenance Manual, John Vernon, 1983 (Van Nostrand Reinhold Co., NY).

Illustrated Guide to House Clocks, Anthony Bird, 1973 (Arco Publishing Co., NY).

Horological Hints and Helps, F.W. Britten, 1977 (Antique Collectors' Club, Woodbridge, Suffolk, England).

Making and Repairing Wooden Clock Cases, V.J. Taylor and H.A. Babb, 1986 (David & Charles, North Pomfret, VT).

Re-Covering Cuckoo Clock and Bird Cage Bellows, John J. Goggin, 1986 (16 Jones Lane, Huntington, NY 11743).

Repairing & Restoring Pendulum Clocks, John Plewes, 1984 (Blandford Press, Poole, Dorset, England).

Repairing Antique Clocks, Eric P. Smith, 1974 (Arco Publishing Co., NY).

Repairing Old Clocks & Watches, Anthony J. Whiten, 1979 (NAG Press, London).

Striking and Chiming Clocks, Eric Smith, 1985 (Arco Publishing Co., NY).

Clothing & Accessories

Collecting vintage clothing is a fairly recent hobby. Many cities have shops that specialize in old clothing that can be worn every day. There is usually someone at these shops who can repair old clothing or furnish the trim and material needed for repairs. A few bridal and antiques shops also sell old fabrics, lace, or dresses. Check the Yellow Pages of the telephone book under "Clothing Bought & Sold" or "Second Hand Stores" to locate the dealers who sell and repair old clothes.

Dirt and sunlight do more harm to old fabrics than cleaning. Most fabrics can be gently washed in pure soap, not detergent, or they can be carefully dry-cleaned. The rules for old fabrics are the same as those for modern ones. Some stains may be permanent, but the overall soil should be cleaned away. Repairs to rips should be made before the pieces are cleaned. This avoids more damage. Loose beading and lace trim should be repaired as soon as damage is noticed.

See also the section on Textiles.

Sources

King's Storehouse, Judith Anderson, R.R. 1, Box 42, Prairie du Rocher, IL 62277, 618-284-7278. Handmade 18th-century-style men's and women's shoes. Buckles for shoes, pants, belts. Brochure.

The Simple Machine, Cathy and Stephen Racine, 18 Masonic Hill Road, Route 31 South, Charlton, MA 01507, 508-248-6632, 11:00 a.m.-7:00 p.m. Repair and restoration of sewing machines; instruction manuals, needles, bobbins, bobbin cases, leather belts for antique treadle sewing machines. Cabinet restoration done May to September, other work done all year. Mail order.

Uncle Sam Umbrella Shop, 161 West 57th Street, New York, NY 10019, 212-582-1977, 9:30 a.m.-6:00 p.m. New and old umbrellas and canes repaired. Parts repaired or replaced, material on old frames replaced.

Coin-operated Machines, Jukeboxes & Slot Machines

"Coin-ops" include arcade and amusement machines, jukeboxes, scales, slot machines, vending machines, and a special group of old machines called "trade stimulators." These were games that encouraged the sale of cigarettes, cigars, drinks, and other products or services. A slot machine was made to pay out money from the machine, while the trade stimulator rewarded the player with products or free games. It was an easier machine to make, but often had many of the other features of a slot machine.

Jukeboxes gained favor as collectibles during the 1970s. There are several good books that give the history of jukeboxes and list the models and stores that sell parts or repair existing machines. Reprints of some of the original instruction books can be found.

Buying parts for any of the coin-operated machines requires some ingenuity. Machines can be found in special shops and shows, but some of the best buys are made by smart collectors who follow their local newspaper's classified section. A machine in very poor condition is still useful for parts to be used to repair other machines. There are specialists who fix slot machines and jukeboxes.

Sources

A.M.R. Publishing Company, P.O. Box 3007, Arlington, WA 98223, 206-659-6434, Mon.-Fri. 9:00 a.m.-5:00 p.m.; fax 206-659-5994. Books, service and parts manuals for jukeboxes and player pianos. Catalog $2.

Ancient Slots and Antiques, 3127 Industrial Road, Las Vegas, NV 89109, 702-796-7779, 800-228-SLOT, 8:30 a.m.-5:00 p.m.; fax: 702-796-4389. Slot machine parts, service, and restorations.

Antique Amusements Co., 14502 Ventura Boulevard, Sherman Oaks, CA 91403, 818-995-8537, 11:00 a.m.-5:00 p.m., 818-995-8546; fax: 805-987-3654. Wurlitzer jukeboxes and parts.

Antone's Buy & Sell Shop, 735 Harlem Road, West Seneca, NY 14224, 716-826-8502 or 716-649-6285, 8:30 a.m.-11:00 p.m. Coin-operated machines restored. Serving western New York State and northwestern Pennsylvania. Mail order.

Brass & Copper Polishing Shop, Don Reedy, 251 West Patrick Street, Frederick, MD 21701, 301-663-4240, 8:00 a.m.-4:00 p.m. Gumball and peanut machines repaired. Brass and copper pieces repaired, lacquered, and polished. Serving the Maryland-Virginia-Pennsylvania area.

Evans and Frink, 7999 Keller Road, Cincinnati, OH 45243-1037, 513-891-6841, 6:00 a.m.-10:00 p.m. Reproduction slot machine reel strips and award cards. Mail order. Catalog $1.

Falcum Service, 550 Route 110, Amityville, NY 11701, 516-842-1065, 24 hours a day. Pinball machines, arcade games, and video games repaired. Serving New York State, New Jersey, and Connecticut. Parts by mail order.

Home Arcade Corp., 1108 Front Street, Lisle, IL 60532, 708-964-2555, Mon.-Fri. 10:00 a.m.-6:00 p.m. Service of coin-operated machines for homes. Parts by mail, including tubes, needles, jukebox parts, and reproduction Coke machine parts.

Jukebox Junction, Inc., P.O. Box 1081, Des Moines, IA 50311, 515-981-4019 or 515-981-0245, Mon.-Fri. 8:30 a.m.-5:00 p.m.; fax: 515-981-4657. Restoration parts and manuals for 1930s-1950s jukeboxes. Complete restoration on selected models. Mail order worldwide. Catalog $2.50, refundable with first order.

Jukebox Junkyard, P.O. Box 181, Lizella, GA 31052, 912-935-2721, 9:00 a.m.-6:00 p.m. Jukeboxes, parts, reproduction parts, accessories, supplies, restoration. Parts and supplies available through mail order worldwide.

Just Slots, 46 Ellerker Rise, Willerby, Hull HU10 6EY, England, 0482-655504 or 0836-767575, 9:00 a.m.-9:00 p.m. Repair and restoration of old slot machines, bandits, and jukeboxes.

New England Amusements, 77 Tolland Turnpike, Manchester, CT 06040, 203-646-1533, 11:00 a.m.-7:00 p.m. Specializing in Seeburg and Wurlitzer jukebox parts and service. Serving the New England, New York State, and New Jersey area. Mail order.

Orange Trading Company, 57 South Main Street, Orange, MA 01364, 508-544-6683, Mon.-Sun. 9:00 a.m.-6:00 p.m. Restoration of coin-operated machines.

Paul's Chrome Plating Inc., 198 Mars-Valencia Road, Mars, PA 16046, 412-625-3135, 800-245-8679, Mon.-Fri. 8:00 a.m.-5:00 p.m. Custom-plating of coin-operated machines. Custom show plating, die-cast restoration, aluminum polishing, gold, brass, and cadium plating.

Paul's Pinball, Paul M. Kunik, R.D. 2, Box 18, Berkshire, NY 13736, 607-657-8097, evenings. Repair and restoration of coin-operated machines, specializing in electromechanical and mechanical pinball machines (no solid state). Will also repair other amusement machines, jukeboxes, shuffleboards, shooting galleries. Upstate New York area. No mail order.

Pinball Wizard, Chance and Elaine Tess, 21934 John R. Road, Hazel Park, MI 48030, 313-399-6438, weekdays after 5:00 p.m., weekends after 9:00 a.m., answering machine other times. Jukebox amplifiers of the 1950s-1960s repaired, by mail or locally; pinball machines serviced, within a reasonable distance of Detroit; digital boards and displays repaired, by mail or locally. Pinball backglasses and parts.

Rock-ola Jukebox Service, Charles Maier, 3016 Derry Terrace, Philadelphia, PA 19154-2519, 215-637-2869, 6:00 p.m.-midnight. Jukebox and audio systems service; factory trained on Rock-Ola jukeboxes. Jukebox literature, reprints of service manuals and advertising brochures. Mail order. Catalog $2.

Saint Louis Slot Machine Co., Tom Kolbrener, 2111 South Brentwood Boulevard, St. Louis, MO 63144, 314-961-4612, Mon.-Fri. 9:00 a.m.-5:00 p.m., Sat. 9:00 a.m.-2:00 p.m. Coin-operated machines repaired. Books. Mail order. Catalog $3.

Sandler Vending Co., 236 Girard Avenue North, Minneapolis, MN

55405, 612-377-1140. Bally pinballs, Rock-Ola jukeboxes and parts. No mail order.

Speed & Sport Chrome Plating, Craig Bierman, 7477 SW Freeway, Houston, TX 77074, 713-981-1440, Mon.-Sat. 10:00 a.m.-6:00 p.m. Chrome-plating of jukeboxes, slot machines, and scales. Gumball machine globes, candy scale scoops and parts.

Tim Nabours Novelty, Route 2, Box 73, Annandale, MN 55302, 612-274-5953, anytime. Service, parts, and supplies for pinball machines, jukeboxes, shuffle alleys, and video games. In-home service within 100-mile radius of Annandale. Mail order.

Two-Bit Score, Bob Sokol, 11600 Manchaca Road, Suite 305, Austin, TX 78748, 512-282-9369, Mon.-Fri. 9:00 a.m.-5:00 p.m. Parts and service on pinballs manufactured after 1977.

Vic-Clar Antique Juke Boxes, 9313 Rose Street, Bellflower, CA 90706, 213-866-7106, 8:00 a.m.-6:00 p.m. Jukebox restoration and parts, specializing in Golden Era jukeboxes.

Vintage Vending, Tom & Louise Tolworthy, Box 146, Noblesville, IN 46060, 317-887-1266, evenings until 10:00 p.m., answering machine during day. Restoration decals for Coke or Pepsi machines, advice on restoration and decal placement. Mail order.

Wiesner Radio & Electronics, 149 Hunter Avenue, Albany, NY 12206, 518-438-2801 or 518-371-9902, 4:30 p.m.-11:00 p.m. Jukebox amplifiers rebuilt, parts for obsolete electrical equipment. Mail order.

Bernie Berten, 9420 Trumbull, Chicago, IL 60642, 708-499-0688, 8:00 a.m.-9:00 p.m. Complete parts service for antique slot machines; repair and restoration. Send two first class stamps for catalog.

Frank Brunette, 5318 Stranahan Drive, Cross Lanes, WV 25313, 304-776-6175, anytime. Restore slot machines, jukeboxes, Coke and Pepsi machines, gumball machines, and penny arcade games.

Ken Durham, 909 26th Street NW, Washington, DC 20037, 202-338-1342, evenings. Books and catalogs on coin-operated machines. Mail order.

D.B. Evans, 7999 Keller Road, Cincinnati, OH 45243, 513-891-6841, evenings. Reproduction reel strips and award cards for antique slot machines. Mail order only. Send four first class stamps for catalog.

Jim Farago, P.O. Box 6313, Minneapolis, MN 55406, 612-772-0708, anytime. Overhaul of any tube-type jukebox amplifiers, 1930-1965. Schematic copies of amplifiers sold, $3 plus SASE. Mail order worldwide.

Tucker Flandrena, Box 378, Arnold's Park, IA 51331, 712-332-7286, 7:00 p.m.-10:00 p.m. Parts for pinball, baseball, and bingo machines. Mail order only.

Patrick Hamelet, P.O. Box 10557, Chicago, IL 60610, 708-362-6255, 10:00 a.m.-6:00 p.m. Pinball machines serviced, Chicago area.

Donnie Kueller, 841 Robinwood Road, Washington Township, Westwood, NJ 07675, 201-664-5479, 9:00 a.m.-8:00 p.m. Jukeboxes from the 1940s-1960s serviced and restored. Specializing in Rock-Olas. Parts for Rock-Olas, AMI, and Seeburg "trashcans." Reproduction Rock-Ola parts.

Donal Murphy, c/o E.W.I., 2015 North Kolmar Avenue, Chicago, IL 60639, 312-235-3360. Pinball backliners and sunburst "when lit" caps, used on 1960s pinball games.

Bob Nelson, 1426 Murray Court, Wichita, KS 67212, 316-722-4090, 8:00 a.m.-10:00 p.m. Glasses, parts, schematics, and operating instructions for console slots, pinballs, arcades, and jukeboxes. Jukeboxes, console slots, and pinballs restored and reproduced. Mail order. Inventory lists $2.

Chris Pokorny, 4728 Via San Andros, Las Vegas, NV 89103, 702-367-8994, anytime. Jukeboxes, slot machines, and other coin-operated machines repaired. Service area limited to 100-mile radius of Las Vegas. Mail order.

Ted Salveson, P.O. Box 602, Huron, SD 57350, 605-352-3870. Coin-operated machine parts and supplies. Salgo All-purpose Coin Machine cleaner.

R. Shaw, 1142 Scotland, Cupertino, CA 95014, 408-255-9178, 8:00 a.m.-5:00 p.m. Jukeboxes and reproduction parts for jukeboxes. Mail order.

Jan and Ed Stevens, 4820 North Troy, Chicago, IL 60625, 312-478-3535, 9:00 a.m.-9:00 p.m. Specializing in the restoration of 1950s Seeburg jukeboxes.

Jack Weber, 434 Nold Avenue, Wooster, OH 44691, 216-264-6897, evenings. Coin-operated machines repaired.

Craig Willardson, P.O. Box 8296, Dept. K, Spokane, WA 99203, 509-624-0772, 6:00 p.m.-midnight. Repair and restoration of early coin-operated machines. Decals, labels, instructions sheets. Mail order. Catalog $1.

Steve Young, 46 Velie Road, R.D. 3, Lagrangeville, NY 12540, 914-223-5613, evenings and weekends. Pinball parts, supplies, schematics, restoration aids, service information, and backglass preservative. Pinball repair and restoration. Mail order service. Serving the mid-Hudson Valley and western Connecticut.

Books

American Premium Guide to Coin Operated Machines, Jerry Ayliffe, 1981 (Crown Publishers, NY). (Information on restoration and repair.)

Slot Machines, Marshall Fey, 1983 (Nevada Publications, Box 15444, Las Vegas, NV 89114).

Slot Machines of Yesteryear: Operator's Companion, Mills of the Thirties, Herbert S. Mills, 1979 (Post-Era Books, Box 150, 119 South First Avenue, Arcadia, CA 91006).

Slot Machines of Yesteryear: Operator's Companion, Mills of the Forties, 1980 (Post-Era Books, Box 150, 119 South First Avenue, Arcadia, CA 91006).

Slot Machines of Yesteryear: Operator's Companion, Watling, 1979 (Post-Era Books, Box 150, 119 South First Avenue, Arcadia, CA 91006).

Coins, Tokens & Other Numismatic Items

The value of rare coins, perhaps more than for any other type of collectible, is determined by condition as well as rarity, beauty, and history. For this reason, coin collectors, or numismatists, are particularly careful about handling, storing, or cleaning coins. The perspiration from a hand will eventually damage a coin. It should always be handled with gloves or by the edges. Never store coins in bags where they might rub against each other. Try storing them in an area where they will not tarnish. Keep them away from damp places, too much direct sunlight, off floors, and away from rubber bands, tape, metal, and cardboard. The sulfur in the rubber or cardboard will eventually damage the coins. There are many types of holders with spaces for specific coins, or envelopes and filing boxes that are made for coin storage.

Never clean your coins. If it must be done, consult an expert. There are dips, cleaning cloths, and other products made to clean coins, but they may cause damage if not used correctly.

Many types of tokens are collected under the general heading of "non-money" in coin catalogs. They are special metal or wooden pieces that served as a medium of exchange at a company store or as advertising for a regular store. They were not legal tender produced by a government. Information on coin and related collecting can be found in any library. Never clean a token or a medal; it lowers the value. Handle the pieces as little as possible and wear white cotton gloves. The perspiration from your hand can mark the metal.

Checks and credit cards are the newest types of money substitutes to be collected. They should be stored or restored in the same way as any paper or plastic items.

Sources

Lin Terry, 59 East Madison Avenue, Dumont, NJ 07628, 201-385-4706. Coin mounts, currency holders, coin tubes, envelopes, and other supplies and literature.

Stock Search International, Inc., Micheline Masse, 16855 West Bernardo Drive, Suite 207, San Diego, CA 92127-1627, 619-592-0362, 800-537-4523, 8:00 a.m.-5:00 p.m.; fax: 619-592-0366. Traces stock market certificates, recovers intrinsic funds on behalf of clients, provides collector value appraisals of researched certificates. Mail order. Phone for brochure.

Comic Art

Collectors have recently become serious about comic art. Although comic books have been collected for years, the original art for movie cartoons and comic strips surprisingly had been ignored. Most of these materials are now of enough historic importance to be found in universities and museums. The strips and "cels" (celluloid pictures used for movie cartoons) were not made to be permanent, and they fade and deteriorate easily. Watch out for excess light, heat, or humidity because they will quickly damage the materials. There are restorers for many of these items, but the restoration is expensive.

See also the sections on Movie Memorabilia, Paper, and Photographs.

Source

Restorations, 563 North Pine Street, Nevada City, CA 95959, 916-477-5527, 8:00 a.m.-4:00 p.m. Mylar bags, restoration supplies, including ink touch-up kits, tape removal and stain removal kits, and adhesives. Restoration services. Restoration techniques video. Mail order.

Book

Collecting Comic Books, Marcia Leiter, 1983 (Little, Brown & Co., Boston).

Videotape

Comic Restoration Techniques, Restoration, J. Dennis Saunders (563 North Pine Street, Nevada City, CA 95959).

Decoys

Collectors of hunting decoys are often as interested in modern decoys of top quality as they are in older, used ones. Waterfowl decoys are the most popular but many collectors also want fish decoys. This is a special field of collecting, with clubs, publications, auctions, and other events that are separate from the general antiques market. Talk to local collectors to learn about events in your area. Those who make modern decoys can often restore old ones.

See books listed in the Furniture section.

Source

G. Schoepfer Inc., 138 West 31st Street, New York, NY 10001, 212-736-6934 or 212-736-6939, 9:30 a.m.-3:30 p.m.; fax: 212-736-6934. Glass and plastic eyes for duck decoys. Mail order worldwide. Send SASE and specify project to get list.

Dolls

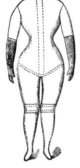

Doll collectors judge their collections by beauty, rarity, age, and condition. Examine your old doll carefully. Has it been repainted? Is the body original? Are the arms and legs undamaged? Is the surface of the face uncracked? Doll heads can be professionally mended. Many of the same restorers who mend porcelains will repair a china-headed doll (see the section on Pottery & Porcelain). Composition dolls and doll heads often crack with age and heat, but can be restored. Bodies can be restored or replaced. Old and new clothing is available, as are patterns for period doll dresses. A restored doll is worth more than a damaged doll, but much less than an all-original one. The sound mechanisms of old dolls and stuffed animals can be repaired, but the restoration is expensive. To replace the voice in a "talking Barbie," the entire head must be removed and split, the voice mechanism's rubber parts replaced, the head reglued, and the joint repainted. It is sometimes less expensive to buy a new doll, but there are times when emotional attachment to a doll makes restoration a good idea.

If you are taking a doll to be repaired, there are a few rules that must be followed to assure you and the doll hospital a happy transaction. Photograph the doll and the damaged parts. Take pictures of the marks, body, hair, and clothes. Get a written estimate of the cost of the repair and the work that is to be done before agreeing to the work. It is often easy to remember an old doll as more glamorous than it actually was, and sometimes when the restored doll is returned it appears unfamiliar. We often hear complaints that a head or body was replaced or that the repairs were more extensive than expected. The pictures and estimate will help solve these problems. Other sources can be found in the section on Toys.

Sources

A. Ludwig Klein & Son, Inc., P.O. Box 145, Dept. 13, Harleysville, PA 19438, 215-256-9004, Tues.-Fri. 10:00 a.m.-5:00 p.m., Sat. 10:00 a.m.-2:00 p.m. Repairs and restorations, missing parts resculpted. Mail photo of doll and blank audio cassette tape to receive instructions on how to repair your doll yourself.

Antique Replica Dolls, 2780 Mill Creek Road, Mentone, CA 92359, 714-794-2686, 9:00 a.m.-5:00 p.m. Replacement arms and legs for china and bisque dolls. Antique bisque arms and legs for bisque dolls 10 inches and under.

Appel Restorations, 87 Bradford Road, Rochester, NY 14618-2912, 716-442-9807. Restores dolls through the mail only. Free estimates.

Chili Doll Hospital & Victorian Doll Museum, Linda Greenfield, 4332 Buffalo Road, North Chili, NY 14514, 716-247-0130, Tues-Sat. 10:00 a.m.-4:30 p.m., Sun. 1:00 p.m.-4:30 p.m. Doll restoration, wigs, and costumes. Write before sending doll. Victorian doll museum on premises.

Collectible Doll Company, 1421 North 34th Street, Seattle, WA 98103, 206-634-3131, Mon.-Fri. 9:00 a.m.-5:00 p.m.; order desk 800-HOT-DOLL; fax: 206-634-3131. Molds for doll bodies and parts, doll eyes, mohair, paints, brushes, video on doll painting, doll clothes, antique doll and children's furniture and accessories. Classes on making antique reproduction porcelain or wax dolls taught throughout the country. Catalog $5.

Colorado Doll Faire, 3307 South College Avenue, Fort Collins, CO 80525, 303-226-3655, Mon.-Sat. 10:00 a.m.-6:00 p.m. Repair kits for composition dolls.

Create-A-Doll, 146 East Chubbuck Road, Chubbuck, ID 83202, 208-238-0433, 10:00 a.m.-5:00 p.m. Leather doll bodies, porcelain arms and legs.

Dean's China Restoration, 131 Elmwood Drive, Cheshire, CT 06410, 203-271-3659, Mon.-Fri. 9:00 a.m.-5:00 p.m. Repair and restoration of dolls. Invisible repairs, undetectable by black light. China restoration seminars. Mail order.

Dempsey & Baxter, Sherri and Jack Dempsey, 1009 East 38th, Erie, PA 16504, 814-825-6381, 10:00 a.m.-5:00 p.m. Doll restoration and books.

Doll Cellar, Gloria McCarty, 2337 46th Avenue SW, Seattle, WA 98116, 206-938-4446, 9:00 a.m.-9:00 p.m. Repairs and accessories. Mail order.

Doll City, 2040 North Trustin Avenue, Orange, CA 92665, 714-998-9384,

10:00 a.m.-4:45 p.m. Doll-making supplies, replacement parts, molds, patterns, and collectible dolls. Mail order, store sales. Mold Pattern catalog $3.50. *Doll City U.S.A. Newsletter* $2.

Doll Connection, 117 Market Street, Portsmouth, NH 03801, 603-431-5030, 10:00 a.m.-4:00 p.m. Antique dolls restored. Doll parts, eyes, wigs, clothes, and shoes.

Doll House, Nanci Zigler, 1263 North Parker Drive, Janesville, WI 53545, 608-752-7986, 1:00 p.m.-10:00 p.m. Custom-made kid bodies, German styles, French fashion bodies, reproduction cloth bodies, Bye-Lo bodies, porcelain hands, cloth bodies with china limbs, custom leather arms and legs. Brochure, price list.

Doll Lady Doll Hospital, 94 Pent Road, Branford, CT 06405, 203-488-6193, 8:00 a.m.-6:00 p.m. Dolls repaired and missing parts replaced. Papier-mâché and ball-jointed bodies, china parts, doll clothes, and leather shoes. Catalog $2.25. Repairs by appointment only.

Doll Repair Parts, Inc., 9918 Lorain Avenue, Cleveland, OH 44102, 216-961-3545, 10:00 a.m.-5:00 p.m. Parts, supplies. Mail order service available.

Doll Shop Enterprises USA, P.O. Box 6776, Marietta, GA 30065, 404-422-9184, 8:00 a.m.-6:00 p.m. Mail order doll supplies, including wigs, eyes, and bodies.

Doll World, Cynthia Bows, 1008B Oak Hill Road, Lafayette, CA 94549, 415-283-2299, 10:00 a.m.-4:00 p.m., 415-827-5540, evenings. Doll repair and doll clothes. Mail order.

Doll's Nest, 1020 Kenmore Boulevard, Akron, OH 44314, 216-753-2464. Doll making and repair supplies. Doll stands, wigs, eyes, eyelashes, shoes, accessories, tools, and books. Catalog.

Dolls Reborn, 3833 Lake Mary Center, Lake Mary, FL 32746, 407-333-0886, Mon.-Fri. 10:00 a.m.-5:00 p.m., Sat. 10:00 a.m.-3:00 p.m. Doll hospital, retail shop. Restoration, repair, handmade clothes, seminars. Eyes repaired and made movable, bisque heads, fingers and toes repaired, hair restyled, clothing restored.

Dollspart Supply Co., 46-50 54th Avenue, Maspeth, NY 11378, 718-361-1833, 9:00 a.m.-5:00 p.m., 800-336-DOLL outside New York; fax: 718-361-5833. Doll wigs, eyes, stands, bodies, clothing, and accessories. Doll-making kits, supplies, and tools. Mama double voices, pull-string talking unit, teddy bear eyes and noses. Books on dolls and teddy bears. Mail order. Catalog $3.

Dr. Re's Doll Clinic, Main Street, Elm City, NC 27822-0846, 919-236-3144, anytime. Dolls repaired, restored, and redressed. Supplies and classes. Porcelain dolls, kits, blanks.

Enchanted Doll House, P.O. Box 3001, Manchester Center, VT 05255, 802-362-3030 for orders, 802-362-3037 for customer service. Doll and teddy bear accessories, stands, display cases, glass domes, plastic covers. Acid-free paper for wrapping dolls. Books. Brochure.

Fabric Specialties, Glendolyn Alkas, 6623 San Pedro, San Antonio, TX

78216, 512-344-4885 or 512-344-0227, 8:30 a.m.-10:00 p.m.; fax: 512-344-8000. Paperweight eyes, doll bodies, French human hair wigs, vintage/antique lace, fabrics, and costuming supplies. Catalog $3.

Freda's Doll Repair & Supplies, 6204 Monterey Drive, Klamath Falls, OR 97603, 503-882-2204 8:00 a.m.-10:00 a.m. Wigs, eyes, shoes, hats, patterns, minor repairs. Oregon, northern California area. By appointment.

G. Schoepfer Inc., 138 West 31st Street, New York, NY 10001, 212-736-6934 or 212-736-6939, 9:30 a.m.-3:30 p.m.; fax: 212-736-6934. Glass and plastic eyes for dolls and other projects or restorations. Mail order worldwide. Send SASE and specify type of project to get list.

Grady Stewart, Expert China Restoration, 2019 Sansom Street, Philadelphia, PA 19103, 215-567-2888. Doll repair.

Hamilton Eye Warehouse, Box 450, Dept. K, Moorpark, CA 93021, 805-529-5900, 8:00 a.m.-6:00 p.m. Glass paperweight eyes, acrylic eyes, hollow blown glass eyes, all sizes, 2mm to 30mm. Mail order, telephone orders, trade shows. Catalog $1.

Happy Hearts, Route 1, Box 164, Lexington, MO 64067, 816-259-4422, 9:00 a.m.-5:00 p.m., 816-259-4706, evenings. Accessories for dolls. Buttons, lace, fabric, ribbons, feathers, ostrich plumes, hair combs, pocket watches, and more. Catalog $2. Worldwide mail order business.

J & H China Repairs, 8296 St. George Street, Vancouver, BC V5X 3C5, Canada, 604-321-1093, 9:00 a.m.-4:00 p.m. Restoration of dolls.

Joyce's Doll House of Parts, 20188 Williamson, Mt. Clemens, MI 48043, 313-791-0469, 8:00 a.m.-4:00 p.m. Replacement parts for dolls, including porcelain limbs for all-bisque and shoulder-head dolls, wigs, eyes, doll stands, glues, paints, porcelain for making replacement limbs, shoes, trims. Mail order worldwide.

Kandyland Dolls, 7600 Birch Avenue, P.O. Box 146, Grand Ronde, OR 97347, 503-879-5153, 9:00 a.m.-7:00 p.m. Doll restoration and repair, custom sewing. Will work on all types of dolls. Mail order.

Kaney Made Doll Shoes, 2171 1/2 East Colton Avenue, Mentone, CA 92359, 714-794-6771. Doll shoes available in several sizes; custom shoes made. Send SASE for color samples.

Kleinhans Restorations, T.A. Kleinhans, P.O. Box 93082, Rochester, NY 14692, 716-624-4685, 9:00 a.m.-8:00 p.m. Restoration of dolls. Mail order.

KSG, 2073 North Oxnard Boulevard, #112, Oxnard, CA 93030-2964, 805-487-6927, 8:00 a.m.-5:00 p.m. Doll stands. Mail order.

Ledgewood Studio, 6000 Ledgewood Drive, Dept. RTK 89, Forest Park, GA 30050, 404-361-6098, 10:00 a.m.-4:00 p.m. Dress patterns, fabrics, ribbons, trims for costuming antique dolls. Wholesale prices on quantity orders. Mail order service to North America and South America, Western Europe, New Zealand, and Australia. Catalog $2. Send double stamped SASE.

Les Bebe De Bea, 24302 West Warren, Dearborn Heights, MI 48127,

313-563-0775, Mon.-Wed., Fri. 10:00 a.m.-4:00 p.m., Thurs. 10:00 a.m.-7:00 p.m. Complete line of doll-making supplies, including composition bodies, glass eyes, bell porcelain, molds, and patterns. Doll repairs. Lessons in making reproduction dolls. Mail order.

Lyn Alexander Designs, P.O. Box 8341 K, Denver, CO 80201. Dress, hat, and shoe patterns for antique, reproduction, and cloth dolls. Books: *Pattern Designing for Dressmakers* and *Make Doll Shoes!*, Workbooks I & II. Mail order. Catalog $2.50.

Mary's Attic, Mary Lambeth, 2806 Regency Drive, Winston-Salem, NC 27106, 919-725-1533. Dolls and painted heads. Mail order.

McDowell Laboratories, Robert McDowell, Route 1, P.O. Box 15A, Aldie, VA 22001, 703-777-6644. Restoration of bisque, Parian, and porcelain doll heads; wooden limbs. Mail order worldwide.

Merrily Supply, 8542 Ranchito Avenue, Panorama City, CA 91402, 818-894-0637, 10:30 a.m.-4:00 p.m. Supplies and tools for making and repairing dolls and teddy bears. Mail order only. Catalog $2.

Monique Trading Corporation, 1369 Rollins Road, Burlingame, CA 94010, 415-347-3737, 800-621-4338, 8:30 a.m.-5:00 p.m.; fax: 415-347-7407. Doll supplies, wigs, shoes, clothes, acrylic and glass eyes, parts for doll making, and accessories. Worldwide.

Morgan's Collectibles, 831 SE 170th Drive, Portland, OR 97233, 503-252-3343, 8:00 a.m.-8:00 p.m. Restoration of dolls, papier-mâché toys. Doll restoration taught. Write for information. Mail order.

New York Doll Hospital, Inc., 787 Lexington Avenue, New York, NY 10021, 212-838-7527, 9:30 a.m.-6:00 p.m. Restoration of antique dolls and animals. Parts, doll clothes, wigs. Mail order.

Paradise Doll Part Supply, 576 Roberts Road, Paradise CA 95969, 916-877-1670, 9:00 a.m.-5:00 p.m. Porcelain arms and legs, sawdust body parts for antique dolls. Seeley distributor. Brochure.

Rivendell, Inc., 8209 Proctor Road, Painesville, OH 44077, 216-254-4088 or 216-946-9544 in Cleveland, Mon.-Thurs. 11:00 a.m.-7:00 p.m., Fri.-Sat. 10:00 a.m.-4:00 p.m. Wholesale and retail distributors of doll-making supplies, including porcelain molds, composition bodies, eyes, shoes, patterns, and costumes. Catalog.

Seeley's Ceramic Service, Inc., P.O. Box 669, Oneonta, NY 13820-0669, 607-433-1240, weekdays 8:00 a.m.-5:00 p.m.; fax: 607-432-2042. Doll-making supplies, parts, for porcelain dolls only, including paperweight eyes, molds, composition bodies, patterns, wigs, shoes, brushes, porcelain slip, tools, instruction books. Seminars. Mail order. "Catalog and Guide for Dollmakers," $6.

Ship's Treasures, P.O. Box 590-EM, Milton, MA 02186, 617-964-8010, anytime. Adjustable doll stands.

Sierra Studios, 37 West 222, Route 64, Suite 103, St. Charles, IL 60175, 708-683-2525. Restoration of doll's heads, china, bisque, Parian, and porcelain art objects. Mail order.

Vernal Restorations, 3625 Lyric Avenue, Wayzata, MN 55391, 612-471-0015, 612-438-6058 for answering service. Porcelain restoration and antique bisque doll restorations.

Viv's Ribbons & Laces, 212 Virginia Hills Drive, Martinez, CA 94553, 415-937-0909, Mon.-Fri. 9:00 a.m.-5:00 p.m. Ribbons, fabrics, straw, cotton laces, patterns for dolls of all sizes. Wholesale/retail. Mail order only. Catalog $3.50, $2 refunded with purchase.

Wonderful Things, P.O. Box 536, Van Brunt Station, Brooklyn, NY 11215, 718-965-4515, evenings, 10:00 p.m.-11:00 p.m. Dolls, bears, and related items repaired.

Yesteryears Museum, P.O. Box 609, Sandwich, MA 02563, 508-888-2788 (winter), 508-888-1711 (summer), Mon.-Sat. 10:00 a.m.-4:00 p.m. Doll hospital, collector's shop, and antique doll, toy, and miniature museum. Restoration of cloth, kid, and other dolls. No porcelain repairs. Mail order.

Helen Barglebaugh, 118-01 Sutter Avenue, Jamaica, NY 11420, 718-641-1220, Tues.-Sat. 9:00 a.m.-5:00 p.m. Eyelet kit for doll shoes or corsets, replacement eyelets, shoe buckles. Mail order.

E. Black, 6130 SW 12th Street, Miami, FL 33144, 305-266-0177, after 4:00 p.m. Doll restoration. composition, bisque, and china doll repair, restoration, restringing, replacement parts. Porcelain bisque and china reproduction parts. Authentic costuming. Mail order.

Sheryl Garcia, 11 North Beverly Avenue, Youngstown, OH 44515, 216-792-0549. Doll clothes, underwear, French dresses, bonnets. Underwear made to order to meet special requests.

L. Hulphers, 3153 West 110th Street, Inglewood, CA 90303, 213-678-1957, noon-9:00 p.m. Doll parts and supplies. Mail order.

Robert MacDowell, Oakwood, Aldie, VA 22201, 703-777-6644. Doll restoration. Mail order.

Doris Price, 4 North Point Road, Lincroft, NJ 07738, 201-842-2676 evenings. Doll repair and supplies, wigs, shoes, clothing. Display at Red Bank Antique Center, Bldg. 3, 226 West Front Street, Red Bank, NJ 07701, Fri.-Mon. afternoons or by appointment. Mail order.

Mary Radbill, 4512 Eden Street, Philadelphia, PA 19114, 215-632-4606, 9:00 a.m.-5:00 p.m. Doll supplies, including all products necessary to complete a doll or restore an antique doll. Wigs, eyes, paperweight eyes, shoes, stockings. Mail order only. Catalog $4.

Madeline Sansom, 5838 Huntington Avenue, Richmond, CA 94804. Old out-of-print crochet patterns for doll costumes. Mail order only. International. Catalog $1.

Books

How to Collect French Bébé Dolls, Mildred & Vernon Seeley, 1985 (HP Books, P.O. Box 5367, Tucson, AZ 85703).

How to Collect French Fashion Dolls, Mildred & Vernon Seeley, 1985 (HP Books, P.O. Box 5367, Tucson, AZ 85703).

Videotapes

Colemans on Doll Collecting, Dorothy, Elizabeth, and Evelyn Coleman (Concept Associates, 4809 Morgan Drive, Chevy Chase, MD 20815).
Jean Nordquist's Collectible Doll Video: Doll Painting Technique and Philosophy (Collectible Doll Company, 1421 North 34th, Seattle, WA 98103).

Fans

Most of the organizations for fan collectors are interested in electric fans. So be sure to determine which kind of fan--the hand-held ladies' fan or the commercial electric fan--is the subject of fan publications and clubs. Restorers are listed in these publications which can be found in *Kovels' Guide to Selling Your Antiques & Collectibles*.

Source

Fan Man, Kurt House, 4614 Travis, Dallas, TX 75205, 214-559-4440, 9:00 a.m.-6:00 p.m. Electric fan parts, rewinding service, reproduction antique fans. Catalog.
Light Ideas, 1037 Taft Street, Rockville, MD 20850, 301-424-LITE, Mon.-Sat. 10:00 a.m.-5:00 p.m., fax: 301-424-5791. Electric fan repair and parts. Mail order, store. Brochure.

Fireplace Equipment

An old fireplace had many pieces of equipment: a set of tools, fireback, andirons, coal basket, fender, and such aids as bellows or match holders.

All of these are considered collectibles and enjoy tremendous popularity. Some imagination is needed to repair these items. Look in your local phone book for firms that make iron fences or decorative metal pieces. Companies that replate metal often repair. See also Metals.

Sources

Authentic Lighting, 558 Grand Avenue, Englewood, NJ 07631, 201-568-7429, Mon.-Fri. 9:00 a.m.-5:00 p.m. Fireplace tools and equipment refinished.

The Brass Knob, 2311 18th Street NW, Washington, DC 20009, 202-332-3370, 10:30 a.m.-6:00 p.m. Old fireplace mantels and equipment sold and restored. Brochure.

Fine Finishes, Kenneth Miltner, Route 176, Box 248, Brooksville, ME 04617, 207-326-4545, 8:30 a.m.-5:00 p.m. Fireplace hardware restored. Brass refinishing, antiquing, polishing, and lacquering; pewter and copperware restored.

Lemee's Fireplace Equipment, 815 Bedford Street, Bridgewater, MA 02324, 508-697-2672, Mon.-Sat. 9:00 a.m.-5:00 p.m. Fireplace equipment, firebacks, dutch oven doors, cleanout doors, bellows, cranes, brackets, grates, cast-iron utensils, accessories.

New England Firebacks, P.O. Box 162, Woodbury, CT 06798, 203-263-4328, anytime. Reproduction cast-iron firebacks. Mail order. Brochure. Extra charge for shipping west of Mississippi. Showroom at Woodbury Blacksmith & Forge Co., 161 Main Street South, Woodbury, CT, Mon.-Fri. 9:00 a.m.-5:00 p.m., or by appointment.

Pine & Palette Studio, 63 Ventura Drive, Danielson, CT 06239, 203-774-5058, 9:00 a.m.-9:00 p.m. Antique bellows repair, leather replacement, refinishing. Handcrafted fireplace bellows with reproductions of designs found on bellows of the 1800s. Brochure.

Thomas Loose, Blacksmith-Whitesmith, Route 2, Box 2410, Leesport, PA 19533, 215-926-4849 or 215-926-4849, 8:00 a.m.-5:00 p.m. Hand-forged iron for home and hearth. Reproduction hearth cooking utensils. Send double stamped SASE for information. Mail order.

Floorcloths

The 18th-century American home was more likely to have a heavy, painted sailcloth rug, called a floorcloth, than any type of fabric covering used today. Floorcloths were painted with geometric borders, flowers, or patterns that resembled marble, carpet, or wood floors. Only small pieces of original canvas floorcloths have survived, but it is possible to buy a modern reproduction of an old floorcloth.

Good & Co. Floorclothmakers, P.O. Box 497, Dublin, NH 03444, 603-672-0490, 10:00 a.m.-5:30 p.m., 603-563-8021 evenings. Custom-stenciled and hand-painted floorcloths, hall and stair runners. Mail offer through P.O. Box 497. Retail shop at Salzburg Square, Route 101, Amherst, NH. Catalog $2.

Handpainted House, 2272 West 29th Place, Los Angeles, CA 90018, 213-733-5459, anytime, leave message. Floorcloths, murals, painted and stained floors. Design done from photos of fabrics, book illus-trations, or clippings. Restoration.

Olde Virginea Floorcloth & Trading Co., P.O. Box 3305, Portsmouth, VA 23701, 804-488-7299, Mon.-Fri. 8:00 a.m.-noon. Hand-painted canvas floorcloths, 18th-century to contemporary designs. Preprimed canvas and supplies. Free brochure. Catalog $4 in U.S., $5 outside.

Folk Art

There is an ongoing argument among experts over what is folk art. For the purposes of this book, folk art is whatever is called that by some experts. It may have been made in the 18th, 19th, or 20th century. It may be naive art by an untrained artist, or an old advertisement, or carnival figure. This is one collecting field with few hard and fast rules of quality, condition, and age. Beauty is in the eye of the beholder, and what seems primitive to one may be considered superior by another. Some collectors prefer pieces with worn paint and rough wooden edges; others want pristine paint. Don't do any restoration unless the piece is so badly damaged that it would be useless without restoration. If you think your folk art piece is of value, be sure to ask an expert before any work is done.

Restoration should be done by a craftsman in the appropriate field. A painted figure might be restored by a carousel-figure expert or a furniture-restoration firm. Paper, glass, or metal pieces require other specialists. We once had a tin chimney replaced on a folk art house by the man putting metal heat ducts in our room addition, and painted by the house painter who worked on the walls.

Sources

Copper House, Route 4, R.F.D. 1, Epsom, NH 03234, 603-736-9798. Weathervane parts and repair. Sat. noon-5:00 p.m., Sun. 10:00 a.m.-5:00 p.m., or by appointment or mail order. Catalog $2.

G. Schoepfer Inc., 138 West 31st Street, New York, NY 10001, 212-736-6939 or 212-736-6934, Mon.-Fri. 9:30 a.m.-3:30 p.m.; fax: 212-736-6934. Eyes for dolls, teddy bears, toys, carousel horses, decoys, ceramic figures, taxidermy, etc. Over 3 million in stock. Eyes sent worldwide. Send measurements in millimeters and SASE for reply. Mail order. Brochure and price list.

Ruth S. Szalasny, 3048 Belknap Road, Eden, NY 14057, 716-992-9102, 10:30 a.m.-8:00 p.m. Patterns for theorem painting. Instruction booklet: "Theorem Painting for Beginners." Mail order only.

Furniture

Refinishing and restoring furniture has been discussed in dozens of books. For precise information on what to do, how to do it, and what finishes are best, we suggest that you go to your local hardware or paint store or library and study the products, books, and methods. Local experts are listed in the Yellow Pages of your telephone book. We have listed a few of the major books and included sources for many of the materials. You may find additional sources in the hardware section.

The general rule for refinishing an antique is less is better. Never strip a piece that can be restored. Never remove a painted surface that can be saved. If you want furniture with a natural wood finish, don't buy an antique with an original finish that was painted. For many years collectors used a polish made with boiled linseed oil. This finish darkens with age and cannot be removed. Certain early paints made with buttermilk, blood, and other pigments are almost impossible to remove from wood pores. Many pieces of furniture are made of a variety of woods, so stripping and refinishing may result in a hodgepodge of colors.

Our ancestors seem to have delighted in surrounding themselves with chairs. Inventories of homes from the late 18th century list over a dozen chairs even in small bedrooms. We often wonder how they found room for all of them. Whatever their reason, the chair is still one of the most popular pieces of furniture in a home. An odd chair from a different period can often be placed in a room as a special accent.

Refinishing and restoring chairs can be handled by most amateurs. Recaning, upholstering, and other more complicated parts of refinishing may require a few special lessons, but many adult education centers and schools offer this type of instruction. Libraries are filled with books that furnish detailed refinishing information. Most of these services are available through local decorating shops or services. Look in the Yellow Pages under "Caning," "Furniture Repairing & Refinishing," and "Upholsterers."

Sometimes a wooden chair needs minor "tightening." The glue has dried and the parts wobble. Special products found in hardware stores can solve this problem. Just squirt a bit of the special glue into the loose joints. If the parts are very loose, you may have to take the arm or leg off the chair, clean the pegs or posts and holes, and reglue them with modern wood glue.

Some people hesitate to buy antique beds because they worry about technical problems, such as special mattress sizes and special restoration techniques. The problems can be solved in various ways:

1. Measure an antique bed carefully before buying it. Make sure the bed is not too high for your ceiling, because surgery on bedposts reduces the bed's value.

2. Rope "springs" are satisfactory, but they must be properly laced and tightened periodically. A box spring can also be used if it is supported by metal brackets. Standard brackets can be screwed to the frame, but the best solution is to have six or eight hanging supports custom made by an ornamental ironworker. They do not harm the frame or reduce the value of the bed. If the box spring combined with a standard mattress is too high,

a thinner foam-rubber mattress can be substituted.

3. Odd-sized mattresses and box springs can be custom-made in most major cities or ordered by mail.

4. Antique-style bed hangings and rope springs are also available.

It is best to be sure your bed is one of the standard sizes in use today if you plan to use easily available sheets and bedspreads. Brass beds require special care; restoration for these is discussed in the section on Metals.

Sources

Abend Metal Repair, Delavan Center, 501 West Fayette Street, Syracuse, NY 13204, 315-478-2749, Mon.-Fri. 9:00 a.m.-5:30 p.m.; answering machine other times. Repair and restoration of aluminum, brass, bronze, cast iron, steel, stainless steel, or white metal. Custom welding, polishing, patina restoration, cast reproductions.

Abercrombie & Co., 9159A Brookville Road, Silver Spring, MD 20910, 301-585-2385, weekdays 9:00 a.m.-5:00 p.m., Sat. 9.00 a.m.-1:00 p.m. Metal refinishing. Brass beds repaired, polished, and lacquered.

Able to Cane, 67 Main Street, P.O. Box 429, Warren, ME 04864, 207-273-3747, 9:00 a.m.-5:00 p.m. Chair seating. Natural and fiber rush, splint, cane, and Shaker tape seating. Wicker repair. Serving Northeastern U.S. Mail order nationwide. Catalog.

Alexandria Wood Joinery, George & Judy Whittaker, Plumer Hill Road, P.O. Box 92, Alexandria, NH 03222, 603-744-8243, 10:00 a.m.-5:00 p.m. Furniture repair, cane chair seats, Shaker tape, fiber rush, custom furniture, reproductions. Serving New England.

Anderson-Williams House, Joseph Williams, 47 Mohican Road, Cornfield Point, Old Saybrook, CT 06475, 203-388-2587, 8:00 a.m.-8:00 p.m. Seat weaving, using natural materials, such as rush, cane, splint, and Shaker listing (woven tape). Serving the New England area, New York, New Jersey, and Pennsylvania.

Antique Furniture Workroom, Inc., 225 East 24th Street, New York, NY 10010, 212-683-0551, 8:00 a.m.-4:00 p.m.; fax: 212-696-1561. Restoration, French polishing.

Armor Products, P.O. Box 445, East Northport, NY 11731, 516-462-6228, 9:00 a.m.-5:00 p.m. Specialty hardware for furniture. Tools and finishing supplies.

Artistic Finishers East, Wade Denson, 2350 East Javelina Avenue, Mesa, AZ 85204, 602-892-6348, 9:00 a.m.-5:00 p.m.; fax: 602-892-3576. Antique wood furniture restoration and conservation. Touch-ups, repairs, and refinishing.

Barap Specialties, 835 Bellows, Frankfort, MI 49635, 616-352-9863, 8:30 a.m.-5:00 p.m. Decorative head nails, drawer slides, hardware, upholstering tools, and supplies.

Bedpost, Inc., 32 South High Street, East Bangor, PA 18013,

215-588-4667 or 215-588-3824, 8:00 a.m.-4:00 p.m. weekdays. Replacement parts for brass or iron beds. Scroll bending. Catalog.

Bob Morgan Woodworking Supplies, 1123 Bardstown Road, Louisville, KY 40204, 502-456-2545. Veneers, decorative inlays, embossed wood moldings, tools, hardwood finishes. Catalog.

Cambro Enterprises, 109 First Avenue North, Franklin, TN 37064, 615-790-8873, 9:00 a.m.-5:00 p.m., 615-790-9664. Stripping, repairing, and restoring furniture. Send SASE for information, order form for Cambro furniture cleaner.

Cane & Basket Supply Company, 1238 South Cochran Avenue, Los Angeles, CA 90019, 213-939-9644, 8:30 a.m.-5:00 p.m., Mon.-Fri. fax: 213-939-7237. Pressed fiber replacement seats and chair caning supplies. Catalog.

Caning Shop, 926 Gilman Street, Berkeley, CA 94710, 415-527-5010, 800-544-3373, Tues.-Fri. 10:00 a.m.-6:00 p.m., Sat. 10:00 a.m.-2:00 p.m. Repairing woven furniture; chair caning supplies and pressed fiber seats. Catalog $1, refundable with order.

Chair Shop, Lawrence Nelson, 101 South Street, Chagrin Falls, OH 44022, 216-247-2126. Furniture restoration and repair. Cane, rush, splint weaving. Danish cord, flat-oval reed weaving. Old finishes restored, patio furniture relaced.

CHILIAD, Susan L. Wilson, Principal, 6 Ottawa Street, Toronto, ON M4T 2B6, Canada, 416-928-0659, evenings. Furniture conservation, collection assessment, and planning for preserving collection. Ontario and Northeastern U.S.

Clark Manufacturing Company, Dorothy Clark, 1301 Southwind Drive, Raymore, MO 64083, 816-331-6851, leave message on answering machine. Custom-made pierced tins for pie safes, kitchen cabinets, etc. Nine designs available. Orders sent UPS within 2 weeks. Brochure.

The Clayton Store, Sue Connell, Star Route, Southfield, MA 01259, 413-229-2621, 9:00 a.m.-5:00 p.m. Restoration of painted and decorated furniture. "Smalls" repaired. Will travel.

Cohasset Colonials, 648JX Ship Street, Cohasset, MA 02025, 617-383-0110, 8:00 a.m.-4:30 p.m. Hand-tied cotton canopies, fabrics, trundle mattresses. Catalog.

Country Accents, P.O. Box 437, Montoursville, PA 17754, 717-478-4127, 9:00 a.m.-4:00 p.m., Mon.-Fri. Pierced-tin panels, custom sizes, for kitchen cabinets. Pie safe kits, tin piercing kits and patterns. Catalog $5; with set of metal sample swatches $15.95.

Derby Desk Company, 140 Tremont Street, Brighton, MA 02135, 617-787-2707, Mon.-Sat. 10:30 a.m.-5:00 p.m. Restores desks made between 1860 and 1890. Send photo.

DHM Cabinetmakers, P.O. Box 173, Route 4, Floyd, VA 24091, 703-745-3875, 8:30 a.m.-4:30 p.m.; fax: 703-745-3875. Repair of antique furniture.

Farmerstown Furniture, 3155 S.R. 557, Dept. K, Baltic, OH 43804, 216-893-2464, Mon., Tues., Thurs., Fri. 8:30 a.m.-4:30 p.m., Wed.

& Sat. 8:30 a.m.-11:30 p.m. Hardware for Morris chairs, Hoosier cabinets, iceboxes, etc. Brass, iron bed parts, pressed fiber seats, oak highchair trays, replacement runners and curved seats for rockers, spool cabinet decals, brass and wood specialty items. Catalog $2.

Fine Finishes, Kenneth Miltner, Route 176, Box 248, Brooksville, ME 04617, 207-326-4545, 8:30 a.m.-4:00 p.m. Brass beds refinished, repaired, restored.

George G. Whitmore Co., Inc., 311 Farm Hill Road, Middletown, CT 06457, 203-346-3492, Mon.-Fri. 9:00 a.m.-4:00 p.m. Restoration. Serving the New England area.

GST Designs, 3 Russell Road, Stratford, CT 06497, 203-375-3807, 8:00 a.m.-8:00 p.m. Furniture repair and custom turnings. Match and repair wood-turned antiques, such as chairs and balusters. Flyer available.

Isabel Brass & Metal Furniture, 200 Lexington Avenue, New York, NY 10016, 212-689-3307, 800-221-8523; fax: 212-684-7132. Brass beds restored and repaired. Custom-made beds. Mail order. Catalog.

J.M. Gray, Inc., 509 West Fayette Street, Syracuse, NY 13204, 315-476-1003, 9:00 a.m.-5:00 p.m., 315-475-9498, evenings. Wood and wrought iron repair and reproduction. Missing parts replaced. Serving Northeastern U.S. Call first.

Jack's Upholstery & Caning Supplies, 52 Shell Court, Oswego, IL 60543, 312-554-1045, Mon.-Fri. 8:00 a.m.-5:00 p.m., Sat. 8:00 a.m.-noon. Upholstery and caning supplies for chairs. Mail order. Catalog $2, refundable with first purchase.

Julius Lowy Frame and Restoring Co., 28 West End Avenue, New York, NY 10023, 212-586-2050 or 212-861-8585, 8:30 a.m.-5:00 p.m.; fax: 212-489-1948. Gilded furniture restored. Brochure.

Levine's Restorations, 4801 7th Street North, Arlington, VA 22203, 703-525-4009, 9:00 a.m.-6:00 p.m. Furniture restoration, 100-mile radius of shop.

Marlborough Cottage Arts & Interiors, Jeff Von-Er, SR 70, Box 144, New Marlborough, MA 01230, 413-229-2170, weekdays 8:00 a.m.-8:00 p.m. Gold leaf restoration, fancy paint finishes, conservation work done on frames, mirrors, furniture, and interiors.

Medusa, 236 Prospect Street, Cambridge, MA 02139, 617-776-6667, 9:00 a.m.-5:00 p.m. Furniture painted with unique finishes. Faux marbre, faux bois, stencils, trompe l'oeil, glazes.

Meeting House Furniture Restoration, John T. Schechtman, 11 Waterman Hill, Queechee, VT 05059, 802-295-1309, 8:00 a.m.-9:00 p.m. Conservation, restoration, repair, and refinishing of wooden heirlooms and furniture. Specializing in replication of missing carvings, replacement of missing veneers and inlays. Can reproduce pieces of furniture to complete a set. House calls throughout Eastern U.S.

Nininger & Co., Gallery, 4 Main Street (Route 6 at Route 47), Woodbury, CT 06798, 203-266-4661, 10:30 a.m.-5:00 p.m., closed Tues. Antique restoration and custom furniture. Brochure.

Original Woodworks, 360 North Main, Stillwater, MN 55082,

612-430-3622. Restoration of antique furniture and architectural elements. Mirror resilvering. Classes, tools, and supplies. Catalog $3.

Pat's Etcetera Company, Inc. (PECO), P.O. Box 777, 810 East First Street, Smithville, TX 78957, 512-237-3600, Mon.-Fri. 10:00 a.m.-3:00 p.m. Pressed fiber replacement chair seats. Pressed from 1890s dies, trimmed to fit. Curved glass for china cabinets. Mail order. Brochure.

Paxton Hardware Ltd., P.O. Box 256, 7818 Bradshaw Road, Upper Falls, MD 21156, 301-592-8505, Mon.-Fri. 9:00 a.m.-5:00 p.m.; fax: 301-592-2224. Cane, pulls, knobs, locks, hinges, casters, supports, and other furniture hardware. Mail order. Mini catalog free. Complete 75-page catalog $4.

Period Furniture Hardware Co. Inc., 123 Charles Street, P.O. Box 314, Charles Street Station, Boston, MA 02114, 617-227-0758, 8:30 a.m.-5:00 p.m. Reproduction brass furniture hardware, cabinet and door hardware. Mail order. Catalog $4.50.

Phyllis Kennedy Restoration Hardware, 9256 Holyoke Court, Indianapolis, IN 46268, 317-872-6366, 9:00 a.m.-6:00 p.m. Restoration hardware for antique furniture. Mail order. Catalog $2.

R. Wagner Company, 1231 NW Hoyt, Studio 401, Portland, OR 97209, 503-224-7036, 9:00 a.m.-5:00 p.m.; fax: 503-274-1057. Painted finishes, wall glazing, trompe l'oeil, stenciling, gilding. Seminars in painted finishes and painted furniture.

R. Wayne Reynolds, Ltd., R. Wayne Reynolds, 3618 Falls Road, Baltimore, MD 21211, 301-467-1800, Mon.-Fri. 9:00 a.m.-5:00 p.m. Conservation of gold leaf frames and furniture. Mail order.

R.G. Brown & Associates, Ron Brown, 7530 East Hinsdale Place, Englewood, CO 80112, 303-721-6514, 9:00 a.m.-6:00 p.m. Embossed wood carvings, decorative ornaments, and moldings, designs from the 1880s-1960s. Mail order. Catalog $4.

The Re-Store, Jim Johnson and Teri Browning, Route 25 at 25A, Wentworth, NH 03282, 603-764-9395, 10:00 a.m.-5:00 p.m. Antiques and furniture restored and repaired. Restoration of roll-top desks. Free on-site estimates. New England area. Brochure.

Regency Restorations, Ltd., 220 West 19th Street, Floor 9, New York, NY 10011, 212-989-0780, Mon.-Fri. 8:30 a.m.-5:00 p.m. Restoration, preservation of furniture, veneering, gilding, painted finishes, inlay, carving, polishing, and turning. Custom reproductions. Serving greater New York City area.

Renaissance Restorations, Ltd., Wilmington, VT 05363, 802-464-2343, 7:00 a.m.-6:00 p.m. Antique furniture repair, specializing in Shaker, early American, and European furniture. No mail order.

Renovator's Supply, 149 Northfield Road, Millers Falls, MD 01349, 413-659-3152 Hardware and leather replacement seats. Catalog.

Restore-it Supply Co., P.O. Box 10600, White Bear Lake, MN 55110, 612-429-2222, Thurs.-Sat. noon-5:00 p.m. Restoration products, including cane, rush, decals, handles, pulls, casters, veneers, tools, and hard-to-find items. Serving five-state area. Catalog $3.

Restorers of America, R.D. 4, Box 382, Wynantskill, NY 12189, 518-283-5317, Mon.-Fri. 9:00 a.m.-5:00 p.m.; fax: 518-283-5380. Furniture restoration and repair, done in your home. Serving the Albany-Schenectady-Troy area.

Sack Conservation Co., Inc., 15 East 57th Street, New York, NY 10022, 212-753-6069, Mon.-Fri. 9:30 a.m.-5:00 p.m.; fax: 212-753-9252. Furniture conservation and restoration of 17th-, 18th-, and early 19th-century American furniture. No mail order service.

Sawdust Room, P.O. Box 327, Stevesville, MI 49127, 616-429-5338, 9:00 a.m.-9:00 p.m. Canopy beds, spinning wheels, and other furniture and antiques repaired. Custom wood products, cylindrical lathe duplications, chair rungs, rockers, spokes. Mail order.

Shaker Shops West, P.O. Box 1028, Concord, MA 01742, 415-669-7256, 11:00 a.m.-5:00 p.m.; fax: 415-669-7327. Replacement Shaker chair seat tape. Reproductions of Shaker furniture, woodenware, and crafts. Reseating of Shaker or similar chairs. Mail order. Catalog $2.50.

Shaker Workshops, P.O. Box 1028, Concord, MA 01742, 617-646-8985, Mon.-Sat. 9:30 a.m.-5:00 p.m.; fax: 617-648-8217. Replacement Shaker chair seat tape, parts for Mt. Lebanon Shaker rockers, repairs and reweaving for original Shaker furniture, paints and stains. Mail order worldwide. Catalog $1.

Sleep Tite Mattress Company, 8 Moore Street, Middletown, OH 45042, 513-422-9206, 8:00 a.m.-5:00 p.m. Custom-made mattresses and box springs for odd-sized and antique beds. Foam mattresses, institutional bedding, mattresses for any specialty purpose. Mail order.

Society of Gilders, 42 Maple Place, Nutley, NJ 07110, 201-667-5251. List of gilders; lectures, workshops, classes. Newsletter.

Stanton Furniture Restoration Supply, Box 640003, El Paso, TX 79904-0003, 915-755-0763, Mon.-Fri. 9:30 a.m.-5:00 p.m., Sat. 9:30 a.m.-noon. Antique and reproduction parts, glass ball feet, brass labels. Matching service for furniture parts. Mail order.

Studio Workshop, Ltd., 22 Bushy Hill Road, Simsbury, CT 06070, 203-658-6374, 8:00 a.m.-6:00 p.m. Restoration of furniture, specializing in turn-of-the-century.

Thomas H. Kramer, Inc., 805 Depot Street, Commerce Park, Columbus, IN 47201, 812-379-4097 or 812-342-3443, Mon.-Sat. 10:00 a.m.-5:00 p.m. Wooden turned knobs, feet, legs. Porcelain, brass knobs. Catalog.

Timothy G. Riordan Inc., 423 West 55th Street, New York, NY 10019, 212-581-3033, Mon.-Sat. 10:00 a.m.-8:00 p.m. Antique furniture restoration and sales. On-site French polishing in tristate area.

Tromploy Inc., 400 Lafayette Street, New York, NY 10003, 212-420-1639, 10:00 a.m.-5:00 p.m. All types of faux finishes and murals for furniture. Trompe l'oeil, faux marbre, faux bois, and stencils. Mail order. Murals can be done in studio and mailed anywhere.

William Hunrath Company, 153 East 57th Street, New York, NY 10022,

212-758-0780, Mon.-Fri. 9:00 a.m.-5:30 p.m., Sat. 9:00 a.m.-4:00 p.m. Furniture hardware, pulls, knobs, fasteners; cabinet hardware. Mail and phone orders. Flyers available.

Wise Company, 6503 St. Claude Avenue, P.O. Box 118, Arabi, LA 70032, 504-277-7551, 9:00 a.m.-5:00 p.m. Reproduction hardware for antique furniture, including keys, pulls, hinges, passageway sets. Refinishing products, chair cane and wooden parts. Mail order, shop sales, wholesale and retail. Catalog.

Wood & Leather Craft, H.C.R. 3, Box 9, Callicoon, NY 12723, 914-887-4241, 8:00 a.m.-6:00 p.m. Leather tabletops, gold-tooled, period designs. Trace pattern for leather top on brown paper and send with exact measurements of area to be covered. Will send price quote and leather samples with gold tooling by return mail.

Wood Finishing Supply Co., Inc., 100 Throop Street, Palmyra, NY 14522, 315-986-4517, 9:00 a.m.-5:00 p.m. Finishing supplies, related items. Reproduction brass hardware, gold leaf and gilding supplies, books.

The Woodworkers' Store, 21801 Industrial Boulevard, Rogers, MN 55374-9514, 612-428-2899, customer service, 612-428-2199, credit card orders, Mon.-Fri. 8:00 a.m.-8:00 p.m. Supplies, hardware, tools. Furniture hardware and trim, wood parts, cane and leather seating supplies, veneers, wood products, tools, books. Catalog.

Y & J Furniture Co., P.O. Box 1361, 1612 East Geer Street, Durham, NC 27702, 919-682-6131, 8:00 a.m.-5:30 p.m. Restoration, repairing, refinishing, and reupholstering. Serving the North Carolina-East Coast area. No mail order.

Randy Armstrong, Box 85, Riverside Road, Bluff City, TN 37618, 615-538-7686, 8:00 a.m.-5:00 p.m. Furniture restoration, refinishing, caning, weaving, veneering. Parts replaced, mirrors resilvered, metal beds refinished. Veneer repaired. Will pick up pieces. Serving eastern Tennessee, southwest Virginia.

Manton Bancroft, Box 236, Windham, CT 06280, 203-456-1530. Restoration of fine American and English furniture, structural repair and conservation of original or desirable old finish, inlays, carvings, veneer. Brochure.

Deborah Bigelow, 177 Grand Street, Newburgh, NY 12550, 914-561-6011, anytime. Furniture and gilt decorative arts conservation.

Joseph Biunno, 129 West 29th Street, New York, NY 10001, 212-629-5630 or 212-629-5636, 9:00 a.m.-5:00 p.m.; fax: 212-268-4577. Furniture restoration and repair. French polishing, wood turning, hand carving, gilding, and metalwork. Replacement keys and locks.

Richard Blaschke, 670 Lake Avenue, Bristol, CT 06010, 203-584-2566. Curved glass for china cabinets. Mail order.

Ronald DuCharme, 742 Charlton Road, Ballston Lake, NY 12188, 518-399-1246, 5:00 p.m.-8:00 p.m. Antique furniture conservation and restoration, gold leaf repaired and releafed, French polishing.

Conservation of gilded objects, polychrome wooden objects, and frames. Reproduction of missing elements.

Giordano Grazzini, 86 Regan Road, Ridgefield, CT 06877, 203-431-8726, 8:30 a.m.-5:30 p.m. Restoration of antique furniture, specializing in restoration of carving and gold leafing.

R. Bruce Hamilton, 551 Main Street, P.O Box 587, West Newbury, MA 01985, 508-363-2638 or 508-729-1569, Tues.-Fri. 8:00 a.m.-5:00 p.m. Restoration of furniture and wood finishes, French polish, leather and cloth surfaces replaced, carving, duplication of missing parts. Tray and box stands made to order.

Kenneth R. Hopkins, 3001 Monta Vista, Olympia, WA 98501, 206-943-1118, anytime. Furniture restoration. Stenciling, reproductions. Mail order.

M.D. King, 403 East Montgomery , Knoxville, IA 50138, 515-842-6394, 8:00 a.m.-10:00 p.m. Curved glass for china cabinets and secretaries.

Susan Riley, 1 Ireland Street, West Chesterfield, MA 01084, 413-296-4061, 9:00 a.m.-5:00 p.m. answering machine, 5:00 p.m.-7:00 p.m. in person. Seat weaving, specializing in natural rush. Chairs reglued. Serving Northeastern U.S.

Mario Rodriguez, Cabinetmaker, 419 Manhattan Avenue, Brooklyn, NY 11222, 718-387-6685, 8:00 a.m.-4:00 p.m. Restoration, replacement parts, moldings, bun feet, knobs, leaves for tables. Brochure $3.50.

Floyd J. Rosini, Route 22 North, Millerton, NY 12546, 518-789-3582, 8:00 a.m.-4:30 p.m.; fax: 518-789-6386. Period furniture restoration and conservation. Distributor of Rosini's Rejuvenator, Briwax, and Simichrome Polish. Mail order. Brochure.

Dr. Michael A. Taras, 5 South Craggmore Drive, Salem, SC 29676, 803-944-0655 after 5:00 p.m., 803-656-2432 daytime. Identification of wood.

William Therry, Furniture Conservation Laboratory, Unionville, PA 19375, 215-347-1684, 8:00 a.m.-6:00 p.m. Period furniture conservation.

Regina Wenzek, 2966 Briggs Avenue, Bronx, NY 10458, 212-733-5040, 9:00 a.m.-5:00 p.m. Specializing in restoration of Oriental lacquer, painted furniture, and gold leaf. By appointment only.

Robert Whitley, Laurel Road, Bucks County, Solebury, PA 18963, 215-297-8452, 8:00 a.m.-11:30 a.m., 1:30 p.m.-4:00 p.m. Furniture restoration, repairing, and refinishing. Veneer, inlay work, and carving. Old finish preservation.

Books and Leaflets

Art of Painted Finish for Furniture & Decoration, Isabel O'Neil, 1971 (William Morrow & Co., NY).

Wicker Furniture:Restoring & Collecting, Richard Saunders, 1990 (Crown Publishers, NY).

Complete Book of Furniture Repair & Refinishing, Ralph Parsons Kinney, 1981 (Charles Scribner's Sons, NY).

Complete Book of Furniture Restoration, Tristan Salazar, 1982 (St. Martin's Press, NY).

Conservation and Restoration of Antique Furniture, Stan Learoyd, 1983 (Sterling Publishing Co., NY).

Early American Decoration, Esther Stevens Brazer, 1961 (Pond-Ekberg Company, Springfield, MS).

Emyl Jenkins' Appraisal Book, Emyl Jenkins, 1989 (Crown Publishers, NY).

Furniture Care and Conservation, Robert F. McGiffin, Jr., 1983 (AASLH, 172 Second Avenue North, Suite 102, Nashville, TN 37201).

How to Gold Leaf Antiques and Other Art Objects, Donald L. Chambers, 1973 (Crown Publishers, NY).

Keeping It All Together, Marc A. Williams, 1988 (Ohio Antique Review, Inc., 12 East Stafford Avenue, Worthington, OH 43085).

Knock on Wood, Bruce E. Johnson, 1984 (G.P. Putnam's Sons, NY).

Manual of Traditional Wood Carving, Paul N. Hasluck, 1977 (Dover Publications, NY).

Preserving Your Investment, Marc A. Williams, 1983 (Furniture Conservation Services, 572 Washington Street, Haverhill, MA 01830).

Windsor Chairmaking, Michael Dunbar, 1976 (Hastings House Publishers, NY).

Wood Polishing and Finishing Techniques, Aidan Walker, 1985 (Little, Brown & Co., Boston).

Woodframe Furniture Restoration, Alan Smith, 1985 (Little, Brown & Co., Boston).

How-to Guide, leaflet, Savogran Company (259 Lenox Street, Norwood, MA 02062).

Videotapes

Refinishing Furniture with Bob Flexner (Taunton Press, 63 South Main Street, Newtown, CT 06470).

Repairing Furniture with Bob Flexner (Taunton Press, 63 South Main Street, Newtown, CT 06470).

Traditional Gilding & Contemporary Metallics (Art Essentials of New York, 3 Cross Street, Suffern, NY 10901).

Glass

Glass collecting covers many glass types, including stained glass, bottles, paperweights, cameo glass, art glass, carnival glass, and such 20th-century ware as Heisey, Fenton, Paden City, Tiffin, Depression glass, and more. A new glass-collecting area called "modern collectibles" includes new pieces such as Pairpoint cup plates or artist-made free-form figures.

Many glass replacement parts for doors and windows are included in this chapter. Reproductions of many of the glass products can be found, so be cautious when you buy. Publications and price guides often list the well-known reproductions. Fake glass marks are often seen, as it is simple to acid-stamp, etch, or sandblast a name on a less desirable piece of glass to raise the value of it for the unsuspecting.

Glass should never be kept in a sunny window. Old glass (before 1900) was made of a slightly different mixture and may turn colors. Any glass can magnify the sun and cause scorch marks on furniture or carpets, or even start a fire.

Chipped glass can be ground down. A local glass-repair shop can be located through the Yellow Pages. New epoxy mixtures can be used to make repairs on glass that are almost impossible to detect without the use of a black light. This type of repair is expensive and only a few restorers offer the service. Any glass can be polished, including the insides of small-necked bottles. There is a danger of breakage and it is a very specialized job. Stained glass can be cleaned and restored. Look for a restorer in the Yellow Pages under "Glass, Stained & Leaded." See also the section on matching services in *Kovels' Guide to Selling Your Antiques & Collectibles.*

Sources

A. Ludwig Klein & Son, Inc., P.O. Box 145, Dept. 13, Harleysville, PA

19438, 215-256-9004, Tues.-Fri. 10:00 a.m.-5:00 p.m., Sat. 10:00 a.m.-2:00 p.m. Repair and restoration, missing parts resculpted. Mail photo of object and blank audiocassette tape; will send instructions on how to repair glass yourself. Book, *Repairing and Restoring China and Glass* by William Karl Klein. Brochure available.

Atlas Minerals & Chemicals, Inc., Farmington Road, Mertztown, PA 19539, 215-682-7171, 8:00 a.m.-4:30 p.m.; fax: 215-682-9200. Master Mending Kit includes products and instructions for making repairs on china, porcelain, pottery, glass. Brochure and price list.

Backstrom Stained Glass & Antiques, 71 Airline Road, P.O. Box 2311, Columbus, MS 39704, 601-329-1254, Mon.-Fri. 8:00 a.m.-noon, 1:00 p.m.-5:00 p.m., Sat. 9:00 a.m.-noon. Stained, etched, beveled glass, tools, supplies. Repairs, custom orders, classes. Old glass repaired.

Bevel-Rite Manufacturing Co., 3434 Highway 9, Freehold, NJ 07728, 201-462-8462, 9:00 a.m.-5:00 p.m.; fax: 201-409-6601. Bevelers of glass, mirrors, tabletops, and special shapes. Custom work.

Blue Colt Collectibles, P.O. Box 154, Marietta, OH 45750, 614-373-8677, anytime. Chrome-plated tops for glass saltshakers. Imperial, Cambridge, Fostoria. Mail order worldwide.

Butterfly Shoppe, 637 Livernois, Ferndale, MI 48220, 313-541-2858, Mon.-Wed. 10:30 a.m.-4:00 p.m., Thurs. until 7:00 p.m. Repair and restoration of glass. Chips removed from goblets. Will repair everything except wood.

Castle's Fair, Lawrence and Sara Castle, 885 Taylor Avenue, Ogden, UT 84404-5270, 801-393-8131, before noon or after 8:00 p.m. Antique glass restoration, specializing in marbles, paperweights, and bottles. Chips removed from glasses and vases, bottles polished inside and out, fractures in paperweights and marbles healed. Custom-made jewelry from broken antique glass. Mail order only.

Crystal Cave, 1141 Central Avenue, Wilmette, IL 60091, 312-251-1160, Mon.-Sat. 9:00 a.m.-5:00 p.m., fax: 312-251-1172. Glass restoration and engraving. Contact before sending item.

Crystal Mountain Prisms, P.O. Box 31, Westfield, NY 14787, 716-326-3676, anytime. Replacement glass prisms for chandeliers and lamps. Glass chains, Czechoslovakian cut balls, pendalogues, bobeches. Mail order only.

Crystal Workshop, Edward D. Poore, P.O. Box 475, 10 Eleanor Avenue, Sagamore, MA 02561, 508-888-1621, 8:00 a.m.-5:00 p.m. Repair and restoration of stemware, art glass, cut glass. Stoppers fitted. Glass engraving of custom panels, sidelights, and presentation pieces. Bull's-eye panels, salt liners, and other items made to order.

CW Design, Inc., 1618 Central Avenue, NE, Minneapolis, MN 55413, 612-789-5685, 8:30 a.m.-5:00 p.m., fax: 612-789-0124. Etched, carved, chipped, color-enhanced, and stained glass. Custom decorative flat glass for dividers, door panels, ceilings, and mirrors. Catalog.

David Jasper's Glass Clinic, R.R. 3, Box 330X-13, Sioux Falls, SD 57106, 605-361-7524, 9:00 a.m.-5:00 p.m. Repair, restoration of glass, lamps, other objects of art. Chips removed. Brochure.

Dean's China Restoration, 131 Elmwood Drive, Cheshire, CT 06410, 203-271-3659, Mon.-Fri. 9:00 a.m.-5:00 p.m. Repair and restoration of glass. Mail order.

Delphi Stained Glass, 2116 East Michigan Avenue, Lansing, MI 48912, 800-248-2048 or 800-322-3336, 8:00 a.m.-6:00 p.m. Wholesale and retail stained glass supplies. Bevels, etching supplies, kits, chemicals, tools, books, lamp bases and supplies. Catalog.

Drehobl Brothers Art Glass Company, 2847 North Lincoln Avenue, Chicago, IL 60657, 312-281-2022, 9:30 a.m.-5:00 p.m. Restoration of glass.

Dunhill Restoration, c/o Lee Upholstery, 2250 Lee Road, Cleveland Heights, OH 44122, 216-921-2932. Chipped and broken glass repaired. Leave message on answering machine.

Eastern Art Glass, P.O. Box 341, Wyckoff, NJ 07481, 201-447-5476, 800-872-3458. Glass etching supplies and accessories. Mail order.

England Associates, Ronald W. England, P.O. Box 4241, Martinsville, VA 24115, 703-638-6284, 8:00 a.m.-5:00 p.m. Philadelphia glass, handmade, mouth-blown glass parts for reproduction and antique furniture and historic restoration.

Glass Arts Inc., 119 Braintree Street, Boston, MA 02134, 617-782-7760, Mon.-Fri. 8:30 a.m.-5:00 p.m.; fax: 617-787-8912. Ornamental glass for architectural use. Leaded, etched, beveled, and stained glass. Repair and restoration of leaded and stained glass, wooden doors and window sashes. Brochure $3.

Glass Doctor, Ross Jasper, 3126 Fairview Street, Davenport, IA 52802, 319-322-5512, 800-344-0479, Mon.-Fri. 9:00 a.m.-5:00 p.m. Figurines and chipped glass restored.

Glass Restoration, 308 East 78th Street, New York, NY 10021, 212-517-3287, Mon.-Fri. 9:30 a.m.-5:00 p.m. Glass restoration and repairs; custom glass cutting, polishing, drilling, and engraving.

Glass Studios Ltd., Thomas E. Matthews, P.O. Box 87, Lompoc, CA 93438, 805-735-1763 or 805-736-1729, 8:00 a.m.-5:00 p.m. American brilliant period cut glass restored. Scratches polished, pattern and teeth recut if necessary, "sick" decanters restored, new stoppers made to fit your bottle, paperweights resurfaced. No crack mending or gluing. Call or write for information on shipping.

The Glassman, 10516 Old Katy Road, Suite D, Houston, TX 77043, 713-468-3183, Mon.-Fri. 10:00 a.m.-4:30 p.m., Sat. 11:00 a.m.-6:00 p.m., Sun. 2:00 p.m.-5:00 p.m. Glass stoppers for decanters, perfumes, cruets, and bottles. Glass restoration. Chips ground down and glass polished. Engraving.

Great Panes Glassworks, 2861 Walnut Street, Denver, CO 80205, 303-294-0927, Mon.-Fri. 8:00 a.m.-5:00 p.m. Custom sandblasted glass and stone; standard patterns available, also. Large restorations and new building projects.

Greg Monk Stained Glass, 98-027 Hekaha Street, Bldg. 3, Aiea, HI

96701, 808-488-9538, Mon.-Sat. 10:00 a.m.-6:00 p.m. Repairs of stained-glass windows, lamps, door panels, skylights, room dividers in leaded, foiled, etched, painted, or dalle de verre. Serving Pacific area and Western states.

Hand Blown Glass, Michael Kraatz and Susan Russell, R.F.D. 2, Canaan, NH 03741, 603-523-4289 until 8:00 p.m. Bull's-eye glass suitable for windows, sidelights, and transoms, leaded glass panels for doors, window, and walls.

Hudson Glass Co. Inc., 219 North Division Street, Peekskill, NY 10566, 914-737-2124, 9:00 a.m.-5:00 p.m.; fax: 914-737-4447. Bent glass for china cabinets and mirrors, beveled and polished edge glass, restoration glass, stained glass, and stained glass supplies. Serving New York, New Jersey, Connecticut, Massachusetts, and Pennsylvania. Nationwide mail order sales of stained glass and supplies. Catalog $3.

Kalesse, Fine Arts Bldg., 1017 SW Morrison Street, 507-C, Portland, OR 97205. Restoration of glass, crystal, and related objets d'art. Mail order service worldwide.

LaRoche Stained Glass, 441-43 Fulton Street, Medford, MA 02155, 617-395-5047, 8:00 a.m.-5:00 p.m. Repair, restoration of stained glass and glass lampshades. Bend glass. Serving New England area.

Lid Lady, Virginia Bodiker, 7790 East Ross Road, New Carlisle, OH 45344. Glass, metal, plastic, and zinc stoppers and salt and pepper lids. Mail order. Open by appointment.

Lyn Hovey Studio, Inc., 266 Concord Avenue, Cambridge, MA 02138, 617-492-6566, 617-492-4603, or 617-492-4606, Mon.-Fri. 9:00 a.m.-5:00 p.m. Stained and art glass restoration and repair. Reproduction and custom work for windows, skylights, glass curtain walls, mirrors, and lighting. Brochure.

Manor Art Glass, 20 Ridge Road, Douglaston, NY 11363, 718-631-8029, 8:00 a.m.-6:00 p.m. Stained glass repair, restoration, new stained glass, carved and etched glass. No mail order. Serving New York tri-state area.

McCurley Glass Repair, Don and Joyce McCurley, Route 1, Box 738, Big Pine Key, FL 33043, 305-872-2359, 9:00 a.m.-10:00 p.m. Glass and crystal repaired. Chips removed, teeth on cut glass bowls reshaped. Glass and crystal replacement parts. Specializing in stoppers for all kinds of bottles.

Neon Alley, Inc., Bobbie Lafone, 1437 Second Street Drive NE, P.O. Box 9698, Hickory, NC 28601, 704-328-9917, Mon.-Fri. 9:00 a.m.-5:00 p.m. Custom neon glass restoration and fabrication. Mail order.

Old Hickory Stained Glass Studio, 215 State Street, La Crosse, WI 54601, 608-782-4384, 800-658-9084 for ordering supplies, 9:00 a.m.-5:00 p.m. Repair and restoration. Stained glass tools and supplies. Mail order supplies. Catalog.

Origina Luster, Box 2092, Dept. K, Wilkes-Barre, PA 18703. Origina Luster is a product that will cure "sick" glass. Glass repair kits, portable ultraviolet long-wave black lights. Mail order only.

Pat's Etcetera Company, Inc. (PECO), P.O. Box 777, 810 East First Street, Smithville, TX 78957, 512-237-3600, Mon.-Fri. 10:00 a.m.-3:00 p.m. Curved glass for china cabinets, oval convex picture-frame glass. Mail order. Brochure.

Pleasant Valley Services, Joe Howell, 1725 Reed Road, Knoxville, MD 21758, 301-432-2721, 9:00 a.m.-9:00 p.m. Restoration of glass. Mail order.

Pocahontas Hardware & Glass, Box 127, Pocahontas, IL 62275, 618-669-2880. Etched glass for doors, windows, transoms, and cabinets. Safety glass used for entrance doors, plate glass for picture window lights and transoms, double-strength glass for cabinet doors, transoms, windows, and ornamental hangings. Catalog $2.

R & K Weenike Antiques, Roy H. Weenike, Route 7, Box 140, Ottumwa, IA 52501, 515-934-5427, anytime. Grinding and polishing of glass. White deposit cleaned from vases, cruets, and bottles. Mail order.

Restorations By Linda, Linda M. Peet, 9787 Townsend Road, Maybee, MI 48159, 313-529-5414. Repair of crystal and cut glass. Glass grinding, polishing, cement work. Free estimates. Mail order worldwide. Also contact at P.O. Box 265, Milan, MI 48160.

RGS Glass & Frame Corp., 138 East 30th Street, New York, NY 10016, 800-735-7667, anytime. Bent glass for china cabinets, tabletops, mirrors, insulated glass, plastics, and supplies. Mirrors resilvered.

Stained Glass Associates, P.O. Box 1531, Raleigh, NC 27602, 919-266-2493, 8:00 a.m.-5:00 p.m., 919-833-7668 evenings. Repairs to Tiffany and other glass shades, restoration of stained-glass windows. Custom designs. Mail order or on site. Booklet "Conservation and Restoration of Stained Glass: An Owner's Guide" $3.65.

Studio Workshop, Ltd., 22 Bushy Hill Road, Simsbury, CT 06070, 203-658-6374, 8:00 a.m.-6:00 p.m. Restoration of stained glass, specializing in turn-of-the-century.

Sunburst Stained Glass Co., Inc., 20 West Jennings, Newburgh, IN 47630, 812-853-0460, Mon.-Fri. 9:00 a.m.-5:00 p.m., Sat. 10:00 a.m.-4:00 p.m. Glass restoration and repair. Stained, etched, and beveled glass, new and restored. Custom designs, mirror and plate glass, lamps, custom storm protection. Architectural enhancements, wood entries, sidelights, transoms. Mail order.

Tops and Bottoms Club, Madeleine France, P.O. Box 15555, Plantation, FL 33318, 305-584-0009 or 305-584-0099, 9:00 a.m.-5:00 p.m.; fax: 305-584-0014. Lalique perfume bottle matching service. Mail order.

Universal Glass Co., P.O. Box 2097, Alma, AR 72921, 800-466-5504, ext. 1, anytime; fax: 501-667-3198. Curved china cabinet glass, glass nuggets, hand-painted vases, and novelties. Mail order worldwide. Brochure.

Venerable Classics, 645 Fourth Street, Suite 208, Santa Rosa, CA 95404, 707-575-3626, Mon.-Fri. 10:00 a.m.-5:00 p.m. Restoration of fragile objects, including crystal. "Impossible smithereens our specialty." Serving northern California and Western U.S. Mail order. Brochure.

Whittemore-Durgin Glass Co., Box 2065LT, Hanover, MA 02339, 617-871-1743, 617-871-1744, 617-871-1790, or 617-871-1803, Mon.-Fri. 8:00 a.m.-5:00 p.m.; fax: 617-871-5597. Stained glass supplies, bent panels and other parts for lampshades. Repairs to stained-glass lamps and windows. Catalog $2, deducted from first order.

Yesteryears Antiques Inc., R.D. 2, Box 227, Route 272, Reinholds, PA 17569, 215-484-0444, Sat. noon-8:00 p.m., Sun. 8:00 a.m.-6:00 p.m. Curved glass for china cabinets. Mail order, retail store at hours listed, by chance or appointment.

Rosemary Barrows, 9 Liberty Avenue, Hicksville, Long Island, NY 11801, 516-938-5643. Glass restoration and polishing; chips ground down. Stemware and cut glass a specialty.

David Lee Colglazier, Old Sturbridge Village, Sturbridge, MA 01566, 508-347-3362, Mon.-Fri. 9:00 a.m.-5:00 p.m.; fax: 508-347-5375. Glass restoration and conservation.

Raymond Errett, 281 Chestnut Street, Corning, NY 14830, 607-962-6026, 7:00 p.m.-9:00 p.m. Repair, restoration of crystal. Chips removed from wineglasses, tumblers, vases. Send photo, SASE for estimate.

H.W. Kopp, Glass Grinding, 26 State Street, Skaneateles, NY 13152, 315-685-5073, 9:00 a.m.-5:00 p.m. Glass repair and restoration, teeth cut, stoppers removed and fitted, small beveling for clocks, hole drilling. Works at antiques shows and at home.

Mike Meshenberg, 2571 Edgewood Road, Beachwood, OH 44122, 216-464-2084, anytime. Repair and restoration of glass.

Joan Meyer, 104 Colwyn Lane, Bala Cynwyd, PA 19004, 215-664-3174 or 215-664-2183, 9:00 a.m.-9:00 p.m. Restoration of Tiffany lamps and windows. U.S. or Europe.

Shay O'Brien, R.D. 2, Box 223K, Acme, PA 15610, 412-547-4618, 8:00 a.m.-10:00 a.m., 6:00 p.m.-8:00 p.m., answering machine 10:00 a.m.-6:00 p.m. Repairs of American cut glass.

Peter Owen, 29 Murray Street, Augusta, ME 04330, 207-622-3277, anytime. Slag-glass panel replacement, stained-glass lamp, window, and panel repair. Bent-glass replacement panels. Mail order.

Jim Rupert, 3851 West Main Street, P.O. Box 195, New Waterford, OH 44445, 216-457-2813, 9:00 a.m.-9:00 p.m. Glass grinding, chips removed from crystal and marbles. Marbles polished. Mail order.

Don and Lynne Wormland, 36777 Mapleridge, Mt. Clemens, MI 48043, 313-791-9191. Restoration of brilliant cut glass, crystal, elegant, and Depression glass. Chips removed.

Leaflets

Conservation and Restoration of Stained Glass: An Owner's Guide, Stained Glass Associates (P.O. Box 1531, Raleigh, NC 27602).

How to Care for Steuben Glass (Fifth Avenue at 56th Street, New York, NY 10022).

Glass Gilding--Vol. I , Wild Bill Betz (Art Essentials of New York Ltd.,
3 Cross Street, Suffern, NY 10901). (Preparation of glass, choosing
size brush and gilders tip.)

Glass Gilding--Vol. II, Wild Bill Betz (Art Essentials of New York Ltd.,
3 Cross Street, Suffern, NY 10901). (Professional glass work done by
head artist featured in trade magazines.)

Hardware

Some collectors want examples of old doorknobs or iron latches to display
as part of a collection, but most people want to use the old hardware.
When using old doorknobs, you must be sure the measurements correspond
to the thickness of your door. Old doors are sometimes thicker than
newer doors.

Hardware for old furniture is difficult to match but relatively easy to
replace. When possible, match existing hardware--some designs are still
being made. A few companies will make a copy of your hardware from the
sample you submit. If the hardware is not original or can't be matched,
replace it with old or new pieces. Be sure to get hardware of the correct
style and period.

When replacing hardware, try buying pieces that will cover the old
screw holes. Special hardware for old refrigerators, trunks, doors, and
windows can be found. Old hardware for doors may not fit in new doors
without alterations.

For more information, see Furniture, Metals, and Pottery & Porcelain
sections.

Sources

Acorn Manufacturing Co., Inc., 457 School Street, P.O. Box 31, Mansfield, MA 02048, 508-339-4500, 800-835-0121, 8:00 a.m.-4:00 p.m.,
fax: 508-339-0104. Reproduction colonial hardware and accessories,

including hinges, door knockers, handles, pulls, switch plates, and bath accessories. Catalog.

Anglo-American Brass Co., Box 9487, 4146 Mitzi Drive, San Jose, CA 95157, 408-246-0203, 8:00 a.m.-4:30 p.m.; 800-222-7277 outside California; fax: 408-248-1308. Solid brass reproduction hardware. Box locks, door locks, keys, hinges, knobs of oak, porcelain, brass, and glass. Custom reproductions made by lost-wax casting. Catalog.

Antique Bath and Kitchens, 2220 Carlton Way, Santa Barbara, CA 93109, 805-962-8598, noon-5:00 p.m. Reproduction plumbing fixtures, including pull-chain toilets, pedestal sinks, bathtubs, copper kitchen sinks, faucets, and parts. Catalog $2.

Antique Hardware Co., P.O. Box 1592, Torrance, CA 90505, 213-378-5990. Furniture replacement parts. Catalog $3.

Antique Hardware Store, R.D. 2, Box A, Kintnersville, PA 18930, 215-847-2447, 800-422-9982, 8:00 a.m.-6:00 p.m.; fax: 215-847-5628. Old-style plumbing fixtures and hardware, including claw-foot tub supplies and shower conversion, chair seats, weathervanes, lighting, and gingerbread trim. Mail order service available. Catalog $3.

Arden Forge, 301 Brintons Bridge Road, West Chester, PA 19382, 215-399-1530, Mon.-Sat. 9:00 a.m.-5:00 p.m. Antique and reproduction 18th- and 19th-century hardware. Duplication of existing hardware, restoration, and repair. Showroom open by appointment. Mail order.

Armor Products, P.O. Box 445, East Northport, NY 11731, 516-462-6228, 9:00 a.m.-5:00 p.m. Specialty hardware for furniture and clocks. Door harp supplies. Tools and finishing supplies. Catalog.

Barap Specialties, 835 Bellows, Frankfort, MI 49635, 616-352-9863, 8:30 a.m.-5:00 p.m. Hardware, wood products, tools, and supplies.

Bona Decorative Hardware, 3073 Madison Road, Cincinnati, OH 45209, 513-321-7877, 9:30 a.m.-5:30 p.m.; fax: 513-321-7879. Decorative hardware. Mail order.

Brass Anvil, Inc., Jim Horack, 186 North DuPont Highway, Bldg. 30, Airport Industrial Center, New Castle, DE 19720, 302-322-7679, 9:00 a.m.-5:30 p.m.; 302-733-0617 evenings. Metal antiques restored and repaired. Polishing and lacquering service, custom range hoods, planters, brass railings for bars, hardware.

The Brass Knob, 2311 18th Street NW, Washington, DC 20009, 202-332-3370, 10:30 a.m.-6:00 p.m. Authentic architectural antiques, period hardware, and lighting. Stairway parts, claw-foot tubs, pedestal sinks, fireplace mantels and equipment. Brochure.

The Broadway Collection, 250 North Troost, Olathe, KS 66061, 800-766-1661, 8:00 a.m.-5:00 p.m.; fax: 913-782-0647. Brass hardware, door and cabinet hardware, switch plates, faucetry, bath accessories.

Cirecast, Inc., 380 Seventh Street, San Francisco, CA 94103, 415-863-8319, 8:30 a.m.-5:00 p.m.; fax: 415-863-7721. Custom Victorian restoration hardware made using the lost-wax casting method. Doorknobs, key plates, latches, hinges, etc. Brochure.

Colonial Lock Co., 172 Main Street, Terryville, CT 06786, 203-584-0311, 7:00 a.m.-4:00 p.m. Iron-Guard rim deadbolt lock. Will custom-make wood-covered locks. Brochure.

Conant Custom Brass, P.O. Box 1523A, 270 Pine Street, Burlington, VT 05402, 802-658-4482 or 802-658-9978, 8:00 a.m.-5:00 p.m. Complete metal restoration and repair, custom fabrication, plating, hardware, light fixtures, brass dust corners, and more. Brochure.

D.E.A. Bathroom Machineries, 459 Main Street, P.O. Box 1020, Murphys, CA 95247, 209-728-2031. Victorian-style plumbing fixtures, shower parts, claw foot tubs and accessories, pedestal sinks, and hardware. Catalog.

Doug Poe Antiques, 4213W 500N, Huntington, IN 46750, 219-356-4859, 800-348-5004, 8:00 a.m.-5:00 p.m. Antique restoration hardware, including cast brass and stamped brass pulls, knobs, keys, and keyholes. Price list available.

DS Locksmithing Company, 220 East Sixth Street, Jacksonville, FL 32206, 904-356-5396. Reproduction antique locks, designed to provide high security. Padlocks, door locks, window locks, rim locks, mortise locks, and cabinet locks. Keys made for antique locks, ornamental cabinet keys. Miscellaneous hardware. Mail order worldwide. Specify particular needs or send for 1,000-page "Blockbuster" Compendium of Catalogs, available on 30-day loan for $6 shipping plus $44 refundable deposit.

18th Century Hardware Company, Inc., 131 East Third Street, Derry, PA 15627, 412-694-2708, 8:00 a.m.-4:30 p.m. Brass and iron hardware for antique furniture, specialty duplication work. Brass cleaned and repaired. Catalog and price list $3.00

Farm Forge, 6945 Fishberg Road, Huber Heights, OH 45424, 513-233-6751, 6:00 p.m.-10:00 p.m. Reproduction hardware, restoration, and duplication. Balconies, stairs, gates, art metal, cutlery, fireplace equipment, lighting custom made. Catalog $1.

Farmerstown Furniture, 3155 S.R. 557, Dept. K, Baltic, OH 43804, 216-893-2464, Mon., Tues., Thurs., Fri. 8:30 a.m.-4:30 p.m., Wed. & Sat. 8:30 a.m.-11:30 a.m. Reproduction hardware for Morris chairs, Hoosier cabinets, iceboxes, etc. Brass and iron bed parts, pressed fiber seats, oak highchair trays, replacement runners and curved seats for rockers, spool cabinet decals, brass and wood specialty items, Kotton Klenser products, adhesives, and more. Catalog $2.

Fine Finishes, Kenneth Miltner, Route 176, Box 248, Brooksville, ME 04617, 207-326-4545, 8:30 a.m.-4:00 p.m. Fireplace hardware, door hardware, and bath fixtures restored.

Garrett Wade Company, 161 Avenue of the Americas, New York, NY 10013, 212-807-1155 for customer service or information, 800-221-2942 for orders, 24 hours a day; fax: 212-255-8552. Brass hardware, finishing supplies, woodworking tools, machinery, and books. Mail order. Classic hardware catalog $2.

Gaston Wood Finishes, Inc., P.O. Box 1246, 2626 North Walnut Street,

Bloomington, IN 47402, 812-339-9111, 8:30 a.m.-4:30 p.m. Reproduction hardware. Mail order, retail shop. Catalog $2.50.

Granpa Snazzy's Hardware, 1832 South Broadway, Denver, CO 80210, 303-935-3269 or 303-778-6508 anytime. Parts and pieces. Replacement hardware from 72 companies; large selection of old hardware for furniture, doors, windows, etc. Parts fabricated, restoration advice given, locks fixed, keys made.

Hardware Plus, 701 East Kingsley Road, Garland, TX 75041, 214-271-0319, 800-522-7336, Mon.-Fri. 9:00 a.m.-5:00 p.m.; fax: 214-271-9726. Restoration supplies. Parts and hardware for restoring antiques. Basketry materials, bed parts, colonial lighting, dust corners, Hoosier hardware, knobs, platform springs, rocking chair parts, twist doorbells, and wood trims. Mail order. Catalog $3.50, refundable with order of $50 or more.

Harper Hardware Co., 1712 East Broad Street, Richmond, VA 23223, 804-643-9007, 8:30 a.m.-5:00 p.m. Hardware. Mail order.

Historic Housefitters Company, Farm to Market Road, Dept. K, Brewster, NY 10509, 914-278-2427, Mon.-Fri. 9:00 a.m.-5:00 p.m. Hardware, specializing in hand-forged iron 18th-century thumb latches, strap hinges, H and HL hinges, fireplace tools, chandeliers, hooks, and accessory items. Leaded crystal, porcelain, and wood knobs. Handmade copper, brass, and tin light fixtures and lanterns. Mail order shipped worldwide. Catalog $3.

Horton Brasses, Nooks Hill Road, P.O. Box 120Q, Cromwell, CT 06416, 203-635-4400, 8:30 a.m.-4:00 p.m. Reproduction furniture hardware. 17th-, 18th-, 19th- and 20th-century-style brass pulls, cupboard hardware, hinges, clock parts, hand-forged black iron hardware. Mail, telephone orders. Showroom open 8:30 a.m.-3:45 p.m. Catalog $3.

JGR Enterprises, Inc., P.O. Box 32, Route 522, Fort Littleton, PA 17223, 800-223-7112, 8:00 a.m.-4:30 p.m., 717-485-4344, 8:00 a.m.-5:00 p.m., 717-485-4693 after 5:00 p.m. Replacement hardware for doors, windows, lockers; Kennaframe security hardware; hardware for sliding, pocket, bypass, and folding doors. Mail order.

Kayne & Son Custom Forged Hardware, Steve Kayne, 76 Daniel Ridge Road, Candler, NC 28715, 704-667-8868 or 704-665-1988, 8:00 a.m.-11:00 p.m. Custom hand-forged steel hardware, custom cast brass and bronze. Reproduction furniture hardware. Will reproduce any piece of brass, bronze, or copper from customer's original. Repair and restoration. Walk in or mail order. Catalogs: forgings $2, castings $2, both for $3.50.

Lemee's Fireplace Equipment, 815 Bedford Street, Bridgewater, MA 02324, 508-697-2672, Mon.-Sat. 9:00 a.m.-5:00 p.m. Colonial hardware, fireplace equipment, and accessories. Catalog.

M. Wolchonok and Son, Inc., 155 East 52nd Street, New York, NY 10022, 212-755-2168, 9:00 a.m.-5:30 p.m. Reproduction hardware, furniture legs and hardware, bathroom hardware. Mail order.

Monroe Coldren and Sons, 723 East Virginia Avenue, West Chester, PA

19380, 215-692-5651, 8:30 a.m.-5:00 p.m. Original 18th- and 19th-century hardware, including locks, latches, shutter hardware, fireplace accessories, brass, copper items. Hardware reproductions. Mail order.

Muff's Antiques, 135 S. Glassell Street, Orange, CA 92666, 714-997-0243, Tues.-Sat. 11:00 a.m.-5:00 p.m. Furniture hardware, trunk supplies, rolltop desk locks, decorative furniture trim. Restoration and sales, new and old hardware, parts, advice and instructions. Hardware for Hoosiers, trunks, and rolltop desks. Keys made for barrel or pin locks. Mail order worldwide. Restoration hardware catalog and re-creations catalog (pulls and decorative accessories) $4.

North Raleigh Antique Mall, 4410 Craftsman Drive, Dept. K, Raleigh, NC 27609, 919-876-6250, 10:00 a.m.-5:00 p.m. Brass furniture hardware for all periods, door plates, heat grilles, kickplates, unusual door and window hardware. Catalog $3. Mail order sales.

Old and Elegant Distributing, 10203 Main Street Lane, Bellevue, WA 98004, 206-455-4660, Mon.-Sat. 9:00 a.m.-6:00 p.m., Thurs. 9:00 a.m.- 9:00 p.m.; fax: 206-454-6287, use company name. Salvage and reproduction hardware: door, cabinet, plumbing, window, lighting, and architectural.

Paxton Hardware Ltd., P.O. Box 256, 7818 Bradshaw Road, Upper Falls, MD 21156, 301-592-8505, Mon.-Fri. 9:00 a.m.-5:00 p.m.; fax: 301-592-2224. Period reproduction hardware. Casters, table hardware, fasteners, locks, catches, hinges, pulls, supports, bolt covers for beds, rail fasteners, bed bolts, wood, and wrenches. Free minicatalog. Complete 75-page catalog $4.

Period Furniture Hardware Co. Inc., 123 Charles Street, P.O. Box 314, Charles Street Station, Boston, MA 02114, 617-227-0758, 8:30 a.m.-5:00 p.m. Reproduction brass hardware for furniture and home. Reproduction cabinet and door hardware, fireplace equipment, weathervanes. Mail order. Catalog $4.50.

Renovation Concepts, Inc., 213 Washington Avenue North, Minneapolis, MN 55401, 612-333-5766, Mon.-Fri. 8:30 a.m.-5:00 p.m., Sat. 10:00 a.m.-2:00 p.m.; fax: 612-333-5782. Plumbing, hardware, and lighting products. Showroom and mail order. Brochure.

Renovator's Supply, 149 Northfield Road, Millers Falls, MD 01349, 413-659-3152. Hardware, including rimlocks, cabinet hardware, door and window hardware. Catalog.

Restoration Resources, 200 Webster Street, Route 123, Hanover, MA 02339, 617-878-3794, 10:00 a.m.-6:00 p.m. Reproduction cabinet and door hardware in brass, porcelain, and wrought iron.

Restoration Works Inc., P.O. Box 486, Buffalo, NY 14205, 716-856-8000, 9:00 a.m.-5:00 p.m. Decorative hardware and plumbing fixtures, bath accessories, architectural trims, and medallions. Brass products refurbished. Catalog $3.

Ritter & Son Hardware, 38001 Old Stage Road, P.O. Box 578, Gualala, CA 95445-9984, 707-884-3363 or 707-884-3528, 8:00 a.m.-4:30 p.m. Reproduction antique brass furniture hardware, Hoosier hardware, bail sets, keyhole covers, knobs, Morris chair hardware, brass and iron bed parts, kitchen cabinet and icebox hardware, hand-carved oak gingerbread, and more. Mail order. Catalog.

Robinson's Antiques, 170 Kent Street, Portland, MI 48875, 517-647-6155, 9:00 a.m.-9:00 p.m. Antique replacement hardware matching service, 1680-1915. No reproductions. Stripping, refinishing, repairing old parts. Restoration of missing parts. Mail order.

Samuel B. Sadtler, 340 South 4th Street, Philadelphia, PA 19106, 215-923-3714, 8:00 a.m.-8:00 p.m. Box locks, door hardware, cast-iron butt hinges, and shutter strap hinges. Brochure.

Sign of the Crab, Ltd., 3756 Omec Circle, Rancho Cordova, CA 95742, 916-638-2722; fax: 916-638-2725; order desk: 800-THE-CRAB; inside CA: 800-THE-SOTC. Brass hardware: bar rails, brackets, door hardware, pulls, mailboxes, sun dials, wind vanes; plumbing and bath fixtures: drains, faucets, mirrors, towel bars; gifts, accessories: fireplace items, picture frames, candleholders.

Thomas H. Kramer, Inc., 805 Depot Street, Commerce Park, Columbus, IN 47201, 812-379-4097 or 812-342-3443, Mon.-Sat. 10:00 a.m.-5:00 p.m. Porcelain and brass knobs. Wooden turned knobs, feet, and legs. Catalog.

Tremont Nail Company, P.O. Box 111, Dept. K-89, Wareham, MA 02571, 508-295-0038 or 508-295-1365, 7:30 a.m.-5:00 p.m. Manufacturer of old patterned nails, including 19th-century style wrought-head nails. Free mail order catalog.

W.T. Weaver and Sons, Inc., 1208 Wisconsin Avenue NW, Washington, DC 20007, 202-333-4200, 9:00 a.m.-5:00 p.m.; fax: 202-333-4154. Decorative hardware and building supplies, including porcelain and brass furniture hardware, knobs, rim locks, front door hardware, brass switch plates, lavatory bowls, and ceiling medallions. Free literature on ceiling pieces.

William Hunrath Company, 153 East 57th Street, New York, NY 10022, 212-758-0780, Mon.-Fri. 9:00 a.m.-5:30 p.m., Sat. 9:00 a.m.-4:00 p.m. Bathroom fixtures, door hardware, pulls, knobs, brass tubing, fasteners, decorative brass goods, closet accessories, cabinet hardware, door knockers, furniture hardware, and more. Mail and phone orders. Flyers on products available.

Williamsburg Blacksmiths, Inc., Goshen Road, P.O. Box 1776, Williamsburg, MA 01096-1776, 413-268-7341, Mon.-Fri. 9:00 a.m.-5:00 p.m., Sat. 9:00 a.m.-1:00 p.m.; fax: 413-268-9317. Early American wrought-iron reproduction hardware. Catalog $5.

Winchester Brass Hardware, 107 West Pall Mall Street, Winchester, VA 22601, 703-722-2053, 8:30 a.m.-5:00 p.m. Brass reproduction hardware, oak gingerbread replacements, solid brass stamped and cast pulls and knobs, hand-carved brass bed parts. Catalog.

Windy Hill Forge, 3824 Schroeder Avenue, Perry Hall, MD 21128-9783, 301-256-5890, 8:00 a.m.-5:00 p.m. Custom and reproduction hardware for homes and furniture. Colonial box locks and latches, snow irons, cast brackets, restoration parts in iron, brass, lead, and sheet metal. Brochure.

Yesteryears Antiques Inc., R.D. 2, Box 227, Route 272, Reinholds, PA 17569, 215-484-0444, Sat. noon-8:00 p.m., Sun. 8:00 a.m.-6:00 p.m. Brass reproduction hardware for furniture. Mail order and retail store at hours listed, by chance or appointment.

George and Ione Baker, Renninger's Antique Market, Route 441, Mount Dora, FL 37245, Antique iron and brass hardware and lighting.

Joseph Biunno, 129 West 29th Street, New York, NY 10001, 212-629-5630, 212-629-5636, 9:00 a.m.-5:00 p.m.; fax: 212-268-4577. Hand-carved custom drapery hardware including finials, tiebacks, fancy poles and rings, and carved wood tassels.

Ned James, Wrought Metals, 65 Canal Street, Turners Falls, MA 01376, 413-863-8388, 11:30 a.m.-1:30 p.m. Early American wrought-iron hardware. Custom hand-wrought metalwork, repairs, and restoration.

Jim Leonard, Antique Hardware, 509 Tanglewood Drive, Jamestown, NC 27282, 919-454-3583, after 6:00 p.m. Antique hardware, fireplace equipment, and lighting; specializing in wrought-iron door hardware and fireplace equipment. Send 50¢ for photos and price list.

Thomas Loose, Blacksmith-Whitesmith, Route 2, Box 2410, Leesport, PA 19533, 215-926-4849 or 215-926-4849, 8:00 a.m.-5:00 p.m. Hand-forged iron for home and hearth. Reproduction hardware, hearth cooking utensils, and lighting devices. Double stamped SASE for brochure. Mail order.

Horse-Drawn Vehicles

Horse-drawn vehicles, like carriages and sleds, are collected by a small, earnest group with space and, probably, horses. To learn more about horse-drawn vehicles, read the special publications on the subject (listed in *Kovels' Guide to Selling Your Antiques & Collectibles*). Meets, restoration problems, and history are discussed. There are still a few working wheelwrights in rural America who can put an iron band on a wooden wheel and do other repairs. To locate one nearby requires ingenuity and determination. Try calling a local farm paper and ask if they can help. We met a Midwestern wheelwright doing demonstrations at a local "living history" fair.

Source

Carpenter and Smith Restorations, Box 504, Highland Park, IL 60035, 312-831-5047, 8:00 a.m.-5:00 p.m. Repair and restoration of horse-drawn carriages. Mill shop. Serving northern Illinois, southern Wisconsin, and northwestern Indiana.

Indian & Western Artifacts

Indian baskets, pottery, rugs, jewelry, beadwork, and leatherwork have become increasingly popular with collectors. Interest is especially keen in the West, where American Indian culture is more evident. Perfect pieces of American Indian pottery are so rare that the slightly damaged and repaired piece is in demand. If you break a piece of cut glass in half, then glue it together, the resale value drops to about 10 percent of the original value. If you repair a broken piece of American Indian pottery, the resale value is from 50 to 75 percent of the original value. So if you drop your Maria vase, save the pieces and have the vase professionally restored.

Sources

Havran's Navajo Rug Cleaners, 18 North Chestnut, Cortez, CO 81321,

303-565-7977, 8:30 a.m.-5:30 p.m. Navajo rug cleaning and stain removal. Send rugs wrapped in plastic trash bag and securely boxed. Include information on problem spots.

Trail Blazer, 210 West Hill, Gallup, NM 87301, 505-722-5051, 9:00 a.m.-5:00 p.m. Indian jewelry repaired. Mail order. Indian jewelry catalog $2.50.

White Deer Indian Traders, 1834 Red Pine Lane, Stevens Point, WI 54481, Indian culture items repaired. Mail order.

Ivory

Ivory requires special care and cleaning. Never make the mistake that we made many years ago when we carefully washed our first ivory carving, leaving it an undesirable white color. It has been years since we erred and the carving has still not regained the yellow-brown tint or patina preferred by collectors. If a carving is handled, body oils and moisture will eventually help to age it, but that would take more than one lifetime. Never wash old ivory. The proper steps for cleaning can be found in technical books on restoration.

Ivory can be repaired by experts. Minor breaks can be mended by using a good commercial glue. Thin slices of ivory for inlay replacement are available.

Sources

Broken Art Restoration, Michelle and Bill Marhoefer, 1841 West Chicago Avenue, Chicago, IL 60622, 312-226-8200. Restoration of ivory. Invisible repair. Missing parts replaced. Brochure.

Dean's China Restoration, 131 Elmwood Drive, Cheshire, CT 06410,

203-271-3659, Mon.-Fri. 9:00 a.m.-5:00 p.m. Repair and restoration of ivory and jade. Mail order.

Glass Restoration, 308 East 78th Street, New York, NY 10021, 212-517-3287, Mon.-Fri. 9:30 a.m.-5:00 p.m. Ivory restored.

Kalesse, Fine Arts Building, 1017 SW Morrison Street, 507-C, Portland, OR 97205. Restoration of ivory and related objets d'art. Mail order service worldwide.

Restoration & Design Studio, Paul Karner, 249 East 77th Street, New York, NY 10021, 212-517-9742, Mon.-Fri. 10:00 a.m.-5:00 p.m., Wed. 1:00 p.m.-5:00 p.m. Ivory repaired.

Venerable Classics, 645 Fourth Street, Suite 208, Santa Rosa, CA 95404, 707-575-3626, Mon.-Fri. 10:00 a.m.-5:00 p.m. Restoration of fragile objects, jade, and ivory. "Impossible smithereens our specialty." Serving northern California and the Western U.S. primarily. Mail order. Brochure.

Wedgwood Studio, 2522 North 52nd Street, Phoenix, AZ 85008, 602-840-0825, 9:00 a.m.-1:00 p.m. Restoration of figurines, ivory, jade, and cabinet pieces. Mail order. Serving Western U.S.

Bradford Blakely, 6228 SW 32nd Avenue, Portland, OR 97201, 503-245-4534. Restoration of ivory carvings. Missing inlays replaced. Custom carving of netsuke.

David Lee Colglazier, Old Sturbridge Village, Sturbridge, MA 01566, 508-347-3362, Mon.-Fri. 9:00 a.m.-5:00 p.m.; fax: 508-347-5375. Conservation of ivory. Answers questions by mail.

John Edward Cunningham, 1516 Dustin Drive, #1, Normal, IL 61761, 309-454-8256, anytime. Restoration of ivory figurines. Ivory and mother-of-pearl inlays. Missing parts made. Mail order.

Jewelry

Antique jewelry has become very popular during the past few years, particularly Georgian, Victorian, Art Nouveau, Art Deco, costume, and American Indian jewelry. Always be sure when buying old jewelry that you get an all-original piece. Many are changed or "married" (mismatched) or are modern copies.

Repairing old jewelry requires the greatest concern, because repairing or remodeling can destroy the antique value. Repairs should be made in the spirit of the original jewelry. Replace old gems or stones with old stones; if you put a modern cut diamond in a piece with old mine-cut diamonds, the new one will be too bright and look out of place. Replacing earring backs, safety catches, or pin backs or restringing beads does not harm the value of most old jewelry and will definitely help to prevent loss. Many artisans now make necklaces of old and new beads. They may also be able to restring your old beads. Many jewelers will restring pearls and other valued beads.

Many local jewelers know how to appraise and repair old jewelry, but they often consider old jewelry "scrap" and figure the value based on the melt-down of the elements. Be sure to go to someone who understands the problems of old pieces, old methods, and old stones.

Jewelry can and should be cleaned at home. Be particularly careful of pieces with pearls or opals. They can be damaged by incorrect care, oil, and temperature changes. Never store opals or pearls in an airtight bag or bank safe-deposit vault. Lack of air may dull the luster.

Sources

Consortium, 949 North Rush Street, Chicago, IL 60611, 312-943-3600, Mon.-Sat. 10:00 a.m.-7:00 p.m.; fax: 312-943-9434. Estate and antique jewelry repaired.

Dunhill Restoration, c/o Lee Upholstery, 2250 Lee Road, Cleveland Heights, OH 44122, 216-921-2932. Jewelry repairs. Leave message on answering machine.

Myron Toback, Inc., 25 West 47th Street, New York, NY 10036, 212-398-8300, 8:00 a.m.-4:00 p.m.; fax: 212-869-0808. Jewelry findings, beads, roundels, clasp shorteners, chains, settings, cloisonné wire, jewelers' tools, solder, precious metals, and other items necessary to repair jewelry. Warehouse and showroom. Catalog. Mail order worldwide.

N.L. Designs, Box 3792, Oak Park, IL 60303, 708-848-4560, Mon.-Sat. 9:00 a.m.-5:00 p.m. Restringing and knotting of beads, semi-precious stones, and pearls. Bead necklaces redesigned. Mail order.

Richardson's American Indian Art, 3876 East Fedora Avenue, Fresno, CA 93726, 209-222-3300, 9:00 a.m.-6:00 p.m. Jewelry repair. Showroom by appointment only. Mail order service.

Ship's Treasures, P.O. Box 590-EM, Milton, MA 02186, 617-964-8010, anytime. Jewelry supplies.

Thompsons Studio, Inc., Back Meadow Road, R.R. 1, Box 340, Damariscotta, ME 04543, 207-563-5280 or 207-563-5280. Restoration of jewelry of any period. Mail order. Brochure.

Trail Blazer, 210 West Hill, Gallup, NM 87301, 505-722-5051, 9:00

a.m.-5:00 p.m. Indian jewelry repaired. Mail order. Indian jewelry catalog $2.50.

Vogue & Vintage at Grandma's Attic, 187-20 Union Turnpike, Jamaica Estates, NY 11366, 718-454-1033, Mon.-Sat. 10:00 a.m.-5:00 p.m. Complete restoration of jewelry, replacement of pearls and precious stones. Phone or mail orders. Jewelry and giftware store.

WTC Associates, Inc., 2532 Regency Road, Lexington, KY 40503, 606-278-4171; fax: 606-276-1717. Silver jewelry repaired. Hand engraving.

Kitchen Paraphernalia

Anything that was used in an old kitchen, from the cookstove to the eggbeater, is in demand. Collectors should remember that while old items are fine for decorations, they are sometimes not safe to use for food preparation. Some types of pottery had a lead glaze that is poisonous. Copper molds and pots should never be used unless the tin lining is flawless. Companies that re-tin pots are listed in the Metals section. Chipped graniteware could add bits of crushed glass to your food. Woodenwares should only be treated with edible oils and not linseed oil. Iron skillets and baking pans must be properly cured to work well.

Directions and supplies for the care of glass, metals, and pottery and porcelain are listed in other sections.

Sources

Antique Farm, David Caraway, 1315 Dollarway, Ellensburg, WA 98926, 509-925-3527, 7:00 a.m.-9:00 p.m. Sadiron handles, $7 plus postage.

Hormel Corporation, Box 218, 15 Alabama Avenue, Island Park, NY 11558, 516-889-2244, Mon.-Fri. 10:00 a.m.-4:00 p.m.; fax: 516-889-2283. Old thermos-lined ice buckets, carafes, and thermos bottles repaired and relined.

Muff's Antiques, 135 South Gassell Street, Orange, CA 92666, 714-997-0243, Tues.-Sat. 11:00 a.m.-5:00 p.m. Hoosier cabinet restoration, parts, and supplies. Book on Hoosier identification and restoration. Mail order. Catalog $4.

Phyllis Kennedy Restoration Hardware, 9256 Holyoke Court, Indianapolis, IN 46268, 317-872-6366, 9:00 a.m.-6:00 p.m. Restoration hardware for Hoosier cabinets. Replacement sifters, sifter bowls, and flour bins for Hoosier cabinets. Mail order. Catalog $2.

Lorrie Kitchen & Dan Tucker, 3905 Torrance, Toledo, OH 43612, 419-478-3815. Labels for Owens-Illinois and Anchor-Hocking kitchen canisters and cookie jars.

Knives

Knife collecting includes everything from penknives to daggers, regardless of their age. Some of these items are listed in the sections on metals and military memorabilia. Repairs can sometimes be done by companies that repair or sell modern knives.

Sources

New England Country Silver, Inc., Smith Road, East Haddam, CT 06423, 203-873-1314, 9:00 a.m.-3:00 p.m. Repairing, refinishing, replating, and engraving of antique silverware, copper, and brassware. Replacement knife blades. Mail order.

Peninsula Plating Works, 232 Homer Avenue, Palo Alto, CA 94301, 415-326-7825 or 415-322-8806, Mon.-Fri. 8:30 a.m.-6:00 p.m., Sat. 10:00 a.m.-5:00 p.m.; fax: 415-322-7392. Restoration of knife blades and pearl handles. Brochure.

LABELS, see Advertising & Country Store Collectibles; Paper Collectibles & Ephemera

Lamps & Lighting Devices

Lamps and lighting devices are collected for many reasons, the most obvious being that they can light a room. If you are using old lamps in your home, be sure they are restored so they can be safely used. Oil and kerosene lamps have well-known hazards. Always check to be sure that all of the parts are working. Most early lamps can be converted to electricity. The original burner can be replaced with a new electric socket and cord. The unit will fit into the available space of the old lamp and can be removed or added with no damage to the antique value of the lamp. If you do electrify an old lamp, be sure to keep the old parts. The next owner may want an all-original lamp.

The light bulb was invented in 1879. That means that some electric lamps can be over 100 years old. If you are using any electric lamp that is more than 25 years old, be sure it is safe. The cord should not be frayed, and if it is an old-style silk-wrapped cord or a stiff rubber cord, it should be totally replaced. Local lamp shops can rewire any lamp. Look for them in the Yellow Pages of the telephone book under "Lamp-Mounting & Repairing." If the sockets or pull chains need repairing, ask the shop to use as many of the old pieces as possible. Old sockets were made of solid brass, but now most of them are plated. A serious collector will always want the original chain. Some pay extra to get old ones with the acorn-tipped pull chain.

Reproductions of almost all parts of old lamps are available: glass shades, lamp chimneys, sockets, hangers for chandeliers, and more. Old metal lamps can be cleaned or replated. Leaded shades can be repaired. Art glass shades are being reproduced or can be repaired.

The lampshade and lamp finial can often make the difference between an attractive, period-look lamp and an unattractive hodgepodge. Finials with old pieces of jade or porcelain are being offered by decorating services and mail-order houses. More sources are in the Glass and Metals sections.

Sources

Abend Metal Repair, Delavan Center, 501 West Fayette Street, Syracuse, NY 13204, 315-478-2749, Mon.-Fri. 9:00 a.m.-5:30 p.m.; answering machine other times. Repair, restoration of aluminum, brass, bronze, cast iron, steel, stainless steel, or white metal. Custom welding, antique polishing, patina restoration, cast reproductions.

Abercrombie & Co., 9159A Brookville Road, Silver Spring, MD 20910, 301-585-2385, weekdays 9:00 a.m.-5:00 p.m., Sat. 9:00 a.m.-1:00 p.m. Lamp repair, rewiring, replating; parts fabricated. Metal refinishing. Mail order.

Al Bar Wilmette Platers, 127 Green Bay Road, Wilmette, IL 60091, 312-251-0187, Mon.-Fri. 8:00 a.m.-4:30 p.m., Sat. 8:00 a.m.-3:00 p.m. Restoration service, including refinishing, repairs, rewiring of light fixtures; broken or missing pieces reproduced; lacquer coating.

American Lamp Supply Co., Tom Teeter, 51 Vaughans Gap Road, Nashville, TN 37205, 615-352-2357, 9:00 a.m.-3:00 p.m.; fax: 615-352-9423. Aladdin lamps and parts. Catalog $3.

American Period Lighting, 3004 Columbia Avenue, Lancaster, PA 17603, 717-392-5649, Mon.-Sat. 10:00 a.m.-4:30 p.m. Restoration of antique lighting; consulting services. Hand-crafted reproduction lighting fixtures, lanterns, and chandeliers. Retail shops, The Saltbox, in Massachusetts, New York, and Pennsylvania. Mail order. Brochure.

Angelo Brothers Co., 12401 McNulty Road, Philadelphia, PA 19154, 215-671-2000, 8:00 a.m.-4:30 p.m.; fax: 215-464-4115. Parts and supplies, switch plates, chimes, replacement glass, and fan accessories. Mail order.

Antique & Colonial Lighting, 10626 Main Street, Clarence, NY 14031, 716-759-2661, Mon.-Fri. 10:00 a.m.-5:00 p.m., Sat.-Sun. noon-5:00 p.m. Restoration of antique lighting; brass polishing, metal spinning. Odd-size rings or adapters for antique lamps.

Arroyo Craftsman, 2080-B Central Avenue, Duarte, CA 91010, 818-359-3298 or 818-359-7749, 8:00 a.m.-5:00 p.m.; fax: 818-303-1860. Custom-designed lighting fixtures.

Art Directions Inc., 6120 Delmar Boulevard, St. Louis, MO 63112, 314-863-1895, 7:30 a.m.-5:00 p.m.; fax: 314-863-3278. Lighting fixtures, shades in styles from turn-of-the-century to the 1930s. Brochure. Architectural antiques, refurbished lighting fixtures.

Authentic Lighting, 558 Grand Avenue, Englewood, NJ 07631, 201-568-7429, Mon.-Fri. 9:00 a.m.-5:00 p.m. Lighting fixtures repaired, rewired, and refinished; shades made or recovered; crystal chandeliers cleaned and rewired; reproduction and custom lighting.

B & P Lamp Supply Co., Inc., Route 3, McMinnville, TN 37110, 615-473-3016, 7:00 a.m.-5:00 p.m.; fax: 615-473-3014. Manufacturer, importer, and distributor of lamp parts, shades, and reproduction lamps in style of Handel, Tiffany, Aladdin, Emeralite, and Victorian lamps. Catalog, price list.

Barap Specialties, 835 Bellows, Frankfort, MI 49635, 616-352-9863, 8:30 a.m.-5:00 p.m. Lamp parts, tools, and supplies.

Bradford Consultants, P.O. Box 4020, Alameda, CA 94501, 415-523-1968, 10:00 a.m.-5:00 p.m. Reproduction period light bulbs, carbon and tungsten wire filaments. Gaslight mantels, twisted silk-covered lamp cord, old-fashioned figural Christmas lights, bubble lights, and replacement light strings.

Brass 'n Bounty, 68 Front Street, Marblehead, MA 01945, 617-631-3864, 9:00 a.m.-5:30 p.m. Antique lighting restored. Search service available. Mail order.

Brass Anvil, Inc., Jim Horack, 186 North DuPont Highway, Bldg. 30, Airport Industrial Center, New Castle, DE 19720, 302-322-7679, 9:00 a.m.-5:30 p.m., 302-733-0617 evenings. Metal antique chandeliers and lighting fixtures restored and repaired. Polishing and lacquering service.

Brass Light Gallery, 131 South First Street, Milwaukee, WI 53204, 414-271-8300, 800-243-9595, Mon.-Fri. 9:00 a.m.-5:00 p.m., Sat. 10:00 a.m.-1:00 p.m.; fax: 414-271-7755. Restoration of antique lighting fixtures, including polishing, lacquering, rewiring, and electrification of gas wall sconces and chandeliers. Mail order. Catalog.

Campbell Lamps, Bill Campbell, 1108 Pottstown Pike, West Chester, PA 19380, 215-696-8070, 9:00 a.m.-5:00 p.m. Replacement glass shades, student shades, chimneys, and metal parts.

Candle Snuffer, 28 Maple Root Road, Coventry, RI 02816, 401-397-5565, Tues.-Sat. 9:00 a.m.-5:00 p.m. Lighting repair and restoration, lamps, and lamp parts. Old and new electric and oil lamp parts, glass shades and chimneys, fabric shades. No mail order.

Century House Antiques & Lamp Emporium, 46785 Route 18 West, Wellington, OH 44090, 216-647-4092, 10:00 a.m.-5:00 p.m., closed Thurs. Lamp restoration, metal stripping, polishing, and wiring. Decorative antique lighting, old glass shades and parts. No glass repair. Do not ship. Brochure.

Conant Custom Brass, P.O. Box 1523A, 270 Pine Street, Burlington, VT 05402, 802-658-4482 or 802-658-9978, 8:00 a.m.-5:00 p.m. Complete metal restoration and repair, custom fabrication, plating, rewiring, light fixtures, replacement glass shades. Brochure.

Copper House, Route 4, R.F.D. 1, Epsom, NH 03234, 603-736-9798. Copper and brass lighting, lanterns, cupolas, parts and repair. Sat. noon-5:00 p.m., Sun. 10:00 a.m.-5:00 p.m., or by appointment. Mail order. Catalog $2.

Country Fare, Route 188 South, 45 Quaker Farms Road, Southbury, CT 06488, 203-264-7517, Tues.-Sat. 10:00 a.m.-5:00 p.m. Repairs, restoration, parts, custom lamps and shades, custom mounting.

Crystal Mountain Prisms, P.O. Box 31, Westfield, NY 14787, 716-326-3676, anytime. Replacement glass prisms for chandeliers and lamps. Glass chains, Czechoslovakian cut balls, pendalogues, bobeches. Mail order only.

Custom House, 6 Kirby Road, Cromwell, CT 06416, 203-828-6885, Tues.-Fri. 10:00 a.m.-4:00 p.m. Silk lampshades, cut and pierced lampshades, laminated paper or fabric shades.

DS Locksmithing Company, 220 East Sixth Street, Jacksonville, FL 32206, 904-356-5396. Parts for old and new lamps. Reproduction Aladdin lamps, shades, and parts. Pictures, prices available.

Dunhill Restoration, c/o Lee Upholstery, 2250 Lee Road, Cleveland Heights, OH 44122, 216-921-2932, leave message on answering machine. Lamp repair.

18th Century Hardware Company, Inc., 131 East Third Street, Derry, PA 15627, 412-694-2708, 8:30 a.m.-4:30 p.m. Lamps electrified. Brass items cleaned and repaired.

Elcanco Ltd., P.O. Box 682, Westford, MA 01886, 508-392-0830, 9:00 a.m.-5:00 p.m. Hand-crafted electric wax candles, "one-candlepower" bulbs, beeswax candle covers, 6-volt adapter. Can outfit any candle-type fixture. Brochure $1.

Elements Pottery, Linda and Andre Brousseau, 629 North Third Street, Danville, KY 40422, 606-236-7467 or 606-236-1808, Mon.-Sat. 9:00 a.m.-7:00 p.m. Rolled beeswax candles made in 4 sizes, 13 colors. Handmade stoneware pottery. Mail order. Send LSASE for brochure.

Faire Harbour Ltd., 44 Captain Peirce Road, Scituate, MA 02066, 617-545-2465, 8:00 a.m.- 10:30 p.m. Lamp parts, custom design and fabrication, repairs. Specializing in Aladdin kerosene mantel lamps. Mail order. Catalog $2, credited toward purchase of $15 or more.

Fine Finishes, Kenneth Miltner, Route 176, Box 248, Brooksville, ME 04617, 207-326-4545, 8:30 a.m.-4:00 p.m. Repair, restoration, and refinishing of old lighting fixtures; missing parts, glass shades, and globes replaced; gas and kerosene lamps converted to electric; collectibles converted to lamps. Brass refinishing, antiquing, polishing, and lacquering; pewter and copperware restored.

Harvey M. Stern & Co., 6350 Germantown Road, Philadelphia, PA 19444, 215-438-6350, 8:00 a.m.-5:00 p.m.; fax: 215-843-2322. Lighting fixtures refinished, repaired, and rewired. Metal restoration and custom metal finishings. Serving Philadelphia, New Jersey, Delaware, and parts of Maryland and Pennsylvania.

Hexagram, 426 Third Street, Eureka, CA 95501, 707-443-4334 or 707-725-6223, 9:00 a.m.-6:00 p.m. Restoration of antique lighting fixtures. Brass reproduction Victorian lighting, reproduction shades, custom orders, consultation. Retail shop, serving the northern California-Oregon area.

Historic Housefitters Company, Farm to Market Road, Dept. K, Brewster, NY 10509, 914-278-2427, Mon.-Fri. 9:00 a.m.-5:00 p.m. Chandeliers, hooks, accessory items. Mail order worldwide. Catalog $3.

Just Bulbs, 938 Broadway, New York, NY 10010, 212-228-7820, Mon.-Fri. 8:00 a.m.-5:00 p.m.; fax: 212-529-3307. Novelty light bulbs. Mail order.

Lamp Glass, 2230 Massachusetts Avenue, Cambridge, MA 02140,

617-497-0770, Wed.-Sat. 10:00 a.m.-6:00 p.m., Thurs. until 7:30 p.m. Replacement glass shades; reproduction shades for torchières, Gone With The Wind, student lamps, and others. Prisms and other parts. Mail order. Catalog $1.

Lampshades of Antique, Dorothy Primo, P.O. Box 2, Medford, OR 97501, 503-826-9737, Mon.-Sat. 8:00 a.m.-5:00 p.m. Manufacture, restoration, and recovering of Victorian fabric lampshades. Will recover your frame. Catalog $3. Items should be sent UPS to 321 Pruett Road, Eagle Point, OR 97524.

Leacock Coleman Center, 89 Old Leacock Road, Ronks, PA 17572, 717-768-7174, 8:00 a.m.-5:00 p.m., or 717-768-7174. Old Coleman light parts, hard-to-find items. Mail order, U.S. and Canada.

Light Ideas, 1037 Taft Street, Rockville, MD 20850, 301-424-LITE, Mon.-Sat. 10:00 a.m.-5:00 p.m., fax: 301-424-5791. Lamp and fixture repair and parts, replacement glass, specialty wire, beaded fringe for shades. Mail order, store. Brochure.

Littlewood & Maue Museum Quality Restorations, P.O. Box 402, Palmyra, NJ 08065, 609-829-4615, 9:00 a.m.-9:00 p.m. Restoration, metal repair, refinishing; reproduction globes. Identify and restore lighting, locate and refurbish needed objects. Brochure.

Loyal-T-Lites, Inc., 1144 Brooks Hill Road, Brooks, KY 40109, 502-955-9238. Reproduction glow light bulbs with decorative filaments in various designs. Mail order.

Lundberg Studios, P.O. Box C, 131 Marineview Avenue, Davenport, CA 95017, 408-423-2532, 9:00 a.m.-2:00 p.m.; fax: 408-423-0436. Glass shades. Mail order worldwide.

McCurley Glass Repair, Don and Joyce McCurley, Route 1 Box 738, Big Pine Key, FL 33043, 305-872-2359, 9:00 a.m.-10:00 p.m. Chandeliers rebuilt, lamps and lighting fixtures rewired. Glass and crystal parts and repair. Mail order.

Michael J. Dotzel & Son, 402 East 63rd Street, New York, NY 10021, 212-838-2890, 9:00 a.m.-4:00 p.m. Lamps and chandeliers rewired. Metal liners and shades made. Polishing, plating, and metal repair. New York area. Will repair items shipped to shop.

Old Hickory Stained Glass Studio, 215 State Street, La Crosse, WI 54601, 608-782-4384, 9:00 a.m.-5:00 p.m. Repairs, lamp bases and lighting parts for stained-glass lighting. Patterns and books for stained-glass lampshade construction. Mail order supplies.

Old Lamplighter Shop, Route 12-B, Deansboro, NY 13328, 315-841-8774. Restoration of antique lighting fixtures, china shade painting, slag glass, etc. Mail order: Restore-it Supply Co., P.O. Box 10600, White Bear Lake, MN 55110. Phone 612-429-2222.

Original Woodworks, 360 North Main, Stillwater, MN 55082, 612-430-3622. Lamp repair. Classes, tools, and supplies. Catalog $3.

P.A. Stammer Company, 824 L Street, Arcata, CA 95521, 707-822-5424; fax: 707-822-6213. Reproduction glow light bulbs with decorative filaments in various designs. Mail order.

Paxton Hardware Ltd., P.O. Box 256, 7818 Bradshaw Road, Upper Falls, MD 21156, 301-592-8505, Mon.-Fri. 9:00 a.m.-5:00 p.m., fax: 301-592-2224. Lamp parts and supplies, including bushings, chimneys, finials, oil burners, wicks, and more. Parchment, glass, and fabric lampshades. Mail order. Free minicatalog. 75-page catalog $4.

Peninsula Plating Works, 232 Homer Avenue, Palo Alto, CA 94301, 415-326-7825 or 415-322-8806, Mon.-Fri. 8:30 a.m.-6:00 p.m., Sat. 10:00 a.m.-5:00 p.m.; fax: 415-322-7392. Lighting repair and refinishing. Brochure.

Period Furniture Hardware Co. Inc., 123 Charles Street. P.O. Box 314, Charles Street Station, Boston, MA 02104, 617-227-0758, 8:30 a.m.-5:00 p.m. Reproduction lighting. Mail order. Catalog $4.50.

Price Glover Incorporated, 825 Madison Avenue, New York, NY 10021, 212-772-1740, 10:00 a.m.-5:00 p.m. English lighting made for the Indian market in the late 18th, early 19th centuries; exact reproductions of this lighting and of English brass chandeliers and hanging lanterns. Mail order.

Rare & Beautiful Things, P.O. Box 6180, Annapolis, MD 21401, 301-263-2357, 508-487-1974 summer season. Restored light fixtures; parts, pieces, and shades. Will locate antique fixtures or sell appropriate shades or pieces for restoration. Brochure.

Rejuvenation Lamp & Fixture Co., 901 North Skidmore, Portland, OR 97217, 503-249-0774, 7:00 a.m.-5:30 p.m.; fax: 503-281-7948. Reproduction period lighting, including shades and 1920s-style hanging bowls. Custom orders welcome. Mail order. Free catalog.

Renovation Concepts, Inc., 213 Washington Avenue North, Minneapolis, MN 55401, 612-333-5766, Mon.-Fri. 8:30 a.m.-5:00 p.m., Sat. 10:00 a.m.-2:00 p.m.; fax: 612-333-5782. Lighting products. Showroom, mail order. Brochure.

Renovator's Supply, 149 Northfield Road, Millers Falls, MD 01349, 413-659-3152. Lighting fixtures, glass replacement shades. Catalog.

Restoration & Design Studio, Paul Karner, 249 East 77th Street, New York, NY 10021, 212-517-9742, Mon.-Fri. 10:00 a.m.-5:00 p.m., Wed. 1:00 p.m.-5:00 p.m. Restoration and repair, missing parts reproduced.

Riverwalk Lighting, 401 South Main Street, Naperville, IL 60540, 708-357-0200, Mon.-Sat. 9:00 a.m.-5:00 p.m. Restoration of all types of lighting, lamps and shades. Serving the Midwest. No mail order.

Roy Electric Co., Inc., 1054 Coney Island Avenue, Brooklyn, NY 11230, 718-434-7002, 800-366-3347, 9:00 a.m.-9:00 p.m. Antique light fixtures and parts, replacement glass shades for Victorian and turn-of-the-century lighting fixtures. Mail order. Catalog $5.

Rumplestiltskin Designs, 1714 Rees Road, San Marcos, CA 92069, 619-743-5541, 9:00 a.m.-9:00 p.m. Hand-beaded lampshade fringe, assorted patterns and colors. All glass or glass and plastic fringe, rayon fringe for dyeing, gold and silver metallic antique trims. Mail order. Send $1 and SASE for color photos and prices.

Shades of the Past, P.O. Box 206, Fairfax, CA 94930, 415-459-6999,

8:00 a.m.-5:00 p.m. Fringed silk lampshades and brass bases. Catalog. Mail order.

Shady Lady, Marilynn Pinney, 418 East Second Street, Loveland, CO 80537, 303-669-1080, 9:00 a.m.-5:00 p.m. Fringed lampshades, antique shade restoration, lampshade frames recovered. Catalog $3.50.

St. Louis Antique Lighting Company, 801 North Skinker, St. Louis, MO 63130, 314-863-1414; fax: 314-863-6702. Restoration of antique lighting and architectural bronze work, historic preservation consultation services. Catalog.

Stanley Galleries, 2118 North Clark Street, Chicago, IL 60614, 312-281-1614, Mon.-Fri. noon-7:00 p.m.; fax: 312-348-3533 (call first to turn on machine). Antique lighting fixtures and original shades of the period. Some restoration of fixtures. Mail order. Showroom open noon-7:00 p.m., Sundays noon-6:00 p.m..

Theiss Plating Corporation, 9314 Manchester, St. Louis, MO 63119, 314-961-0600, 8:30 a.m.-5:00 p.m. Lighting repairs. Serving the Midwest.

Universal of Georgetown, Inc., 1804 Wisconsin Avenue NW, Washington, DC 20007, 202-333-2460, Mon.-Fri. 8:30 a.m.-5:00 p.m., Sat. 10:00 a.m.-4:00 p.m. Lighting repairs, rewiring, and refinishing. D.C., Maryland, Virginia area.

Victorian Lighting Works, 251 South Pennsylvania Avenue, P.O. Box 469, Centre Hall, PA 16828, 814-364-9577, Mon.-Fri. 8:00 a.m.-6:00 p.m. Restoration of antique lighting fixtures. Mail order sales catalog $5, refundable with first order.

Washington House Reproductions, P.O. Box 246, Washington, VA 22747, 703-675-3385. Restoration of old lighting. Mail order.

William Spencer, Inc., Creek Road, Rancocas Woods, NJ 08060, 609-235-1830, 10:00 a.m.-5:00 p.m. Metal lamps refinished.

Yestershades, 3824 SE Stark Street, Portland, OR 97214, 503-235-5645 Reproduction and custom lampshades, Victorian to 1930s designs. Handmade fringed shades. Catalog $3.50, refundable with first order.

N. Bucki, 7974 Route 98 South, Arcade, NY 14009. Copies of broken lamp tops painted to order. Custom china painting done on several sizes of blank globes.

Kathleen M. Hymes, P.O. Box 243, Santa Monica, CA 90406, 213-395-6360, anytime. Hand-dyed and hand-sewn Victorian-style lampshades. Period fabrics from antique piano shawls often used. Mail order. Catalog $2.50.

Ned James, Wrought Metals, 65 Canal Street, Turners Falls, MA 01376, 413-863-8388, 11:30 a.m.-1:30 p.m. Repair, restoration of lighting.

Thomas Loose, Blacksmith-Whitesmith, Route 2, Box 2410, Leesport, PA 19533, 215-926-4849 or 215-926-4849, 8:00 a.m.-5:00 p.m. Hand-forged iron for home and hearth. Reproduction lighting devices. Double stamped SASE for information. Mail order.

Joan Meyer, 104 Colwyn Lane, Bala Cynwyd, PA 19004, 215-664-3174 or 215-664-2183, 9:00 a.m.-9:00 p.m. Restoration of Tiffany lamps and windows. Works in U.S. or Europe.

Peter Owen, 29 Murray Street, Augusta, ME 04330, 207-622-3277, anytime. Slag glass panel replacement and stained glass lamp repair. Bent replacement panels. Rewiring, lamp bases repaired, Tiffany-style shades repaired. Mail order.

E.W. Pyfer, 218 North Foley Avenue, Freeport, IL 61032, 815-232-8968, anytime. Lamp repairs, parts, and supplies. Brass and metal refurbished, missing parts replaced, old chandeliers restored, oil and gas lamps converted to electricity.

Book

How-to Book of Repairing, Rewiring, and Restoring Lamps and Lighting Fixtures, Rachel Martens, 1979 (Doubleday & Co., NY).

Leather Goods

Leather requires special care. Use only accepted leather cleaners and preservatives. Never use general-purpose waxes and polishes. Most department, furniture, and hardware stores sell suitable leather cleaners. Products such as neat's-foot oil and mink oil, sold in shoe stores, leather shops, and shoe repair shops, are made especially for use on leather. If the leather binding on your book is deteriorating into red crumbles, there is little that can be done. More sources are in the sections on Books and Furniture.

Source

The Leather Factory, 3847 East Loop 820 South, P.O. Box 50429, Fort Worth, TX 76105, 800-433-3201. Leathers, snaps, rivets, findings, saddle hardware, buckles, dyes, kits, tools, and books. Distribution centers throughout the country. Mail order. Catalog.

Limited Editions

Limited editions include many types of newer collectibles. The designation "limited edition" first became popular during the 1960s, even though the first limited-edition plate was the Bing & Grondahl Christmas plate of 1895. Many types of porcelains and silver were made in limited quantities, but the idea of stating the limits before offering the collectible is new. Some pieces are limited to an announced number, some to the number made before a special date. Limited editions can include plates, figurines, eggs, bells, forks, spoons, plaques, boxes, steins, mugs, urns, Christmas ornaments, paperweights, bottles, and thimbles.

Repairs to limited editions are almost useless if you are concerned with value. The slightest chip, crack, or imperfection lowers the value considerably and almost any repair will cost more than the value of the repaired piece. The only exception might be for very rare figurines. Hummels and Royal Doultons are sometimes repaired. When reselling a limited piece, it is best to have the original box and certifying paper. Because of the demand for the original box, some dealers will gladly pay for the rare, empty box. See also Pottery & Porcelain.

LOCKS & KEYS, see Hardware

MAGAZINES, see Paper Collectibles & Ephemera

Marble

The major concern regarding marble is its care and upkeep. Marble should be kept clean. Wipe up any spills as soon as possible or the marble may become etched. If the stain is stubborn, use soap and lukewarm water. Marble should be dusted with a damp cloth and washed with water and a mild detergent about twice a year. You can wax marble with a colorless paste wax, but white marble may appear yellow if waxed.

Minor breaks can be mended with instant epoxy glue. Most marble cutters, cemetery monument makers, tile setters, or windowsill installers have the product. Stains can be removed, but it takes time and requires more information. Check your library or contact a marble worker in your area.

Sources

Multi-Seal, 616 South Marengo Avenue, Alhambra, CA 91803, 818-282-5659, 7:30 a.m.-4:30 p.m.; fax: 818-289-9474. Chemicals for repair and maintenance of marble, granite, travertine, terrazzo, and agglomerates. Cleaner, sealer, polish, poultice, refinisher, and restorer. Technical advice on marble care and restoration. Mail order sales and service, local dealer information available.

New York Marble Works, Inc., 1399 Park Avenue, New York, NY 10029, 212-534-2242 or 212-534-2243, 8:30 a.m.-4:30 p.m. Marble repair, custom fabrication, specialty items, floor tiles, marble care products. Serving Northeastern U.S.

Venerable Classics, 645 Fourth Street, Suite 208, Santa Rosa, CA 95404, 707-575-3626, Mon.-Fri. 10:00 a.m.-5:00 p.m. Restoration of fragile objects, marble. Serving northern California and Western U.S. Mail order. Brochure.

Leaflet

How to Keep Your Marble Beautiful, Marble Institute of America (33505 State Street, Farmington, MI 48024).

Medical & Scientific Collectibles

Antique microscopes, telescopes, medical apparatus, and much more are included in scientific collectibles. Of special interest are quack medical machines. These all require special restoration and repair. Sometimes a local expert who works with modern microscopes or telescopes can help. Scales are listed in their own section.

There is not much that can be done about the weather, but for centuries people have wanted to know when storms are approaching. The barometer was invented by Evangelista Torricelli in Florence, Italy, in the 1640s. It measures the change in air pressure and helps indicate changes in weather. Many 18th- and 19th-century barometers still exist and, like all sensitive scientific instruments, often need repair.

Sources

New York Nautical Instrument & Service Co., 140 West Broadway, New York, NY 10012, 212-962-4522, 9:00 a.m.-5:00 p.m.; fax: 212-406-8420. Repair of nautical instruments. Mail order.

Tele-Optics, 5514 Lawrence Avenue, Chicago, IL 60630, 312-283-7757, 8:00 a.m.-4:00 p.m. Binoculars, telescopes, riflescopes, and barometers repaired.

Neville Lewis, H.C.R. 68, Box 130-L, Cushing, ME 04563, 207-354-8055, 8:00 a.m.-9:00 p.m. Barometer parts, mercury tubes, and thermometers made to order. Repair and restoration. Mail order.

Metals & Cloisonné

Each type of metal requires particular cleaning and care. Some copper, bronze, and brass should be kept polished. Bronze should never be cleaned in any way that might affect the patina. Soap, water, dusting, and even a light waxing are safe for most metal items. There are several tarnish-preventative silicon-based polishes that are safe for metals. Do not use harsh abrasives like scouring powder or steel wool on any metal. Always rinse off all polishes completely. Many polishes are made with acids that continue to "eat" the metal after it has been polished.

Do not keep bronzes in a room that is being cleaned with bleaching powders, disinfectants, or floor-washing products containing chlorine. The chlorine can harm the bronze. Never store bronzes near rubber mats. Some carpet adhesives, paints, and fabrics may contain chemicals that are corrosive.

Iron cooking utensils should be seasoned. Coat an iron pot with edible cooking oil and bake it at 300 degrees for about two hours. Special dull black and rust-resistant paint is available if you want to repaint iron, but it must not be used on utensils that hold food.

Once damaged, enamel and cloisonné are very difficult to repair. Dents and chipped enamel require the attention of an expert. The cost of the repair is often more than the value of the piece. Some minor repairs might be done by a local jeweler or metalsmith.

Radical changes in temperature can crack enamel, so pieces should never be kept in a sunny window or over heat ducts, or washed in very hot or cold water.

Pewter is very soft and can be damaged easily or melted. Never put a piece of pewter near a burner on a stove. Never mechanically buff a piece of pewter; it will permanently change the color of the piece. Never use harsh scouring powder or steel wool to clean pewter. There are several commercial pewter polishes available at jewelry and grocery stores.

Tin and toleware should be kept dry and free of rust. If tin is rusty, try removing the rust with 0000 steel wool. For painted toleware, just touch up the spot, but never paint more than is necessary.

A redecorated piece of toleware is of value as a new item but not as an antique. Once the tin is repainted it has lost its value to the serious collector, but sometimes repainting is the only solution for a severely damaged piece. Serious toleware decorators often look for old pieces with worn paint to redecorate. It is possible to get new tinware made in the same manner as the old. Many restored-village museums have tinshops where tin is made and sold. Dents can be removed from tin and toleware by any competent silverworker or metalsmith.

Never wrap metals in plastic or nonventilated materials. Moisture can collect under the wrap, or the plastic may melt and cause damage.

Check in the Yellow Pages of the telephone book under "Plating" to find shops that replate, polish, and restore metal items. See also the section in this book on Silver & Silver Plate.

Sources

Abend Metal Repair, Delavan Center, 501 West Fayette Street, Syracuse, NY 13204, 315-478-2749, Mon.-Fri. 9:00 a.m.-5:30 p.m.; answering machine other times. Repair and restoration of objects made of aluminum, brass, bronze, cast iron, steel, stainless steel, or white metal. Sculpture repair and restoration. Custom welding, antique polishing, patina restoration, cast reproductions.

Abercrombie & Co., 9159A Brookville Road, Silver Spring, MD 20910, 301-585-2385, weekdays 9:00 a.m.-5:00 p.m., Sat. 9:00 a.m.-1:00 p.m. Metal refinishing; gold, silver, copper, brass, nickel, and tin plating. Filled sterling repairs; combs, mirrors, brushes, files, and letter openers replaced. Hand and machine engraving. Tin-lined copper cookware. Lamp repair and rewiring. Mail order.

Al Bar Wilmette Platers, 127 Green Bay Road, Wilmette, IL 60091, 312-251-0187, Mon.-Fri. 8:00 a.m.-4:30 p.m., Sat. 8:00 a.m.-3:00 p.m. Repair and restoration of metal antiques. Plating, polishing, lacquering. Copper cookware re-tinned.

Arden Forge, 301 Brintons Bridge Road, West Chester, PA 19382, 215-399-1530, Mon.-Sat. 9:00 a.m.-5:00 p.m. Restoration of copper items, including weathervanes. Zinc statues restored.

Authentic Lighting, 558 Grand Avenue, Englewood, NJ 07631, 201-568-7429, Mon.-Fri. 9:00 a.m.-5:00 p.m. Refinishing and replating.

Brass & Copper Polishing Shop, Don Reedy, 251 West Patrick Street, Frederick, MD 21701, 301-663-4240, 8:00 a.m.-4:00 p.m. Brass and copper pieces repaired, lacquered, and polished. Serving the Maryland-Virginia-Pennsylvania area.

Brass Anvil, Inc., Jim Horack, 186 North DuPont Highway, Bldg. 30, Airport Industrial Center, New Castle, DE 19720, 302-322-7679, 9:00

a.m.-5:30 p.m., 302-733-0617 evenings. Metal antiques restored and repaired; chandeliers and lighting fixtures a specialty. Polishing and lacquering service, custom range hoods, planters, brass railings for bars, hardware, custom display cases.

Brass Butler, 585 Cobb Parkway South, Marietta, GA 30062, 404-426-8024, 9:00 a.m.-4:00 p.m. Brass, copper, and metal restoration; brazing, soldering, silver brazing.

Bronze et al, 2544 Mountainview Road, Powhatan, VA 23139, 804-598-5818, 9:00 a.m.-7:00 p.m. Restoration of bronze, brass, copper, and other nonferrous metals; replication of antique patinas and finishes; repair of scratches, dents, and holes; missing parts on sculpture or hardware replaced; wood and plaster art objects restored. Mail order. Will travel for on-site restorations.

Cambridge Smithy, Cambridge, VT 05444, 802-644-5358, anytime. Restoration of wrought-iron pieces, iron and copper weathervanes.

Conant Custom Brass, P.O. Box 1523A, 270 Pine Street, Burlington, VT 05402, 802-658-4482 or 802-658-9978, 8:00 a.m.-5:00 p.m. Complete metal restoration and repair, custom fabrication, plating, re-tinning of copper cooking pots, rewiring; hardware, plumbing fixtures, light fixtures, brass dust corners, and more. Brochure.

Country Accents, P.O. Box 437, Montoursville, PA 17754, 717-478-4127, Mon.-Fri. 9:00 a.m.-4:00 p.m. Pierced-tin panels, custom sizes, for kitchen cabinets, and other decorative uses. Revere lantern kits, pie safe kits, tin piercing kits and patterns. Catalog $5; with set of metal sample swatches $15.95.

Cutrone Casting & Restoration, 2888 Detroit Avenue, Cleveland, OH 44113, 216-621-4448, 7:00 a.m.-5:00 p.m. Design, production, and restoration of metal artwork and ornamentation. Bronze restoration. By appointment only. Call for further information.

Ephraim Forge, 8300 West North Avenue, Frankfort, IL 60423, 815-469-3201, 8:00 a.m.-6:00 p.m. Repair, restoration, reproduction of metalwork: iron, steel, copper, and brass. Small items as well as architectural items, such as gates, grilles, and rails.

Fine Finishes, Kenneth Miltner, Route 176, Box 248, Brooksville, ME 04617, 207-326-4545, 8:30 a.m.-4:00 p.m. Brass refinishing, antiquing, polishing, and lacquering; pewter and copperware restored. Fireplace hardware, door hardware, brass beds, kettles, and bath fixtures restored. Copper cookware re-tinned.

Harvey M. Stern & Co., 6350 Germantown Road, Philadelphia, PA 19444, 215-438-6350, 8:00 a.m.-5:00 p.m.; fax: 215-843-2322. Metal restoration and custom metal finishings. Lighting fixtures refinished, repaired, and rewired. Serving Philadelphia, New Jersey, Delaware, and parts of Maryland and Pennsylvania.

Hiles Plating Company, Inc., 2028 Broadway, Kansas City, MO 64108, 816-421-6450 or 816-421-6450, Mon.-Fri. 9:00 a.m.-5:00 p.m. Restoration of antique sterling silver, silver plate, copper, brass, and pewter. Plating in silver, gold, brass, nickel, and copper. Mail order service. Brochure.

Institute of Metal Repair, 1558 South Redwood, Escondido, CA 92025, 619-747-5978, Mon.-Fri. 10:00 a.m.-5:00 p.m. Restoration, repair, preservation, care of metal. How-to and source books. Write or contact computer bulletin board: 619-480-9641, format: N/8/1.

J & H China Repairs, 8296 St. George Street, Vancouver, BC V5X 3C5, Canada, 604-321-1093, 9:00 a.m.-4:00 p.m. Restoration of enamel, cloisonné, and picture frames.

J.M. Gray, Inc., 509 West Fayette Street, Syracuse, NY 13204, 315-476-1003, 9:00 a.m.-5:00 p.m., 315-475-9498, evenings. Wrought iron repair and reproduction. Bases and pedestals for sculptures. Serving Northeastern U.S. Call first.

JAX Chemical Company, Inc., 78-11 267th Street, Floral Park, NY 11004, 718-347-0057, 9:00 a.m.-5:00 p.m.; fax: 914-668-3502. Metal darkening, coloring, plating, polishing, cleaning solutions. Price list.

Memphis Plating Works, 678-682 Madison Avenue, Memphis, TN 38103, 901-526-3051, Mon.-Fri. 8:00 a.m.-5:00 p.m., Sat. 8:00 a.m.-noon. Silver, gold, copper, brass, nickel and chrome restoration and plating. Broken statues repaired and refinished, pot metal or bronze. Chrome on antique and show cars restored.

Metal Finishing Inc., 41 Sutton Lane, Worcester, MA 01603, 508-754-9904, Mon.-Sat. 9:00 a.m.-6:00 p.m. Metal restoration. Polishing, buffing, electroplating. Repair and specialty finishes for chandeliers, brass beds, fireplace equipment, and hardware. Boston area pickup and delivery. Mail order.

Michael J. Dotzel & Son, 402 East 63rd Street, New York, NY 10021, 212-838-2890, 9:00 a.m.-4:00 p.m. Metalwork and repairs in brass, copper, pewter, and bronze. Polishing and plating. Metal liners and shades made. Lamps and chandeliers rewired. Cast restoration of metal antiques. New York area. Will repair shipped items.

New England Country Silver, Inc., Smith Road, East Haddam, CT 06423, 203-873-1314, 9:00 a.m.-3:00 p.m. Repairing, refinishing, replating, and engraving of silverware, copper, and brass. Replacement knife blades, combs, brushes, mirrors for dresser sets. Mail order.

Orum Silver Company, P.O. Box 805, 51 South Vine Street, Meriden, CT 06450, 203-237-3037, Mon.-Fri. 8:00 a.m.-4:30 p.m. Repair, refinishing, replating of old silver, antiques. Pewter, brass, copper restored and refinished. Gold, silver, nickel, copper, brass plating.

Peninsula Plating Works, 232 Homer Avenue, Palo Alto, CA 94301, 415-326-7825 or 415-322-8806, Mon.-Fri. 8:30 a.m.-6:00 p.m., Sat. 10:00 a.m.-5:00 p.m.; fax: 415-322-7392. Plating on brass, bronze, copper, iron, lead, nickel-silver, pewter, steel, white metal, and zinc. Polishing, soldering, repairing, and refinishing metal items, such as lamps, beds, pots and pans, door handles, fireplace equipment, trays, and antiques. Combs, brushes, knife blades, pearl handles, salad servers, and insulators replaced. Brochure.

Re-tinning & Copper Repair, Inc., 525 West 26th Street, New York, NY 10001, 212-244-4896, Mon.-Fri. 9:00 a.m.-5:00 p.m. Repairs and refinishing of metal antiques and collectibles, including brass beds, chandeliers, lamps, samovars, shelving, wire whips, and fireplace equipment. Copper cookware re-tinned. Mail order.

Thome Silversmiths, 49 West 37th Street, Suite 605, New York, NY 10018, 212-764-5426, 8:30 a.m.-1:00 p.m., 2:30 p.m.-5:30 p.m. Brass polishing, gold plating, pewter repair, polishing, engraving, chandelier polishing, reproduction of pieces or parts. Mail order.

Thompsons Studio, Inc., Back Meadow Road, R.R. 1, Box 340, Damariscotta, ME 04543, 207-563-5280 or 207-563-5280. Repairs, reproductions in sterling silver, coin silver, and gold. Mail order. Brochure.

Universal of Georgetown, Inc., 1804 Wisconsin Avenue NW, Washington, DC 20007, 202-333-2460, Mon.-Fri. 8:30 a.m.-5:00 p.m., Sat. 10:00 a.m.-4:00 p.m. Metal restoration, repairs, polishing, plating. D.C.-Maryland-Virginia area.

Vermont Plating, Inc., 113 South Main Street, Rutland, VT 05701, 802-775-5759, 8:00 a.m.-4:00 p.m. Metal restoration, plating, cleaning, and polishing. Copper, nickel, and chrome plating. Cadmium plating keeps metal from rusting.

William Spencer, Inc., Creek Road, Rancocas Woods, NJ 08060, 609-235-1830, 10:00 a.m.-5:00 p.m. Metal refinished.

WTC Associates, Inc., 2532 Regency Road, Lexington, KY 40503, 606-278-4171; fax: 606-276-1717. Restoration, replating, and repair of silver, gold, brass, and copper. Replacement parts. Hand engraving.

Rocco V. DeAngelo, R.D. 1, Box 187R, Cherry Valley, NY 13320, 607-264-3607, 8:00 a.m.-9:00 p.m. Antique cast iron restoration, sandblasting, painting, fabrication of parts. Serving area within 250 miles of Albany, N.Y.

Ned James, Wrought Metals, 65 Canal Street, Turners Falls, MA 01376, 413-863-8388, 11:30 a.m.-1:30 p.m. Custom hand-wrought metalwork, repairs, and restoration. Lighting, hardware, fireplace accessories, architectural metalwork.

Books and Leaflets

Early American Decoration, Esther Stevens Brazer, 1961 (Pond-Ekberg Company, Springfield, MS).

Early American Decoration Made Easy, Edith Cramer, 1985 (General Publishing, 30 Lesmill Road, Don Mills, ON M3B 2T6, Canada).

IMR Sourcebook (Institute of Metal Repair, 1558 South Redwood Street, Escondido, CA 92025).

Oriental Cloisonné and Other Enamels, Arthur & Grace Chu, 1975 (Crown Publishers, NY).

Painting Galvanized Steel, leaflet (Zinc Institute, 292 Madison Avenue, New York, NY 10017). (Lists metal repairers and restorers, schools, preservation organizations.)

A Quarter Century of Decorating and Teaching Country Painting, Dorothy Dean Hutchings, 1975 (Shandling Lithographing Co., Tucson, AZ).

Computer Programs

IMR Metal-Net (Institute of Metal Repair, 1558 South Redwood, Escondido, CA 92025). (Bulletin board with resource information, networking, and problem solving.) Send two first class stamps for information packet.

Military Memorabilia

Collectors of military memorabilia search for everything from toy soldiers to working guns. Many of these souvenirs are dangerous, and any gun, hand grenade, or other military object that might hold explosives should be checked by local police or other experts. If you have children in a home with military memorabilia, be sure the guns and knives are safely locked up. Old guns should have the barrels filled so it is impossible to accidentally discharge the gun. Old rifles may be unsafe to shoot, and often even safe antiques have a recoil that will surprise the inexperienced. Do not buy or sell a gun without checking the local laws; you might be legally responsible if the gun is later used in a crime. Be sure to register any gun.

Repairs to any sort of weapon should only be done by an expert. Many shops that sell modern firearms have staff members who can repair old guns. Other restorers can be located through the publications which are listed in *Kovels' Guide to Selling Your Antiques & Collectibles.* Because of the problems of shipping guns, repair work must be done locally. See also Knives.

Daniel Cullity Restoration, 209 Old County Road, East Sandwich, MA 02537, 508-888-1147, Mon.-Fri. 8:00 a.m.-4:00 p.m. Firearms restoration. Fabrication of parts; metal and wood repaired, restoration of decorative metalwork. Guns cleaned and repaired.

Miniatures & Dollhouses

Miniatures can include anything from tiny 18th-century silver tea sets to complete dollhouses that are furnished to the period. Dollhouses and furnishings are made in several scales, ranging from one inch to one foot (one-twelfth scale) to one-eighth or two-fifths scale. Most modern dollhouse pieces are being made to the scale of one inch to a foot or the latest size, one half inch to a foot.

There are clubs and shows for collectors of miniatures in most parts of the country. Information about these events can be found in the magazines about miniatures which are listed in *Kovels' Guide to Selling Your Antiques & Collectibles*. Craftsmen who make new miniatures can often repair old ones.

Sources

Happy Hearts, Route 1, Box 164, Lexington, MO 64067, 816-259-4422, 9:00 a.m.-5:00 p.m., 816-259-4706 evenings. Accessories for dolls and miniatures. Buttons, lace, fabric, ribbons, feathers, ostrich plumes, hair combs, pocket watches, and many other items. Catalog $2. Worldwide mail order business.

Manhattan Doll Hospital, 176 Ninth Avenue, New York, NY 10011, 212-989-5220, Tues.-Fri. noon-6:00 p.m. Dollhouse kits, finished dollhouses, miniature furniture and accessories, wood components, electrical parts.

Book

Reproducing Period Furniture and Accessories in Miniature, Virginia Merrill and Susan Merrill Richardson, 1981 (Crown Publishers, NY).

Mirrors & Picture Frames

An antique mirror consists of a frame and the silvered glass. The value is higher if both parts are original. Unfortunately, old mirrors often lose some of the backing and the reflective qualities are diminished. It is possible to "resilver" the old glass or to replace the glass entirely if you do not wish to live with flawed glass.

An inexpensive way to restore some old mirrors with poor "silvering" is to remove the metallic backing from the old glass and put a new mirror behind the old glass. This saves the old glass, yet gives a mirror that reflects properly. Contact local mirror installers located through the Yellow Pages of your phone book.

A painting or print needs a frame--old, new, or restored. Try to re-frame any print or painting with a frame in the same style as the original. It is possible to buy antique frames or copies of antique frames from general antiques shops, modern frame shops, or special firms that deal only in period picture frames.

Some of the workmen listed in the Furniture section also restore mirrors and picture frames.

Sources

Eli Wilner & Co., Inc., 1525 York Avenue, New York, NY 10028, 212-744-6521 or 212-744-6674, Mon.-Sat. 9:30 a.m.-5:30 p.m.; fax: 212-628-0264. Frame restoration. American period frames of 19th and early 20th centuries, custom-designed frames and mirrors, picture-hanging services and advice.

FredEric's Frame Studio, Inc., 1230 West Jackson Boulevard, Chicago, IL 60607, 312-243-2950, Mon.-Fri. 8:00 a.m.-5:00 p.m. Restoration of picture frames. Manufacture of custom frames: carved, 22K gold leaf, acrylic, and metal. Serving the Midwest.

Gold Leaf Studios, Inc., P.O. Box 50156, Washington, DC 20004, 202-638-4660, Mon.-Fri. 9:00 a.m.-5:00 p.m. Gold leaf restoration, interior and exterior architectural gilding, custom frame fabrication, specialty matting, frame search service, will locate period styles. Send photo of object and details for estimate on conservation.

Guido, 118 Newbury Street, Boston, MA 02116, 617-267-0569, 9:30 a.m.-5:00 p.m. Picture frames made or restored. Gold leafing.

J & H China Repairs, 8296 St. George Street, Vancouver, BC V5X 3C5, Canada, 604-321-1093, 9:00 a.m.-4:00 p.m. Restoration of frames.

Julius Lowy Frame and Restoring Co., 28 West End Avenue, New York, NY 10023, 212-586-2050, 8:30 a.m.-5:00 p.m., 212-861-8585; fax: 212-489-1948. Restoration of works of art, including frames. Conservation services. Brochure.

Marlborough Cottage Arts & Interiors, Jeff Von-Er, SR 70, Box 144, New Marlborough, MA 01230, 413-229-2170, weekdays 8:00 a.m.-8:00 p.m. Gold leaf restoration, fancy paint finishes, conservation work done on frames and mirrors.

McKenzie's Art Restoration Studio, Keeta McKenzie, 2907 East Monte Vista Drive, Tucson, AZ 85716, 602-323-1466, Tues.-Sat. 9:00 a.m.-noon, 1:00 p.m.-5:00 p.m. Frames restored. Mail order worldwide.

New England Country Silver, Inc., Smith Road, East Haddam, CT 06423, 203-873-1314, 9:00 a.m.-3:00 p.m. Repairing, refinishing, replating, engraving of antique silverware, copper, and brass. Replacement combs, brushes, and mirrors for dresser sets. Mail order.

Original Woodworks, 360 North Main, Stillwater, MN 55082, 612-430-3622. Mirror resilvering. Classes, tools, and supplies. Catalog $3.

Pat's Etcetera Company, Inc. (PECO), P.O. Box 777, 810 East First Street, Smithville, TX 78957, 512-237-3600, Mon.-Fri. 10:00 a.m.-3:00 p.m. Oval convex picture-frame glass. Mail order. Brochure.

R.G. Brown & Associates, Ron Brown, 7530 East Hinsdale Place, Englewood, CO 80112, 303-721-6514, 9:00 a.m.-6:00 p.m. Custom-made picture frames, finished or unfinished. Embossed wood carvings, decorative ornaments, and moldings, designs from 1880s to 1960s. Mail order. Catalog $4.

R. Wayne Reynolds, Ltd., 3618 Falls Road, Baltimore, MD 21211, 301-467-1800, Mon.-Fri. 9:00 a.m.-5:00 p.m. Repair and restoration of mirror frames. Conservation of gold leaf frames and furniture. American period reproduction frames and original, one-of-a-kind designs for frames. Mail order.

Raphael's Antique Restoration, 655 Atlantic Street, Stamford, CT 06902, 203-348-3079, 8:30 a.m.-4:30 p.m. Antique picture and mirror frames repaired, gold leaf restored, inlays, veneers, carvings, turnings restored, parts replaced, French polishing. No mail order.

Ron's Gallery Supply Co., P.O. Box 1791, New York, NY 10016, 800-735-7667, anytime, leave message. Mirrors resilvered. Beveled mirrors. Frames restored, resized. Museum board, conservation supplies, convex oval glass, UV-absorbing glazing, picture moldings and frames. Picture hanging systems, cordless picture lights, print display racks, tools, supplies.

Randy Armstrong, Box 85, Riverside Road, Bluff City, TN 37618, 615-538-7686, 8:00 a.m.-5:00 p.m. Mirrors resilvered. Serving eastern Tennessee, southwest Virginia.

Ronald DuCharme, 742 Charlton Road, Ballston Lake, NY 12188, 518-399-1246, 5:00 p.m.-8:00 p.m. Gold leaf repaired and releafed, conservation of gilded and polychrome wooden frames. Reproduction of missing elements.

Andrew Hurst, 2423 Amber Street, Knoxville, TN 37917, 615-974-6924 or 615-523-3498, 8:30 a.m.-8:00 p.m. Repair and restoration of picture frames. No mail order. Serving eastern Tennessee.

Dorvan L. Manus, 179 Compo Road South, Westport, CT 06880, 203-227-8602, 8:00 a.m.-10:00 a.m., 4:00 p.m.-6:00 p.m. Restoration of 18th- and early 19th-century items, specializing in smalls, gilt mirrors and frames, trays, painted and papered boxes, and lacquerwork.

Videotape

Antique Frame Restoration, (AFR Services, P.O. Box 16785, Wichita, KS 67216-6785).

Movie Memorabilia

Movie memorabilia is a large field, ranging from movie films, sound-track albums, comic materials, toys, and dolls representing characters in movies, to ceramics commemorating movie characters and related events. It also includes movie posters, lobby cards, press kits, movie stills, costumes, and memorabilia from the stars, such as Joan Crawford's false eyelashes or Judy Garland's ruby slippers.

All this material is rightly considered movie memorabilia and can be found in any shop or show. Specialists should be familiar with the publications and shows that are devoted exclusively to movies. Special groups like the "Star Trek" enthusiasts or fan clubs of deceased stars hold regular conventions and meetings, exchanging information and memorabilia. You can find out about these in the clubs and publications which are listed in *Kovels' Guide to Selling Your Antiques & Collectibles.*

Because movie memorabilia is so recent and so abundant, it does not pay to repair any but the greatest rarities. See the sections on Comic Art, Paper, Photographs, Textiles, and Toys.

Music collectibles range from musical instruments to reproducing pianos. The value of each of these items is in the music it makes, so each piece must be in good working condition. Repairs of mechanical music-making machines are slow. Many of the restorers have two- and three-year waiting lists. If you can fix this type of antique yourself, you can usually make good buys. Be very careful if you buy a machine that needs repairs that you can't do yourself.

Mechanical music boxes have been popular for centuries. They range from tiny singing birds to lavish enameled boxes to the large machines that played steel discs 33 inches in diameter. All music boxes are delicate, intricate mechanisms that require care. Don't try to repair a music box unless you're an expert--it's a job for a professional. Restorers and parts can be found, but they are rare and expensive. You may be lucky enough to find a local music box devotee who restores; contact the Musical Box Society International (Route 3, Box 205, Morgantown, IN 46160) for information. Other restorers are listed here, but they have advised us that they are very busy and repairs may take years.

Minor repairs of instruments are possible in some cities, or through dealers or service shops listed in the Yellow Pages under "Musical Instruments--Repairing."

Sources

A.M.R. Publishing Company, P.O. Box 3007, Arlington, WA 98223, 206-659-6434, Mon.-Fri. 9:00 a.m.-5:00 p.m.; fax 206-659-5994. Books, service and parts manuals for player pianos. Catalog.

The Beehive Reed Organ Studio, P.O. Box 41, Oak Street, Alfred ME 04002, 207-324-0990, weekdays 9:00 a.m.-5:00 p.m. Reed organ repair and restoration. Mail order.

Bryant Stove Works, R.F.D. 2, Box 2048, Thorndike, ME 04986, 207-568-3665, 7:30 a.m.-5:00 p.m. Player pianos repaired.

DB Musical Restorations, Carol & David Beck, 230 Lakeview Avenue NE, Atlanta, GA 30305, 404-237-3556, Mon.-Sat. 9:00 a.m.-9:00 p.m. Cylinder and disc music box mechanisms repaired, cleaned, lacquered, lubricated. Comb teeth replaced and tuned, missing parts replaced.

Horn & Son String Instruments, Inc., 2570 Superior Avenue, Cleveland, OH 44114, 216-579-4337, 9:00 a.m.-5:00 p.m. Repair and restoration of string instruments and ethnic instruments. Bow rehairing, manufacture of cellos and basses.

Inzer Pianos, Inc., John and Hazel Inzer, 2473 Canton Road, Marietta, GA 30066, 404-422-2664, Mon.-Sat. 10:00 a.m.-6:00 p.m. Pianos, player pianos, nickelodeons, and reed organs restored. Parts and supplies for pianos, player pianos, and reed organs. Mail order. Catalog $2.

Johnson Music, 147 North Main Street, Mt. Airy, NC 17030, 919-786-8742, 800-247-5979, Mon.-Sat. 9:00 a.m.-5:00 p.m.; 919-320-2212 home. Antique pump organs rebuilt, restored, and refinished. Bellows recovered. Pump organ supplies, including tabs, buttons, bellows cloth, reeds, felts, leather and sheepskin seals, animal glues. Mail order.

Musical Wonder House, 18 High Street, Wiscasset, ME 04578, 207-882-7163 or 207-882-6373, anytime. Complete mechanical restoration of musical boxes and windup phonographs.

Panchronia Antiquities, Nancy Fratti, P.O. Box 28, Whitehall, NY 12887, 518-282-9770, Mon.-Fri. 9:00 a.m.-6:00 p.m.; fax: 518-282-9800. Repairs, parts, and supplies for music boxes. Digitally recorded cassette tapes and compact discs of antique music boxes. Books on antique music boxes. Mail order. Restoration supply catalog $4, refundable with order. Reproduction tune card catalog $2.50. Free tape/compact disc list.

Phoenix Reed Organ Resurrection, Ned Phoenix, Box 3, Jamaica, VT 05343, 802-874-4173, 7:00 a.m.-9:00 p.m.; fax: 802-257-5117. Reed organs restored. Organ parts, stools, blowers, replacement reeds, reed voicing and tuning. Consulting, presentations, and demonstrations. Purchase unusual and historic reed organs, parts, and reeds. Showroom open every day. Mail order. Organ catalog $1 and LSASE. Write with specific requests and enclose SASE.

Player Piano Co., Inc., 704 East Douglas, Wichita, KS 67202, 316-263-1714, weekdays 8:00 a.m.-5:00 p.m. Restoration supplies for bellows-type player unit, all types of player pianos, and reed organs. Leather, tubing, bellows cloth, tools, reed organ parts, decals, piano action supplies, books. Mail order. Catalog.

Pump and Pipe Shop, 7698 Kraft Avenue, Caledonia, MI 49316, 616-891-8743, anytime. Pump organs repaired; parts.

Schutts' Antique Music Repair, 501 5th Avenue NE, Clarion, IA 50525, 515-532-3459, 6:30 p.m.-9:00 p.m. Repair and restoration of disc music boxes, player pianos, "pianocorder" electronic pianos, reed type pump organs, and mechanical music machines. No wood case or comb repair, but will refer work to others. Serving the Midwest, west of Mississippi River. Call first.

Shrine to Music Museum, 414 East Clark Street, Vermillion, SD 57069, 605-677-5306, 8:00 a.m.-5:00 p.m. Will provide references for restoration requests.

William D. Gilstrap, Route 1, Box 74, Bevier, MO 63532, 816-385-5338, 6:00 a.m.-9:00 p.m. Player piano action rebuilding, specializes in Gulbransen & Schultz and all reproducers. Obsolete and missing components manufactured.

Jandi Goggin, Box 175, Huntington, NY 11743-0175. Repair and restoration of musical birdcages, music boxes, and bellows. Material, tools, and instructions for recovering bellows in singing birdcages and singing bird boxes.

Randolph Herr, 111-07 77th Avenue, Forest Hills, NY 11375, 718-520-1443, 8:00 a.m.-11:00 p.m. Restores player and reproducing pianos, uprights and grands.

Stephen Leonard, P.O. Box 127, Albertson, NY 11507, 516-742-0979, 8:00 a.m.-5:00 p.m. Restoration of singing bird boxes and whistling figures. Mail order worldwide.

George Paladics, 414 Route 523 North, Whitehouse Station, NJ 08889, 201-534-2981, 9:00 a.m.-5:00 p.m. Complete restoration and repair of music boxes. Mail order worldwide.

Bob Pierce, 1880 Termino Avenue, Long Beach, CA 90815. Decals for pianos, $2 each. Almost all makers' names. Enclose cash or check with SASE. Mail order only.

Sal Provenzano, P.O. Box 843, Bronx, NY 10469, 212-655-7021. Repairs singing birdcages, bird boxes, music boxes, and animated figures.

Tom Ross, 230 Mustang Circle, Moncks Corner, SC 29461, 803-761-6327, 9:00 a.m.-6:00 p.m.; fax: 803-761-3030. Pianos repaired. Specializing in locating "hard to find goods," importing and exporting between U.S. and Europe.

Eldred Schutt, 501 Fifth Avenue NE, Clarion, IA 50525, 515-532-3459, 6:00 p.m.-9:00 p.m. Disc music boxes, reed organs, player pianos, phonographs repaired. Old and reproduction discs. Serving Midwest.

Paul N. Smith, 408 East Leeland Heights Boulevard, Lehigh Acres, FL 33936, 813-369-4663, 9:00 a.m.-5:00 p.m. Music boxes repaired.

Donald J. Tendrup, 7 Ashland Gate, Holtsville, Long Island, NY 11742, 516-758-4755, 7:00 a.m.-9:00 p.m., daily. Music boxes restored.

Books

Compleat Talking Machine, Eric L. Reiss, 1986 (Vestal Press, P.O. Box 97, Vestal, NY 13850).

Piano Care & Restoration, Eric Smith, 1982 (Tab Books, Blue Ridge Summit, PA 17214).

Piano Servicing Tuning & Rebuilding, Arthur A. Reblitz, 1976 (Vestal Press, P.O. Box 97, Vestal, NY 13850).

Preservation and Restoration of Sound Recordings, Jerry McWilliams, 1979 (AASLH, 172 Second Avenue North, Suite 102, Nashville, TN 37201).

Rebuilding the Player Piano, Larry Givens, 1963 (Vestal Press, P.O. Box 97, Vestal, NY 13850).

Restoring and Collecting Antique Reed Organs, Horton Presley, 1977 (Vestal Press, P.O. Box 97, Vestal, NY 13850).

Computer Program

Homecraft (P.O. Box 074, Tualatin, OR 97062). (Organize records and music collections.)

ORIENTALIA, see Metals; Pottery & Porcelain

Paintings

Oil paintings require special care. Lightly dust the surface of a good painting. Never wash a painting. Never try any at-home restoration unless you are trained or care very little about the final results. Never entrust a good oil painting to anyone but a competent restorer or conservator. Many pictures have been completely ruined by overrestoration, too much overpainting, or an overzealous cleaning that "skinned" the picture. These procedures may cause problems that can never be rectified.

If you believe that your painting, no matter how dirty, is valuable, take it to your local museum to learn about the artist. Museums will not appraise, but they can tell you if your picture is worth restoring, and can furnish the names of local conservators. In some cities, restorers are listed in the Yellow Pages under "Art Restoration and Conservation" or "Picture Restoring."

We have listed restorers, conservators, and companies using their own descriptions of title, training, and work methods. If you are concerned about the quality of the work or whether the firm is headed by a conservator or a restorer, you must check further. More information can be obtained through the American Institute for Conservation, 1522 K Street NW, #804, Washington, DC 20005.

Sources

Appelbaum & Himmelstein, 444 Central Park West, New York, NY 10025, 212-666-4630, 10:30 a.m.-7:00 p.m. Art restoration, specializing in ethnographic art and paintings.

Balboa Art Conservation Center, P.O. Box 3755, San Diego, CA 92103, 714-236-9702, 8:30 a.m.-5:00 p.m. Conservation of paintings and paper, serving the Southwestern U.S.

Fine Art Restoration, John Squadra, R.F.D. 2, Box 1440, Brooks, ME 04921, 207-722-3464. Restoration of oil paintings. Send photo and size of painting for estimate.

FredEric's Frame Studio, Inc., 1230 West Jackson Boulevard, Chicago, IL 60607, 312-243-2950, Mon.-Fri. 8:00 a.m.-5:00 p.m. Restoration of oil paintings, and works on paper. Serving the Midwest.

Gainsborough Products Co., Ltd., 3545 Mt. Diablo Boulevard, Lafayette, CA 94549, 415-283-4187, 800-227-4187 outside California. Art restoration supplies, including chemicals for restoring oil paintings, frame glazes, canvas lining and facing, cleaning and varnish removal kit. Brochure and price list.

Julius Lowy Frame and Restoring Co., 28 West End Avenue, New York, NY 10023, 212-586-2050 or 212-861-8585, 8:30 a.m.-5:00 p.m.; fax: 212-489-1948. Restoration of works of art, including paintings. Conservation services. Brochure.

Kramer Gallery, 229 East Sixth Street, St. Paul, MN 55101, 612-228-1301, Tues.-Fri. 9:00 a.m.-5:00 p.m. Conservation and restoration of 19th- and early 20th-century oil paintings, watercolors, and graphics.

McKenzie's Art Restoration Studio, Keeta McKenzie, 2907 East Monte Vista Drive, Tucson, AZ 85716, 602-323-1466, Tues.-Sat. 9:00 a.m.-noon, 1:00 p.m.-5:00 p.m. Oil paintings restored. Mail order.

Ron's Gallery Supply Co., P.O. Box 1791, New York, NY 10016, 800-735-7667, anytime. Paintings cleaned, restored. Picture hanging systems, cordless picture lights, display racks, tools, supplies.

Sierra Studios, 37 West 222, Route 64, Suite 103, St. Charles, IL 60175, 708-683-2525. Restoration of oil paintings.

Witherspoon Galleries, 3545 Mt. Diablo Boulevard, Lafayette, CA 94549, 415-283-3342, Tues.-Sat. 10:00 a.m.-6:00 p.m. Restoration of oil paintings and English watercolors from the 19th and early 20th centuries. Custom framing. Serving the San Francisco Bay area.

Eric Gordon, 2101 Lake Montebello Terrace, Baltimore, MD 21218, 301-366-2835, anytime. Conservation of fine art, including paintings, murals, and painted surfaces. Serving the mid-Atlantic states.

Andrew Hurst, 2423 Amber Street, Knoxville, TN 37917, 615-974-6924 or 615-523-3498, 8:30 a.m.-8:00 p.m. Repair and restoration of oil paintings. Special crating of art and antiques. No mail order. Serving eastern Tennessee.

Thomas Portue, 639 Silliman Street, San Francisco, CA 94134, 415-239-5264. Conservation and restoration of fine art paintings, murals, and decorative objects. Specializing in work on WPA murals and American, Western, and modern paintings.

Leonard E. Sasso, Master Restorer, 23 Krystal Drive, R.D. 1, Somers, NY 10589, 914-248-8289, 9:00 a.m.-7:00 p.m. Restoration of oil paintings on canvas and board, watercolors, pastels, and drawings. Serving the New York City-Westchester-Connecticut area.

Books

A Handbook on the Care of Paintings, Caroline K. Keck, 1965 (AASLH, 172 Second Avenue North, Suite 102, Nashville, TN 37201).

How to Take Care of Your Paintings, Caroline K. Keck, 1978 (Charles Scribner's Sons, NY).

Preservation Guide 3: Paintings, Priscilla O'Reilly, 1986 (Historic New Orleans Collection, 533 Royal Street, New Orleans, LA 70130).

Paper Collectibles & Ephemera

SUPERFINE BRISTOL TOBACCO

The proper storage, display, and repair of paper collectibles is both difficult and important if you wish to preserve old maps, handwritten documents, sheet music, or other paper items.

For storage, humidity should range between 45 and 65 degrees. If a room is too dry, the paper can become brittle; if it is too wet, various molds and insects can attack. Never glue or paste any paper items. Transparent mending tape can be especially damaging, as it will eventually react with the paper and make a stain.

Be sure to display printed paper away from strong sunlight or direct heat. The sun will fade paper and the heat will cause damage. Unfortunately, ideal conditions are almost impossible for collectors who wish to hang a Currier & Ives print or an old map as decoration.

Consider the value and the possible damage before framing any paper item. Follow these strict rules: use acid-free matting and always leave a space between the paper and the glass. Seal the back to keep it dust-free.

Instructions for framing and/or storing valuable paper collectibles can be found in most paper preservation books. If your local art supply shop or frame shop is unfamiliar with the proper materials, you can purchase them by mail through the companies listed in Part II under Conservation, Restoration, & Preservation Supplies.

See also the sections on Advertising, Books, Photographs, and Prints.

Sources

Archival Restoration Associates, Inc., P.O. Box 1395, North Wales, PA 19454, 215-699-0165, 24 hours, 7 days a week. Restoration and preservation of items on paper and parchment, watercolors, photographs. Repair and restoration of fine bindings. Paper treated to prevent deterioration. Send items registered, return receipt, insured as works of art. Archival consulting services available.

Document Conservation Center, Harold H. Moore, 1220 Fowler Street NW, Atlanta, GA 30318, 404-872-3626, Mon.-Fri. 9:00 a.m.-5:00 p.m. Restoration of paper documents. Brochure.

George Martin Cunha, Inc., Conservation Consultants, Tanglewood Drive, Lexington, KY 40505, 606-293-5703, 8:00 a.m.-5:00 p.m. Restoration of library, archival materials and works of art on paper. Preventive conservation, disaster prevention and recovery, security measures for libraries and archives. No mail order.

Northeast Document Conservation Center, Gary E. Albright, Abbott Hall, School Street, Andover, MA 01810, 508-470-1010, Mon.-Fri. 8:30 a.m.-4:30 p.m. Nonprofit regional conservation center specializing in treatment of paper-based materials: art on paper, books, maps, documents, photographs, and anything else on paper. Preservation microfilming, duplication of historical photographs, consultation workshops, preservation planning surveys, disaster assistance.

Sandlin's Books & Bindery, 70 West Lincolnway, Valparaiso, IN 46383-5522, 219-462-9922, Mon.-Sat. 9:00 a.m.-6:00 p.m. Books rebound and repaired, deacidification of paper and documents, Mylar encapsulation, handmade linen or leather slipcases and pamphlet folders. Mail order.

Talas, Division of Technical Library Service, Inc., 213 West 35th Street, New York, NY 10001, 212-735-7744, 9:00 a.m.-5:00 p.m. Paper restoration, archival storage products. tools, supplies, equipment, and books. Mail order worldwide. Catalog $5.

Tillapaugh Paper Conservation, Ellen Riggs Tillapaugh, 80 Beaver Street, Cooperstown, NY 13326, 607-547-5646. Conservation of works of art and historic documents on paper.

Wei T'o Associates, Inc., P.O. Drawer 40, 21750 Main Street, Unit 27, Matteson, IL 60443, 708-747-6660, Mon.-Fri. 8:30 a.m.-5:00 p.m. Deacidification sprays and solutions, application equipment, and related products. Wei T'o prevents yellowing and embrittlement and protects documents, books, and works of art. Consultant services. Available through distributors or mail order worldwide.

William P. Bissex Enterprises, 606 Seneca Avenue, Norwood, PA 19074, 215-532-5694, 9:00 a.m.-5:00 p.m. Custom binding, rebinding, repair, and restoration of all kinds of books, including Bibles. Written quotation after inspection of material to be restored. Mail order.

Marjorie B. Cohn, Print Department, Fogg Art Museum, Harvard University, Cambridge, MA 02138, 617-495-2393, Mon.-Fri. 9:00 a.m.-5:00 p.m. Advice on prints, specializing in European and American prints 1450-present.

Bernice Masse Rosenthal, 51 McClellan Street, Amherst, MA 01002, 413-256-0844, 9:00 a.m.-5:00 p.m. Restoration of flat printed paper.

David Lloyd Swift, Paper Preservation, 6436 Brownlee Drive, Nashville, TN 37205, 615-352-0308, 8:00 a.m.-4:00 p.m. Preservation, restoration, deacidification, cleaning, and encapsulation. Mail order.

Nancy Wu, Fine Art Conservation Services, 94 Mercer Street, New York,

NY 10012, 212-966-5513, 9:00 a.m.-6:00 p.m. Conservation of works on paper and photographs. No mail order.

Books

Curatorial Care of Works of Art on Paper, Anne F. Clapp, 1974 (Nick Lyons Books, 31 West 21st Street, New York, NY 10010).
How to Care for Works of Art on Paper, 1971 (Museum of Fine Arts, Boston).
Procedures for Salvage of Water-Damaged Library Materials, Peter Waters, 1975 (Library of Congress, Washington, DC).

Paperweights

Advanced paperweight collectors want French, English, or American weights. The most popular are millefiori, floral, and sulfides of the 19th and 20th centuries. Some modern paperweights are being made in limited quantities by artists like Kaziun or Stankard. They are expensive, with some valued in the hundreds or thousands of dollars. There are less desirable and less expensive American and Chinese weights of similar styles, plus flat advertising weights, snow weights, and many other types. The glass can be repolished to remove scratches and nicks. Cracks cannot be repaired. It is important to be sure the condition of the paperweight is good. Repolishing scratched glass will not lower the value of the item.

See books listed in the Glass section.

Sources

Castle's Fair, Lawrence and Sara Castle, 885 Taylor Avenue, Ogden, UT 84404-5270, 801-393-8131. Antique glass restoration, paperweights. Certain types of fractures in paperweights healed. Mail order only.
George N. Kulles, 115 Little Creek Drive, Route 2, Lockport, IL 60441, 312-301-0996, 8:00 a.m.-8:00 p.m. Restoration, identification, and appraisal of antique paperweights.

Phonographs, phonograph records, radios, and even television sets are popular collectibles. Early phonographs are stocked in some shops, but later models are often ignored. The item must be in good working condition to be of value. "Crossover" examples, those wanted by collectors of another type of antique, are worth more than might be suspected and are worth restoring. For instance, Barbie's Vanity Fair record player sold at auction in 1989 for $760. Repairs can be expensive, slow, and sometimes impossible. If you are able to fix this type of collectible, you can usually make a good buy. Repairs can often cost more than the value of a phonograph in very good condition.

Early phonograph records include many types. There are price books that list thousands of phonograph records, but many record titles are still unlisted. Records cannot be restored and have value only if they are in good playing condition.

Radios have gained in interest since the 1970s. Old tubes and other parts are hard to find, but there are dealers, publications, and clubs that make the search a little easier. Most expensive are the colorful plastic or very Art Deco-styled radios. The slightest crack in the plastic or scratches in the surface will lower the value by over 50 percent. This type of damage cannot be repaired.

Television sets that are wanted are in the most modern styles of the fifties. They include those with round picture tubes above the rectangular set or other unusual designs. These can often be repaired by an old-time TV serviceman, but many of the parts are out of production and difficult to locate.

Sources

A.M.R. Publishing Company, P.O. Box 3007, Arlington, WA 98223, 206-659-6434, Mon.-Fri. 9:00 a.m.-5:00 p.m.; fax 206-659-5994. Books, service, parts manuals for radios, phonographs. Catalog.

Andy's Record Supplies, 48 Colonial Road, Providence, RI 02906, 401-421-9453, 9:00 a.m.-9:00 p.m., 7 days a week. Poly, paper, and resealable Mylar sleeves, replacement cassette and compact disc cases. Flyer with prices, free samples.

Antique Phonograph Supply Company, 32 South Tyson Avenue, Floral Park, NY 11001, 516-775-8605, Mon.-Fri. 9:30 a.m.-5:00 p.m., Sat. 9:30 a.m.-3:00 p.m. Antique mechanical record players rebuilt and restored. Spring motors and reproducers rebuilt, steel mainsprings manufactured, cabinets refinished. Refinishing supplies, parts, accessories for vintage spring-operated phonographs.

Antique Radios Inc., David & Nancy Snow, P.O. Box 6352, Jackson, MI 49204, 517-750-4992, evenings. Antique radios repaired. Battery eliminators for pre-1930s radios, tubes for most radios, repair of pre-1940s radios.

Electrotec, P.O. Box 10004, Winslow, WA 90110, 206-947-9460, 9:00 a.m.-5:00 p.m. Record Restorer, a cleaner that removes surface noise. Mail order only. U.S. and Canada.

free form sales, P.O. Box 116, Willmette, IL 60091, 708-328-7100, 24 hours a day. Record-care products, plastic covers, replacement jackets, and record sleeves. Price list. Mail order only.

The Kays, Antique Radios Rebuilt, George & Julia Kay, 5 Fiske Street, Worcester, MA 01602, 508-755-4880, 8:00 a.m.-8:00 p.m. Old radios rebuilt and cabinets restored.

Maurer TV Sales & Service, Donald S. Maurer, 29 South Fourth Street, Lebanon, PA 17042, 717-272-2481, 10:00 a.m.-6:00 p.m. New and old stock radio and TV receiving tubes. Mail order. SASE for price list.

Musical Wonder House, 18 High Street, Wiscasset, ME 04578, 207-882-7163 or 207-882-6373, anytime. Complete mechanical restoration of music boxes and windup phonographs. Restoration of wooden cases available. Music boxes and recordings of antique music boxes on cassettes and LPs shipped anywhere.

Owl Audio-Video Investigations, Inc., P.O. Box 3122, Linden, NJ 07036, 201-382-4299; fax: 201-499-0635. Products for the restoration of old recordings; services for restoration of older audio and video recordings. Mail order. Brochure.

Puett Electronics, Box 28572, Dallas TX 75228, 214-321-0927 or 214-321-8721, 7:00 a.m.-10:00 p.m. Antique radio tubes, knobs, glass dial covers, tuning dials, etc.; schematic diagrams, manuals, books and other literature on antique radios. Catalog $5, includes $6 discount coupon on orders of $25 or more.

Tesla Electronics, 835 Bricken, St. Louis, MO 63122, 314-822-1748, 9:00 a.m.-6:00 p.m. Mechanical television supplies, dials for Philco cathedral receivers, vacuum tubes, power supply for vintage battery radio sets. Radio restorations, transformer rewinding. Mail order. Catalog.

University Products, Inc., P.O. Box 101, South Canal Street, Holyoke, MA 01040, 800-336-4847, 800-628-1912 outside Massachusetts, 8:30 a.m.-5:00 p.m.; fax: 413-532-9281. Archival supplies and repair materials. Phonographic record storage boxes. Free catalog.

Vintage TV & Radio, 3552 West 105th Street, Cleveland, OH 44111, 216-671-6712, 9:00 a.m.-6:00 p.m. New, old, reproduction parts for radios and TVs. Schematics, tubes, books, parts, refinishing supplies, complete repair services. Mail order. Brochure.

Wiesner Radio & Electronics, 149 Hunter Avenue, Albany, NY 12206, 518-438-2801 or 518-371-9902, 4:30 p.m.-11:00 p.m. Antique radio and amplifier repair, amplifiers rebuilt. Mail order.

Yesterday Once Again, Box 6773, Huntington Beach, CA 92615, 714-963-2474, 8:00 a.m.-9:00 p.m.; fax: 714-963-2195, Attention: Yesterday Once Again. Repair, restoration of hand-cranked phonographs only. Parts, needles, accessories, books, and reprints of original instruction manuals. Free catalog.

Ralph Banta, Highway 62, Route 1, Box 453, Green Forest, AR 72636, 501-437-2855, Mon.-Sat. 8:00 a.m.-10:30 p.m. Antique phonographs restored. Mechanisms, cabinets, Orthophonic reproducers, and Pivots restored. Mail order.

Sam Faust, P.O. Box 94, Changewater, NJ 07831, 201-689-7020, after 7:00 p.m. Parts, supplies, and manuals for radio sets. Mail order.

Bill Hulbert, P.O. Box 151, Adams Center, NY 13606, 315-583-5765, after 5:00 p.m. Car and home radios repaired.

Jerry Madsen, 4624 West Woodland Road, Edina, MN 55424, 612-926-7775, anytime. Reprints of Edison phonograph parts lists, original books, parts, and reproducers. Needle tins, phonograph toys, and records. Mail order worldwide.

Chris Pokorny, 4728 Via San Andros, Las Vegas, NV 89103, 702-367-8994, anytime. Phonographs repaired. Service limited to 100-mile radius of Las Vegas. Mail order.

Randle Pomeroy, 54 12th Street, Providence, RI 02906, 401-272-5560, 6:00 p.m.-9:00 p.m. Reproducers repaired and cleaned. Phonographs restored. Mail order.

Ralph Woodside, The Thomas A. Edison Collection, Sedler's Antique Village (lower level), 51 West Main Street, Georgetown, MA 01833, 508-352-9830, 10:00 a.m.-5:00 p.m., except Mon. & Thurs., 508-373-5947 home. Windup phonographs restored. Send only motor or part for repair, no cases, turntables, or cranks. Antique phonographs, records, piano rolls, sheet music, cylinder records, and music boxes bought and sold. Mail order, U.S. and Canada.

Books

Antique Radios; Restoration and Price Guide, David & Betty Johnson, 1982 (Wallace-Homestead Book Co., Radnor, PA).
Collecting Phonographs and Gramophones, Christopher Proudfoot, 1980 (Mayflower Books, NY).
Player Piano Servicing and Rebuilding, Arthur Reblitz, 1985 (Vestal Press, P.O. Box 97, Vestal, NY 13850).

Photographs & Photographic Equipment

Photographs became popular with collectors during the 1970s. Prices have risen into the thousands of dollars for choice pictures, so that conservation, restoration, and storage have become very important. Many types of photographs can be included in the collector's world. Movies are one special type. The old nitrate film is combustible and it is dangerous to store. If you are fortunate enough to find or own some early movies, have them copied on modern film. The American Film Institute at the Kennedy Center for the Performing Arts, Washington, DC 20566, can help you with this problem. Walt Disney original art done on celluloid for cartoon features, or what the collectors call "cels," are also collected and require careful framing or flat storage. These too can be restored.

All types of photographs, from daguerreotypes and glass-plate slides to stereopticon views, cartes de visite, and modern pictures, are important as art as well as history. Do not try a home-remedy restoration. Many old pictures can be saved if the work is done by an expert.

Old cameras can be restored, but once again expertise is required. Sometimes a local camera shop can have the camera repaired, but most old cameras need special parts that are no longer available. There are often modern photography club members who are interested in antique cameras and photographic equipment, and it is helpful to check with a local professional photographer to see if there is someone in your area who likes to work with old cameras. See also the sections on Comic Art, Movie Memorabilia, and Paper Collectibles.

Sources

Antique Camera Repair, William P. Carroll, 8500 La Entrada, Whittier, CA 90605, 213-693-8421, 10:00 a.m.-11:00 p.m. Repair and restoration of antique and collectible cameras. Shutters repaired, bellows replaced. Books on collectible cameras, history of photography. List available. Worldwide service.

Eblinger Laboratories, Inc., 220 Albert Street, East Lansing, MI 48823, 517-332-1430, 9:00 a.m.-5:00 p.m. Archival reproduction of personal and historical photographs on acid-free, fiber-base paper. Faded or damaged photographs restored. Oil coloring. Mail order.

Filmlife Inc., The Film/Video Hospital, Moonachie, NJ 07074, 201-440-8500, 800-FILM026, 9:00 a.m.-5:00 p.m. Motion picture film cleaned, rejuvenated, protected, preserved. Film-to-tape transfer, editing, reduction printing. Scratched, warped, torn, or water-damaged film restored. Movie film has longer life than video tape, so if you have transferred movies to video tape, don't throw out original movie; can be restored and used to make another video copy.

International Museum of Photography, George Eastman House, Grant Romer, Conservator, 900 East Avenue, Rochester, NY 14607, 716-271-3361. Will answer telephone inquiries regarding photographs and make referrals.

Light Impressions, 439 Monroe Avenue, Rochester, NY 14607-3717, 800-828-9629, 800-828-6216 outside New York State, Mon.-Fri. 9:00 a.m.-7:00 p.m., Sat. 10:00 a.m.-4:30 p.m.; fax: 716-442-7318. Archival supplies, including albums, portfolio boxes, home storage systems for photos, negatives, and slides, encapsulation supplies, deacidification solutions, frames, mats, marbled papers, and more.

Marty Bahn & Company, 1974 NE 149th Street, Miami, FL 33181, 305-940-8871, 9:00 a.m.-5:00 p.m. Film cleaner and conditioner, superwhite screen paint, projectors for film and video, audio-video equipment repairs, splicers, rewinder kit, electric and manual rewinds. Mail order.

Northeast Document Conservation Center, Gary E. Albright, Abbott Hall, School Street, Andover, MA 01810, 508-470-1010, Mon.-Fri. 8:30 a.m.-4:30 p.m. Nonprofit regional conservation center specializing in treatment of paper-based materials including photographs.

Duplication of historical photographs, consultation workshops, preservation planning surveys, disaster assistance.

Romney, 615 Hill Street, Emlenton, PA 16373, 412-867-0314, anytime. Camera repair supplies, tools, and books.

Ron's Gallery Supply Co., P.O. Box 1791, New York, NY 10016, 800-735-7667, anytime, leave message. Restores antique photographs. Conservation supplies.

Nancy Wu, Fine Art Conservation Services, 94 Mercer Street, New York, NY 10012, 212-966-5513, 9:00 a.m.-6:00 p.m. Conservation of works on paper and photographs. No mail order.

Book

Care of Photographs, Siegfried Rempel, 1987 (Nick Lyons Books, 31 West 21st Street, New York, NY 10010).

Plastic

Objects made of all types of plastics, from Parkesine to Lucite, are now being collected. Plastic is fragile, and a scratched or cracked piece is lower in value. Some types of plastic fade in sunlight, scorch if overheated, or are stained by alcohol or other materials. Plastic should be washed with a solution of soap and warm water and a soft cloth. Very hot water and detergents may remove the shine. Never use scouring powder or any form of abrasive. Do not put plastic dishes in the dishwasher unless they are marked "dishwasher safe." They will eventually become dull and, if decorated, may lose the color in the decoration. Removing the old adhesive from price-tag labels can be a problem. Use turpentine but not alcohol, acetone (nail polish remover), or lighter fluid. Novus II is a plastic cleaner that can be found in some stores.

Plastic that is cracked or badly scratched or stained cannot be restored. It is often best to replace the part. One word of warning: celluloid is flammable and must be stored in a well-ventilated area where the temperature is never over 120 degrees Fahrenheit. If the celluloid in a favored old toy is decomposing, it may help to soak it in washing soda (sodium carbonate). After it is dry, coat the item with clear nail polish.

Books

Art Plastic Designed for Living, Siegfried Rempel, 1984 (Abbeville Press, NY) (short chapter on care).
Wallace-Homestead Price Guide to Plastic Collectibles, Lyndi Stewart McNulty, 1987 (Wallace-Homestead Book Co., Radnor, PA) (chapter on care and cleaning).

Political Memorabilia

Political collectibles include all types of buttons, textiles including banners and large handkerchiefs, pottery, porcelain, glass pieces with appropriate decoration, jewelry, lanterns, boxes, and toys. The purist collector only saves buttons and other items that were made for an actual campaign and not those produced for a gift or novelty shop afterward. The American Political Items Collectors (APIC) (Box 340339, San Antonio,

TX 78234) carefully documents actual campaign material each year in the publications sent to its members. Reproductions have been made of many early campaign items. It does not pay to restore the reproductions. Check in other sections for restorers of political memorabilia made of glass, metals, or textiles.

Postcards

Most postcards are made of paper and have all of the storage and care problems of any other paper collectibles. They should be kept out of the heat, away from strong sunlight and damp air, and most of all, they should never be glued or taped. Check in *Kovels' Guide to Selling Your Antiques & Collectibles* for postcard publications. Slight soil can be cleaned off postcards with an art gum eraser. Bent cards can sometimes be ironed flat (see Paper Collectibles & Ephemera). If postcards are glued into an album, it may be possible to soak them free. This requires care and time.

Source

University Products, Inc., P.O. Box 101, South Canal Street, Holyoke, MA 01040, 800-336-4847, 800-628-1912, outside Massachusetts, 8:30 a.m.-5:00 p.m.; fax: 413-532-9281. Archival supplies and repair materials. Postcard protectors and storage boxes. Free catalog.

Pottery & Porcelain

Pottery and porcelain are found in every home. Dishes, figurines, lamp bases, flowerpots, crocks, and garden ornaments may all be made of ceramics--pottery or porcelain. To care for and repair them properly, it is necessary to have some idea of the difference between pottery and porcelain. Pottery is usually heavier than porcelain. It is opaque and chips more easily. Because it is more porous, it may become stained by dark-colored food or dirt. Porcelain is translucent; if it is held in front of a strong light, the light will show through. If it is chipped, the break will be shell-like in shape. Pottery usually cracks on a line. Porcelain is thinner, lighter, more durable, and usually more expensive than pottery. The names stoneware, delft, bone china, majolica, and ironstone all refer to either pottery, porcelain, or similar wares with similar problems.

If your pottery or porcelain dishes are stained, it is possible to bleach them using household laundry bleach. If dishes are cracked or chipped, repairs are possible. Waterproof glues are available in most hardware, art-supply, drug, and builder-supply stores. For a simple break, glue is the best method of repair. If there is further damage and a hole or crack must be filled or if repainting is required, it can still be a do-it-yourself job, but special equipment and instructions are necessary.

Many old sets of dishes have, say, only 11 dinner plates, 10 cups and saucers, and 12 of everything else. It is possible to buy the same pattern of old dishes to fill in the set. Haviland, Castleton, Franciscan, Lenox, Noritake, Oxford, Syracuse, Wedgwood, and other makes are being sold through matching services. To order from a service, you must know the pattern of the dish. There are hundreds of patterns listed in books at your library. Many of the patterns have names included on the back as part of the mark. Identify the pattern name from this information or use this easy method: place a plate face down on a photocopying machine and take a picture. Copy the front and the back. Indicate the colors that appear on the plate and send the photocopies to one of the matching services listed in *Kovels' Guide to Selling Your Antiques & Collectibles.*

To properly identify makers, it may be necessary to check the marks in a special book of marks. For example, "H & Co" is one the marks used by the Haviland Company that can be matched through services. Some patterns are still being made and can be replaced through special orders. Firms such as Wedgwood, Royal Doulton, Spode, and Royal Worcester offer this service for a limited number of their patterns.

Here are a few quick clues for dating your dishes. If the name of the country of origin appears, such as "Spode, England," the dishes were probably made after 1891. Since about World War I, the words "made in England" or "made in France" have been favored. The term "Ltd." as part of a company name for English companies was used after 1880. "RD" in a diamond-shaped cartouche was used in England from 1842 to 1883. The letters "RD" followed by numbers were in use after 1884. The words "22 carat gold" and "ovenproof" were used after the 1930s. "Microwave safe" first appeared in the 1970s. "Made in Occupied Japan" was used only from 1945 to 1952.

Sources

A. Ludwig Klein & Son, Inc., P.O. Box 145, Dept. 13, Harleysville, PA 19438, 215-256-9004, Tues.-Fri. 10:00 a.m.-5:00 p.m., Sat. 10:00 a.m.-2:00 p.m. Repairs and restorations, missing parts resculpted. Mail photo of object to be repaired with blank audio cassette tape and receive instructions on how to repair china yourself. Book, *Repairing and Restoring China and Glass* by William Karl Klein. Brochure available.

Appel Restorations, 87 Bradford Road, Rochester, NY 14618-2912, 716-442-9807. Restores china, bisque, porcelain, through the mail only. Free estimates.

Atlas Minerals & Chemicals, Inc., Farmington Road, Mertztown, PA 19539, 215-682-7171, 8:00 a.m.-4:30 p.m.; fax: 215-682-9200. Master Mending Kit includes products, instructions for repairing china, porcelain, pottery, and glass. Brochure and price list.

Broken Art Restoration, Michelle and Bill Marhoefer, 1841 W. Chicago Avenue, Chicago, IL 60622, 312-226-8200. Pottery and porcelain restoration. Ceramic, ivory, wood, metal, and stone art objects restored. Invisible repairs. Missing parts replaced. Brochure.

Butterfly Shoppe, 637 Livernois, Ferndale, MI 48220, 313-541-2858, Mon.-Wed. 10:30 a.m.-4:00 p.m., Thurs. 10:30 a.m.-7:00 p.m. Repair and restoration of china and glass, Hummel, Lladro, Doulton. Will repair everything except wood.

Connecticut Notary Services, 128 Hall Avenue, Wallingford, CT 06492. Collector plates, figurines, repair, restoration. Mail order.

Coulter's China Repair & Restoration, HC 83, Box 715, Crosslake, MN 56442, 218-543-4006, 8:00 a.m.-5:00 p.m., answering service 24 hours. Pottery, porcelain repair, restoration, missing pieces replaced. Invisible repair of Lladro, Boehm, Hummel. Mail order.

David Jasper's Glass Clinic, R.R. 3, Box 330X-13, Sioux Falls, SD 57106, 605-361-7524, 9:00 a.m.-5:00 p.m. Repair and restoration of bisque, figurines, porcelain, Hummel, and other objects of art. Missing parts replaced. Brochure.

Dean's China Restoration, 131 Elmwood Drive, Cheshire, CT 06410, 203-271-3659, Mon.-Fri. 9:00 a.m.-5:00 p.m. Repair and restoration of china, figurines, and dolls. Invisible repairs, undetectable by black light. China restoration seminars. Mail order.

Dunhill Restoration, c/o Lee Upholstery, 2250 Lee Road, Cleveland Heights, OH 44122, 216-921-2932, leave message on machine. Specializing in repair of Hummel, Doulton, Lladro, porcelain, and pottery. Missing pieces replaced.

Glass Doctor, Ross Jasper, 3126 Fairview Street, Davenport, IA 52802, 319-322-5512, 800-344-0479, Mon.-Fri. 9:00 a.m.-5:00 p.m. Figurines and chipped glass restored.

The Glassman, 10516 Old Katy Road, Suite D, Houston, TX 77043, 713-468-3183, Mon.-Fri. 10:00 a.m.-4:30 p.m., Sat. 11:00 a.m.-6:00 p.m., Sun. 2:00 p.m.-5:00 p.m. Pottery and porcelain restored.

Grady Stewart, Expert China Restoration, 2019 Sansom Street, Philadelphia, PA 19103, 215-567-2888. Repair of all types of pottery, porcelain, stoneware, dolls, Battersea and Peking enamels, etc. Does not work on glass or dinnerware.

Harry A. Eberhardt & Son, Inc., 2010 Walnut Street, Philadelphia, PA 19103, 215-568-4144, Mon.-Fri. 9:00 a.m.-5:00 p.m. Repairs and restoration of objects of art, including glass. Replacement parts, antique cut-glass prisms, bobeches, arms. Mail order.

Hess Restorations, 200 Park Avenue South, New York, NY 10003, 212-741-0410, 212-260-2255, 212-979-1443, 10:30 a.m.-4:00 p.m. Restoration of porcelain and ceramics. Supplies. Mail order.

J & H China Repairs, 8296 St. George Street, Vancouver, BC V5X 3C5 Canada, 604-321-1093, 9:00 a.m.-4:00 p.m. Restoration of pottery and porcelain, figurines, sculptures, stone, and dolls.

Just Enterprises, 2790 Sherwin Avenue, Unit 10, Ventura, CA 93003, 805-644-5837, Mon.-Fri. 8:30 a.m.-5:30 p.m., answering machine other times. Repair and restoration services. Send photo, description of item, and description of damage, plus SASE, for estimate. Mail order worldwide.

Kalesse, Fine Arts Bldg., 1017 SW Morrison Street, 507-C, Portland, OR 97205. Restoration of pottery, porcelain, and related objets d'art. Mail order service worldwide.

Kleinhans Restorations, T.A. Kleinhans, P.O. Box 93082, Rochester,

NY 14692, 716-624-4685, 9:00 a.m.-8:00 p.m. Restoration of pottery, porcelain, bisque, Royal Doulton mugs, and Hummel figurines. Mail order.

Levine's Restorations, 4801 Seventh Street North, Arlington, VA 22203, 703-525-4009, 9:00 a.m.-6:00 p.m. Repair and restoration of pottery and porcelain.

Lid Lady, Virginia Bodiker, 7790 East Ross Road, New Carlisle, OH 45344. Pottery, porcelain, metal, plastic, and zinc stoppers and salt and pepper lids. Mail order. Open by appointment.

McKenzie's Art Restoration Studio, Keeta McKenzie, 2907 East Monte Vista Drive, Tucson, AZ 85716, 602-323-1466, Tues.-Sat. 9:00 a.m.-noon, 1:00 p.m.-5:00 p.m. Repair of bisque, china, porcelain, pottery, earthenware figurines, bisque and china doll heads. Mail order service worldwide.

Nonomura Studios, 3432 Connecticut Avenue NW, Washington, DC 20008, 202-363-4025, Mon.-Sat. 10:00 a.m.-5:00 p.m. Repair and restoration. Mail order.

Pleasant Valley Services, Joe Howell, 1725 Reed Road, Knoxville, MD 21758, 301-432-2721, 9:00 a.m.-9:00 p.m. Restoration of china, figurines, and other objects. Mail order.

Professional Restoration, R. DiCarlo, P.O. Box 16222, Orlando, FL 32861, 407-886-7423, anytime. Restoration of pottery, terra-cotta, Boehm, Cybis, Goebel, Lladro. Does not restore dinnerware.

Restoration Tile Co., 3511 Interlake North, Seattle, WA 98103, 206-633-4866, Mon.-Sat. 9:00-5:00 p.m. Restoration of ceramic tiles, broken tiles repaired, replication of missing tiles. Fireplace and mural installations repaired on site. Send photos and description of damage plus SASE for estimate. Mail order service.

Restorations by Dudley, Inc., Box 345B, West Orange, NJ 07052, 201-731-4449, 10:00 a.m.-5:00 p.m. Restoration of Hummel, Lladro, and all figurines.

Restorations By Linda, Linda M. Peet, 9787 Townsend Road, Maybee, MI 48159 or P.O. Box 265, Milan, MI 48160, 313-529-5414. Porcelain and china restoration, replacement of missing parts. Free estimates. Mail order worldwide.

Restorers of America, R.D. 4, Box 382, Wynantskill, NY 12189, 518-283-5317, Mon.-Fri. 9:00 a.m.-5:00 p.m.; fax: 518-283-5380. Invisible black-light proof repair of pottery, porcelain, figurines, and collectibles. Missing pieces replaced.

Rosine Green Associates, Inc., 45 Barlett Crescent, Brookline, MA 02146, 617-277-8368, Mon.-Fri. 9:00 a.m.-5:00 p.m., Sat. 10:00 a.m.-noon. Repair and restoration of pottery, earthenware, fine china, ceramics, and figurines. Brochure.

Sierra Studios, 37 West 222, Route 64, Suite 103, St. Charles, IL 60175, 708-683-2525. Restoration of R.S. Prussia. Mail order.

T.S. Restoration, J.M. Denson, 2622 North Dobson Road, Chandler, AZ 85224. Repair and restoration. Selective restoration outside Arizona.

The T.S. Guide to Antique Restoration can be purchased with or without supplies. Mail order. Send LSASE for information.

Venerable Classics, 645 Fourth Street, Suite 208, Santa Rosa, CA 95404, 707-575-3626, Mon.-Fri. 10:00 a.m.-5:00 p.m. Restoration of fragile objects, including pottery and porcelain. "Impossible smithereens our specialty." Serving northern California and Western U.S. primarily. Mail order. Brochure.

Vernal Restorations, 3625 Lyric Avenue, Waconia, MN 55391, 612-471-0015, 612-438-6058 for answering service. Porcelain restoration and antique bisque doll restorations.

Wedgwood Studio, 2522 North 52nd Street, Phoenix, AZ 85008, 602-840-0825, 9:00 a.m.-1:00 p.m. Restoration of figurines, vases, and other cabinet pieces, specializing in Boehm. Mail order. Serving Western U.S.

Wonderful Things, P.O. Box 536, Van Brunt Station, Brooklyn, NY 11215, 718-965-4515, evenings 10:00 p.m.-11:00 p.m. Hummels repaired.

Yolanda Studio, Yolanda DiSalvo, 228 Washington Avenue, Elmwood Park, NJ 07407. Pottery, porcelain restoration. Will purchase broken or damaged Hummel, Wavecrest, and Lladro. Write for information.

John Edward Cunningham, 1516 Dustin Drive, #1, Normal, IL 61761, 309-454-8256, anytime. Restoration of art and antiques, specializing in Boehm and Royal Worcester. Missing parts made. Mail order.

Richard George, 45-04 97th Place, Corona, NY 11368, 212-271-2506 or 212-271-2507, 9:00 a.m.-4:00 p.m. Repair and restoration.

Herbert Klug, 303-985-9261. Restoration of pottery and porcelain: classical antiquities, modern limited-edition figurines, European and Oriental porcelain, but not dishes. Instruction in restoration.

Mike Meshenberg, 2571 Edgewood Road, Beachwood, OH 44122, 216-464-2084, anytime. Repair and restoration of pottery and porcelain.

Grady Stewart, 2019 Sansom Street, Philadelphia, PA 19103, 215-567-2888. Porcelain restoration for fine antiques.

Morla W. Tjossem, 911 East Hancock Street, Appleton, WI 54911, 414-734-5463, noon-10:00 p.m. Classes in pottery and porcelain restoration, summer only, at Lawrence University, Appleton.

Donna M. Towle-Rupprecht, 129 Dexter Avenue, Watertown, MA 02172, 617-924-8408, anytime. Repair and restoration of Hummel and Sebastian figurines. Mail order.

Regina Wenzek, 2966 Briggs Avenue, Bronx, NY 10458, 212-733-5040, 9:00 a.m.-5:00 p.m. Porcelain restoration. By appointment only.

Books

How to Mend Your Treasures, Laurence Adams Malone, 1972 (Phaedra).
Repair & Restoration of Pottery & Porcelain, Joan Grayson, 1982 (Sterling).

Repairing and Restoring China and Glass, The Klein Method, William Karl Klein, 1962 (Harper & Row).

Repairing Old China and Ceramic Tiles, Jeff Oliver, 1985 (Little, Brown).

Restorer's Handbook of Ceramics and Glass, Jean-Michel Andre, 1976 (Van Nostrand Reinhold).

Two Sisters' Guide to Antique Restoration & China Repair, Jean Myers and Judy Myers Denson (2622 North Dobson Road, Chandler, AZ 85224).

Prints, Woodcuts, Posters & Calendar Art

Prints range from Currier & Ives lithographs of the 19th century to limited-edition prints of the 1980s. Each type of print requires special research. Your library should have books such as *Currier & Ives Prints: An Illustrated Check List*, revised edition, by Frederic A. Conningham (New York: Crown Publishers, 1983) or books that explain the difference between a lithograph and a woodcut, an etching, and an engraving.

Restoration of any type of paper is very difficult. It is possible to carefully clean dust from a print by using wallpaper cleaner, wadded fresh white bread, or an art gum eraser. Creases can be carefully ironed out with a very cool iron. More ambitious repairs should always be done by a restorer. Do not tape or glue any paper item: the acids in the adhesive will eventually cause damage. Marks from old tape can sometimes be removed by a restorer.

Sources

Archival Conservation Center, Inc., 8225 Daly Road, Cincinnati, OH 45231, 513-521-9858, 8:30 a.m.-3:30 p.m. Repair and restoration of prints and works of art on paper. Removal of water stains, foxing, creases. Prints cleaned. Removal of prints glued to acidic cardboards.

Herman Poster Mount, Inc., 250 West 40th Street, New York, NY 10018, 212-730-7821, 10:00 a.m.-6:00 p.m. Poster restoration. Mail order service.

Robert L. Searjeant, P.O. Box 23942, Rochester, NY 14692, 716-424-2489, 9:00 a.m.-8:00 p.m. Currier & Ives print restoration.

Phil Temple, Magic Circus, P.O. Box 12855, San Rafael, CA 94913-2855, 415-897-5130, 8:00 a.m.-11:00 p.m. Poster restoration and mounting, specializing in vintage magic posters. Mail order service. Send SASE for price list and sample.

Book

A Guide to the Collecting and Care of Original Prints, Carl Zigrosser & Christa M. Gaehde, 1965 (Crown Publishers, NY).

Rugs

Oriental rugs should always be kept clean and in good repair. Repairs should be done by a professional, although some minor work can be accomplished at home. A worn spot can be covered temporarily by coloring the exposed beige backing with crayon or colored ink. A full fringe adds to the value of a rug and should never be trimmed or replaced unless absolutely necessary. There are rug dealers in large department stores or in shops in large cities who can do repairs. If a local restorer is not available, a rug can be shipped to another city. See also Textiles.

Sources

Aladdin Company Ltd., Oriental Rug Specialists, 221 South Elm Street, Greensboro, NC 27401, 919-275-6351, 9:30 a.m.-5:30 p.m. Cleaning and repairing of Oriental rugs. Serving 200-mile radius.

Hooked Rug Restoration, Charles J.P. Quigley, Route 28 at North Road, West Harwich Professional Center, Suite 203, West Harwich, MA 02671-0117, 508-432-0897, 24-hour telephone service; fax: 508-432-7996. Restoration of hooked rugs. Mail order worldwide.

Koko Boodakian & Sons, 1026 Main Street, Winchester, MA 01890, 617-729-2213, Mon.-Fri. 8:00 a.m.-5:00 p.m. Restoration and repair of Oriental, antique hooked, and Navajo rugs. Cleaning, reweaving, renapping, refringing, overcasting, edging, and storage.

Maison Chevalier, 157 East 64th Street, New York, NY 10021, 212-249-3922. Antique tapestries and rugs, sales and conservation.

Shallcross & Lorraine, Holly L. Smith, State House Post Office, Box 133, Boston, MA 02133, 617-720-2133. Invisible restoration, conservation, and maintenance of rugs, tapestries, American Indian textiles, Aubussons, and needlework. Damaged threads replaced, missing sections rewoven. Mail order.

Ann Anderson, Star Route, Box 16, Upper Black Eddy, PA 18972, 215-294-9441, 9:00 a.m.-8:00 p.m. Hooked rugs restored. Mail order.

Stephen T. Anderson, 1071 First Avenue, New York, NY 10022, 212-431-8354, Mon.-Fri. 9:00 a.m.-5:00 p.m. Hooked rug restoration.

Linda Eliason, Box 542, Manchester, VT 05254, 802-867-2252, 8:00 a.m.-5:00 p.m. Hooked rug restoration. Free estimates. Call or write before sending rugs.

Angela B. Lyons, 127 Boston Post Road, Wayland, MA 01778, 508-358-4354, Mon.-Fri. 10:00 a.m.-4:00 p.m. Restoration of hooked rugs. Mail order or walk-in.

Book

Oriental Rugs Care and Repair, Majid Amini, 1981 (Van Nostrand Reinhold Co., NY).

Information about scales is scarce. There are a few books and articles to help you solve problems with early scales. The later drugstore scales that require a penny are discussed in the section on coin-operated machines. Sometimes a large, spring-operated scale can be repaired by a local shop that fixes scales for grocery stores and commercial businesses. Search for these through the "Business to Business" Yellow Pages if that is how your phone books are divided, or look under "Scales" in the regular Yellow Pages.

SCULPTURE, see Marble; Metals; Pottery & Porcelain

Silver & Silver Plate

Silver should be kept clean. Use any good commercial polish, and if you keep the silver on display, use a tarnish-retarding polish. For storage, tarnish-retarding cloths and papers are also available. Never use household scouring powder or instant silver polish on your silver. Never store silver in a nonporous plastic wrap, because the wrap may melt or moisture may collect between the silver and the wrap. Never wrap with rubber bands. Silver will tarnish more quickly if displayed on latex-painted shelves, in oak furniture, or near oak trees. If you use camphor (mothballs) to prevent tarnish, don't let the camphor touch the silver.

Knife blades may separate from hollow handles if they are stored in a hot attic or washed in a dishwasher. They can be repaired by using a nonmelting filler.

Silver that is kept on display and never used for eating, such as a large candelabrum, can be lacquered. This will keep the piece clean almost indefinitely. Any good silver-plater can lacquer a piece.

Antique plated silver may "bleed" (the copper underneath shows through the silver). This is not totally objectionable. Resilvering may lower the value, so check on the age and type of silver plate before you replate. Very early "rolled-on" silver on copper Sheffield pieces should rarely be replated.

Late 19th- and 20th-century plated silver that was originally electroplated can be replated with no loss of value. These pieces are usually marked "silver plate." The handles and feet were often made of britannia metal and will appear black when the silverplate wears off. Local platers are listed in the Yellow Pages under "Plating." For information about silver flatware, see the Matching Services list and the many pattern books found in *Kovels' Guide to Selling Your Antiques & Collectibles*.

See also Metals in this book.

Sources

Abercrombie & Co., 9159A Brookville Road, Silver Spring, MD 20910, 301-585-2385, weekdays 9:00 a.m.-5:00 p.m., Sat. 9:00 a.m.-1:00 p.m. Silver plating; filled sterling repairs; combs, mirrors, brushes, files, and letter openers replaced. Hand and machine engraving. Mail order.

Al Bar Wilmette Platers, 127 Green Bay Road, Wilmette, IL 60091, 312-251-0187, Mon.-Fri. 8:00 a.m.-4:30 p.m., Sat. 8:00 a.m.-3:00 p.m. Restoration and repairs, missing parts reproduced, polishing and replating.

Barron's Art Restorations, 5367B East Mountain Street, Stone Mountain, GA 30083, 404-469-8476, 10:00 a.m.-6:00 p.m. Restoration of oil paintings, porcelain, dolls, glass, chandeliers, etc. Will polish chips out of glass and restore stems.

Brandt & Opis, 145 West 45th Street, New York, NY 10036, 212-245-9237, 8:00 a.m.-5:45 p.m. Conservation of silver.

Hess Restorations, 200 Park Avenue South, New York, NY 10003, 212-741-0410, 212-260-2255, 212-979-1443, 10:30 a.m.-4:00 p.m. Blue glass liners for salts. Mail order.

Hiles Plating Company, Inc., 2028 Broadway, Kansas City, MO 64108, 816-421-6450 or 816-421-6450, Mon.-Fri. 9:00 a.m.-5:00 p.m. Restoration of antique sterling silver and silver plate. Silver plating. Ivory and wood insulators, finials, and handles. Mail order service. Price list available. Brochure.

Memphis Plating Works, 678-682 Madison Avenue, Memphis, TN 38103, 901-526-3051, Mon.-Fri. 8:00 a.m.-5:00 p.m., Sat. 8:00 a.m.-noon. Silver, gold, copper, brass, nickel, and chrome restoration and plating. Broken statues repaired and refinished, pot metal or bronze.

Midwest Coin Exchange, Silverware Division, 4311 NE Vivion Road, Kansas City, MO 64119, 816-454-1990. Sterling, silverplate, and stainless repaired, polished, and matched.

New England Country Silver, Inc., Smith Road, East Haddam, CT 06423, 203-873-1314, 9:00 a.m.-3:00 p.m. Repairing, refinishing, replating, and engraving of antique silverware. Replacement knife blades, combs, brushes, and mirrors for dresser sets. Mail order.

New Orleans Silversmiths, 600 Chartres Street, New Orleans, LA 70130, 504-522-8333, 9:00 a.m.-5:00 p.m.; fax: 504-586-8817. Silver restoration, repair, and replacement of parts. Mail order.

Orum Silver Company, P.O. Box 805, 51 South Vine Street, Meriden, CT 06450, 203-237-3037, Mon.-Fri. 8:00 a.m.-4:30 p.m. Repair, refinishing, replating of old silver, pewter, brass, and copper. Gold, silver, nickel, copper, and brass plating.

Peninsula Plating Works, 232 Homer Avenue, Palo Alto, CA 94301, 415-326-7825 or 415-322-8806, Mon.-Fri. 8:30 a.m.-6:00 p.m., Sat. 10:00 a.m.-5:00 p.m.; fax: 415-322-7392. Sterling and silver plate repaired. Combs, brushes, knife blades, pearl handles, salad servers, and insulators replaced. Brochure.

R & K Weenike Antiques, Roy H. Weenike, Route 7, Box 140, Ottumwa, IA 52501, 515-934-5427, anytime. Repair of pickle castor and bride's basket frames. No plating. Mail order.

Restoration & Design Studio, Paul Karner, 249 East 77th Street, New York, NY 10021, 212-517-9742, Mon.-Fri. 10:00 a.m.-5:00 p.m., Wed. 1:00 p.m.-5:00 p.m. Restoration, repair, missing parts reproduced, silver and gold replated, flatware blades replaced.

Silver Chest, 941 Mandalay Avenue, Clearwater Beach, FL 34630, 813-441-4606, 9:00 a.m.-10:00 p.m. Complete restoration of silver and silver plate flatware. Replating, blades replaced, hollow handle serving pieces made, serving spoons pierced, ice cream forks designed from teaspoons. Matching service. Mail order.

Theiss Plating Corporation, 9314 Manchester, St. Louis, MO 63119, 314-961-0600, 8:30 a.m.-5:00 p.m. Repair and replating of silver plate and brass. Serving the Midwest.

Thome Silversmiths, 49 West 37th Street, Suite 605, New York, NY 10018, 212-764-5426, 8:30 a.m.-1:00 p.m., 2:30 p.m.-5:30 p.m. Restoration of silver. Silver and gold plating, engraving, polishing of chandeliers, reproduction of missing parts. Mail order.

Universal of Georgetown, Inc., 1804 Wisconsin Avenue NW, Washington, DC 20007, 202-333-2460, Mon.-Fri. 8:30 a.m.-5:00 p.m., Sat. 10:00 a.m.-4:00 p.m. Restoration of silver. D.C.-Maryland-Virginia area.

Walter Drake Silver Exchange, Drake Building, Colorado Springs, CO 80915-9988, 719-596-3140, 800-525-9291. Silver repair, removal of dents and monograms, replacement of knife blades.

WTC Associates, Inc., 2532 Regency Road, Lexington, KY 40503, 606-278-4171; fax: 606-276-1717. Silver restoration, replating, and repair. Replacement parts made. Hand engraving.

Jeffrey Herman, P.O. Box 3599, Cranston, RI 02910, 401-461-3156, 8:00 a.m.-5:00 p.m. Silver repair and restoration, corrosion removed, knife blades reset, dresser sets restored. Silver-care products. Mail order only.

Smoking Collectibles

Smoking is bad for your health and for the appearance of your antiques and furnishings, but smoking accessories are popular collectibles. Included are matchbooks, match holders, cigar boxes, cigar bands and labels, cigarette packs and paper, tobacco tags, pipe stoppers, pipes, cigarette and cigar lighters, cigar cutters, and ads for all sorts of tobacco items. It is now possible to have old lighters repaired. Matchbooks should be stored in scrapbooks, but first carefully remove the staple and the matches. The staple may rust and the matches are a fire hazard. Pipes can be restored by any dealer in modern pipes. You will probably want a new, unused stem if you plan to smoke the pipe.

Sources

Authorized Repair Service, 30 West 57th Street, New York, NY 10019, 212-586-0947, 9:00 a.m.-5:00 p.m.; fax: 212-586-1296. Cigarette lighters repaired.

Browns Matchboxes, P.O. Box 43, Montpelier, IN 47359-0043. Wooden display boxes with glass tops, for displaying matchbox collections. Mail order.

Just Enterprises, 2790 Sherwin Avenue, Unit 10, Ventura, CA 93003, 805-644-5837, Mon.-Fri. 8:30 a.m.-5:30 p.m., answering machine other times. Repair and restoration. Send photo, description of item, and description of damage, plus SASE for estimate.

von Erck's Pipe & Repair, P.O. Box 425, 6156 U.S. 41 South, Marquette, MI 49855, 906-249-1672, 8:00 a.m.-5:00 p.m. Pipes repaired. Mail order.

The Whitmore Company, 103 Harbor Avenue, Marblehead, MA 01945, 617-631-1282, anytime. Pipe repair.

Stamp collectors know that condition and storage are important considerations. Most stamps are kept in albums and mounted with either hinges or mounts. Never tape or glue a stamp into an album. Inexpensive or used stamps may be "hinged" using the special stamp hinges made with gum that will not harm the stamps. High-priced and mint, unused stamps should be mounted with stamp mounts, small corners that hold the stamp in place. Hinges, mounts, and albums can be found at your local stamp stores or through the mail-order ads in stamp publications.

Sometimes the stamp is more valuable as part of a "cover" (the special stamped envelope). Unusual cancellation marks, postal marks, written information, handstamps, or decorations on the envelope make a cover valuable. First-day covers should always be left intact.

Sometimes you will want to soak a stamp off an envelope. If the envelope is colored or there is ink writing or heavy postmarks, you must test to be sure nothing will fade or run. Brightly colored envelopes from Christmas cards should not be soaked; the color could run and ruin the stamps. Soak white envelopes with stamps in a large dish of warm (room-temperature), not hot, water. A turkey roaster is about the right size. Stir gently. The stamps will float away from the paper. Sometimes a drop of detergent should be added to the water. Gently rub the back of the stamp with your fingers to remove any remaining glue. Never leave a stamp in the water for more than an hour. Dry the stamps on white absorbent paper, newspaper, or terrycloth towels. When almost dry, press the stamps flat under a heavy weight or place them in a drying book made of blotters. Let the stamps dry at least four days before you mount them as part of your collection.

There are products that remove marks from tape or adhesives, ink, grease, and other disfiguring blotches. There are also experts who restore stamps, but only rare and valuable stamps make the expenditure worthwhile.

Store stamps in a dry, not too warm place, out of direct sunlight. Do not remove the selvage edge around a mint or used stamp. Especially important is a selvage with plate numbers and markings. Don't tear stamp groups apart. Blocks and sets are collected in a different way than single stamps. Check your local library for books on stamps. Many contain information on care and conservation.

Sources

Lin Terry, 59 East Madison Avenue, Dumont, NJ 07628, 201-385-4706. Stamp collecting supplies and literature.

University Products, Inc., P.O. Box 101, South Canal Street, Holyoke, MA 01040, 800-336-4847, 800-628-1912 outside Massachusetts, 8:30 a.m.-5:00 p.m.; fax: 413-532-9281. Archival supplies and repair materials. Albums, mounts, Mylar sheet protectors. Free catalog.

Stencils

Stenciling was a popular form of decoration during the 19th century. Walls, floors, chairs, tinware, and glass clock panels were often painted with stencil decorations. Complete pictures called "theorems" were made by schoolgirls, who used a variety of appropriate stencils. Most theorems pictured a large bowl of fruit and flowers. They are valued as folk art and should not be restored by anyone who is not museum-trained. Painted furniture and stenciled walls can be restored. Ready-to-use stencils are available. An art supply store can furnish stencil designs, paper, cutting knives, and paints. Designs not available from a store can be copied from existing stencils or by tracing a stencil from a book. The Dover Publishing Company has printed a series of books offering patterns from classic to Art Deco. There are also many how-to-stencil books. We have listed a few, but your library may have many more.

Stenciling a wall or a floor is very time-consuming and you may wish to hire an expert. Most experts work only within easy distance of their homes. We have listed only those who indicated they would travel out of town. The Historical Society of Early American Decoration (19 Dove Street, Albany, NY 12210) could probably help you find someone in your area. See also the sections on Floorcloths and Textiles.

Sources

Decorative Arts Studio, R.R. 1, Box 136, Route 30, Dorset, VT 05251, 802-867-5915. Restoration of old stenciled walls, reproductions of old stencils, and precut stencils. Books, brushes, fabric paints. Commission work, including design and execution. Work on walls, floors, floorcloths, furniture, woodenware, and fabrics. Catalog.

Hand-Stenciled Interiors, 590 King Street, Hanover, MA 02339, 617-878-7596, anytime. Custom-cut stencils, patterns, and stenciled interiors. Mail order or will travel. Send $1 for information.

Judith Hendershot and Associates, 1408 Main Street, Evanston, IL 60202, 708-475-6411, 9:00 a.m.-5:00 p.m. Decorative stenciling of walls, ceilings, and floors.

Rasa Arbas Design, 306 22nd Street, Santa Monica, CA 90402, 213-395-5529, 8:00 a.m.-5:00 p.m.; fax: 619-436-8189. Stencils, watercolors, hand-painted fabrics. Specializing in botanicals.

Adele Bishop, P.O. Box 3349, Kinston, NC 28501, 800-334-4286, 7:30 a.m.-5:30 p.m.; fax: 919-527-4189. Decorative stencils, stencil paints and brushes. How-to books and seminars. Mail order. Catalog $2, refundable with first order.

Kenneth R. Hopkins, 3001 Monta Vista, Olympia, WA 98501, 206-943-1118, anytime. Restoration of stencils and 18th- and 19th-century decorative arts.

Sara H. Hopkins, 3005 SW Westwood Drive, Portland, OR 97225, 503-292-8114, 9:00 a.m.-5:00 p.m. Restoration of stenciled ceilings, walls, and floors. Primarily Pacific Northwest area.

Carol Nagel/Gerri Sproesser, P.O. Box 832, Richboro, PA 18954, 215-322-7823. Precut Mylar stencils. Will stencil or paint wall murals. Mail order sales of stencils. Catalog $4.

Books

Art of Decorative Stenciling, Adele Bishop & Cile Lord, 1976 (Viking, NY).

Early New England Wall Stencils, Kenneth Jewett, 1979 (Harmony Books, NY).

Traditional Tole Painting, Roberta Ray Blanchard, 1977 (Dover Publications, NY).

Stocks and bonds require special treatment. They are different from any other collectible in this book. Be sure to check whether or not the company issuing the paper might still be redeeming it. Call your local stockbroker or one of the services that search for out-of-business companies. The cash value of a stock may be more than its value as a decorative piece of paper. The value of an unredeemable stock is in the engraving or the autograph. The industry pictured, the artistic worth of the picture, the fame of the company, and the signer all add to the value.

Take care of your stocks and bonds like other paper items. Never use glue or tape to mount the paper unless you feel the item is of minimal value. Old stock certificates used to paper walls can rarely be removed and sold. See Paper Collectibles & Ephemera.

Antique cooking and heating stoves have gained popularity in recent years. Be sure that your stove, as well as your chimney, is in safe working condition if you plan to use it. Old parts are available through many of the dealers who sell antique stoves. New parts can be purchased or made for most old stoves.

An amateur should never restore or install an old stove that is to be used. Many communities have strict fire code laws that require permits plus an inspection of any working stove after installation. Local workmen can safely install your stove; their addresses can be found in the Yellow Pages of your phone directory.

Sources

Antique Stove Information Clearinghouse, 417 North Main Street, Monticello, IN 47960, 219-583-6465, late evening. Manufacturers' catalogs, books on antique stoves, restoration information.

Barnstable Stove Shop, Inc., Box 472, Route 149, West Barnstable, MA 02668, 508-362-9913, 9:00 a.m.-5:00 p.m. Restoration, parts, and sales of wood, coal, and gas cookstoves and parlor stoves. Stove parts, nickel plating, foundry casting, sandblasting, welding, mica.

Bryant Stove Works, R.F.D. 2, Box 2048, Thorndike, ME 04986, 207-568-3665, 7:30 a.m.-5:00 p.m. Restoration of antique wood, coal, gas, and electric stoves. Will ship stoves and stove parts anywhere in the U.S. Brochure and price list.

Country Comfort Stove Works, Union Road, Wales, MA 01081, 413-245-7396, 8:00 a.m.- 8:00 p.m. Stove parts and restoration. Electric cooktops put in antique cookstoves. SASE for information. Brochure $2.

Heckler Brothers, 4105 Stuebenville Pike, Pittsburgh, PA 15205, 412-922-6811, Mon.-Fri. 8:00 a.m.-4:30 p.m. Coal stove parts. Mail order.

Macy's Texas Stove Works, 5515 Almeda Road, Houston, TX 77004, 713-521-0934 or 713-528-1297, 9:30 a.m.-6:30 p.m.; fax: 713-526-9090. Reconditioning, restoration, and parts fabrication. Specializing in Chambers ranges and O'Keefe & Merritt, Maytag, Anderson, and others. Mail order.

Stanley Iron Works, 64 Taylor Street, Nashua, NH 03060, 603-881-8335, Mon.-Fri. 8:30 a.m.-4:30 p.m. Restoration of wood parlor and cook stoves; gas and electric conversions of antique stoves. Mail order.

Tomahawk Foundry, Inc., 2337 29th Street, Rice Lake, WI 54868, 715-234-4498, 7:00 a.m.-4:00 p.m. Will make anything in cast iron. Specializing in duplicating parts for antique stoves, such as firebowls, grates, lids, and liners. Catalog.

Telephone Collectibles

Many types of old telephones can be repaired and used. Old dial phones can even be converted to push-button phones through the addition of an extra box or by another method. Contact your local phone company for exact information about the types of equipment that will work. Old phones often require more power to ring the bell, and sometimes too many phones on one line can cause a mysterious problem. We learned about this the hard way when we tried to install an answering machine. A normal house line can handle "five ringers," we were told; some new phones are only half ringers, but old phones can be more than one ringer. Reproduction phones and phone parts are also available.

Sources

Billiard's Old Telephones, 21710 Regnart Road, Cupertino, CA 95014, Wall telephones and parts, restoration. Mail order. Catalog $1.

Chicago Old Telephone Co., P.O. Box 189, Lemon Springs, NC 28355, 919-774-6625, 800-843-1320, 8:00 a.m.-5:30 p.m. Old telephones, restored to work on modern service. Catalog.

House of Telephones, 15 East Avenue D, San Angelo, TX 76903, 915-655-4174, 8:00 a.m.-5:00 p.m.; fax: 915-655-4177. Antique telephones and parts. Restoration of antique telephones. Parts. Mail order.

Just Enterprises, 2790 Sherwin Avenue, Unit 10, Ventura, CA 93003, 805-644-5837, Mon.-Fri. 8:30 a.m.-5:30 p.m., answering machine other times. Repair and restoration. Send photo, description of item and damage, plus SASE, for estimate. Mail order worldwide.

Phone Wizard, 10 South King Street, P.O. Box 70, Leesburg, VA 22075-0070, 703-777-0000, 703-689-1118 in Washington, D.C. area, Mon.-Sat. 10:00 a.m.-5:00 p.m.; fax: 703-777-1233. Restore and repair antique telephones and parts. Conversions. Catalog.

Phoneco, Route 3, Galesburg, WI 54630, 608-582-4124. Antique telephones repaired and restored. Decorator phones, old phone booths, parts.

Textiles

Textiles include everything from rugs, coverlets, and quilts to lace and needlework. Care is especially important for all of these, as they are perishable. The greatest harm to a fabric can come from strong sunlight and dirt. A small piece of fabric can be successfully displayed if it is washed and stitched to unbleached muslin with unbleached pure cotton thread. It should be mounted on acid-free backing and framed under glass. Never hang it in full sunlight. It is often safer to wash or clean a quilt than to store it as found. Proper washing and hanging is important if you plan to display the quilt on a wall. Be sure that the quilt is hung from a rod held by a tunnel of cloth that supports the entire weight of the quilt and does not cause tears. The Abby Aldrich Rockefeller Folk Art Center, P.O. Box C, Williamsburg, VA 23185, identifies quilts and sells books about their care and display. Rugs can also be hung from rods. Instructions for this type of display can be found in how-to books. Lace should be laundered, stretched, repaired, and either used or framed. Stores that sell old clothing may be able to help with repairs.

Cleaning a rug or quilt requires care and the proper supplies. Use Orvus WA Paste (found at stores that have supplies for horses and farm animals) or Woolite. Always test the colors first to be sure that they will not run. Rinse thoroughly, dry, and either use or store on rolls. This is not too difficult a project for the careful amateur, but be sure to follow directions. Many modern quilt makers will repair old quilts. Some even have supplies of old fabrics. Sources of the many types of supplies needed are listed in the book *Considerations for the Care of Textiles and Costumes* by Harold Maitland (Indianapolis: Indianapolis Museum of Art, 1980). If not in your local library, it should be available through interlibrary loan.

Most rug dealers also clean and repair rugs, so you may be able to find a local expert by checking the Yellow Pages of your local telephone book.

Sources

Appelbaum & Himmelstein, 444 Central Park West, New York, NY 10025, 212-666-4630, 10:30 a.m.-7:00 p.m. Specializing in restoration of deteriorated silk textiles.

Carter Canopies, Box 808, Troutman, NC 28166, 704-528-4071, 8:00 a.m.-6:00 p.m.; fax: 704-528-6437. Hand-tied fishnet canopies, dust ruffles, and coverlets. Custom-made dust ruffles, hand-tied fringe, hand-tied valances, and quilt racks. Catalog. Mail order, retail and wholesale.

Etcetera Shoppe, Route 87, on the Green, P.O. Box 68, Lebanon, CT 06249, 203-642-6847, Mon.-Sat. 10:00 a.m.-4:00 p.m. Repair, restoration of vintage clothing, lectures on fans, reuse of "worn" and "torn" linens. Costume research for theater productions. Serving eastern Connecticut.

Key Tassels, 1314 21st Street NW, Washington, DC 20036, 202-775-9460, 11:00 a.m.-6:00 p.m. Imported handmade cotton tassels. Mail order.

Linens Limited, 240 North Milwaukee Street, Milwaukee, WI 53202, 414-223-1123, 800-637-6334, 8:00 a.m.-5:00 p.m.; in New York

City, 212-838-0650; fax: 414-223-1126. Repair and restoration of fine linens, laundering and finishing. Mail order. Brochure.

Schachter's, 85 Ludlow Street, New York, NY 10002, 212-533-1150, Sun.-Thurs. 9:00 a.m.-4:00 p.m. Quilts renovated and recovered, sleeping pillows renovated and sterilized, sofa cushions renovated and restuffed. Mail order.

Shallcross & Lorraine, Holly L. Smith, State House Post Office, Box 133, Boston, MA 02133, 617-720-2133. Invisible restoration, conservation, and maintenance of rugs, tapestries, American Indian textiles, Aubussons, and needlework. Damaged threads replaced, missing sections rewoven. Mail order.

Stephen & Carol Huber Inc., 82 Plants Dam Road, East Lyme, CT 06333, 203-739-0772, 9:00 a.m.-8:00 p.m. Conservation of antique needlework. Mail order.

Testfabrics, Inc., P.O. Box 420, Middlesex, NJ 08846, 201-469-6446, 9:00 a.m.-4:00 p.m.; fax: 201-469-1147. Textile goods and services for conservation and restoration, including piece goods without dyes or resins, flame-retardant fabrics, and natural cotton tapes. Catalog.

Textile Conservation Center, 800 Massachusetts Avenue, North Andover, MA 01845, 508-686-0191, 9:00 a.m.-5:00 p.m. Preservation and conservation of textiles, including cleaning, stabilization, documentation, and display systems. Lectures, workshops, and consultations. No mail order. Brochure.

Textile Conservation Workshop, Patsy Orlofsky, Main Street, South Salem, NY 10590, 914-736-5805, 9:30 a.m.-5:00 p.m. Conservation and restoration of all textiles. Consultations, lectures, information on new conservation methods. Developing a registry of American textiles as a resource for historians. Brochure.

Textile Restoration, Robin Greeson, R.D. 1, Box 276, Snydertown Road, Craryville, NY 12521, 518-851-7979, 8:00 a.m.-8:00 p.m. Restoration of hooked rugs, Navajo blankets, and quilts.

Thanewold Associates, P.O. Box 104, Zieglerville, PA 19492, 215-287-9158, 8:00 a.m.-10:00 p.m. Restoration and conservation of samplers and other decorative needlework. Dealer and lecturer on decorative arts. Serving the Eastern Seaboard.

Unique Art Lace Cleaners, 5926 Delmar Boulevard, St. Louis, MO 63112, 314-725-2900, 9:00 a.m.-4:00 p.m. Wedding dresses, fine tablecloths, and antique textiles cleaned and mended. Estimate for repairs $15, applied to work if done. Mail order.

Books

Art of Crewel Embroidery, Mildred J. Davis, 1962 (Crown Publishers, NY).

Collecting Costume; The Care and Display of Clothes and Accessories, Naomi Tarrant, 1983 (Allen & Unwin, Winchester, MA).

Considerations for the Care of Textiles and Costumes, Harold F. Mailand, 1980 (Indianapolis Museum of Art, 1200 West 38th Street, Indianapolis, IN 46208).

Encyclopedia of Embroidery Stitches Including Crewel, Marion Nichols, 1974 (Dover Publications, NY).

How to Wet-Clean Undyed Cotton and Linen, No. 478 (Smithsonian Institution Press, Washington, DC).

Legacy of Lace, Kathleen Warnick and Shirley Nilsson, 1988 (Crown Publishers, NY).

TIN & TOLEWARE, see Metals

Tools

Tool collectors are divided on the subject of care and restoration. Some think waxing or treating the wood lowers the value of a tool, while others feel such treatment enhances it. Tools should be kept clean and in working condition. Metal parts should be rust-free and usually require oil or another preservative.

The restoration of tools requires the knowledge of a woodworker, a metalworker, and an expert on tools. Local shops dealing with tools may be able to help, but many antique tools are beyond the skill and knowledge of the modern toolworker.

Source

Just Enterprises, 2790 Sherwin Avenue, Unit 10, Ventura, CA 93003, 805-644-5837, Mon.-Fri. 8:30 a.m.-5:30 p.m., answering machine other times. Tools repaired and restored. Send photo and description of item and damage, plus SASE, for estimate. Mail order worldwide.

Toys

Many toys are found in poor condition because of the love they received from the children who were their original owners. Teddy bear collectors cherish old worn bears, but few other toys are valuable if in very poor condition. Collectors judge condition severely and a pristine tin toy is worth a great deal more than the same toy in damaged or restored condition. Carefully examine an old toy. Has it been repainted? Are there replacement parts? Does it work? It is not advisable for the amateur to make many types of repairs. Never repaint or restore a metal toy if there is any way to avoid it. It is now possible to find reproduced parts for old toys, especially cars and trucks. Decals, wheels, and other parts are available. An old toy that is missing its paint is usually worth more than a toy from the same period that has been repainted. The exception to this rule seems to be pedal cars. Collectors of these, just like collectors of full-sized cars, seem to prefer a "new" look. A fine restoration will add to the value.

If you want a cast-iron bank that looks like a new one, buy a reproduction, but don't paint an old one. The working parts of old toys are very difficult to replace unless you are mechanically inclined. Key-wind mechanisms and power sources for trains are complicated and must often be replaced. Some toys can never be totally repaired. The battery-driven mechanical toys of the 1950s that featured a cigarette-smoking bartender or monkey can be made to smoke again if you add a drop of oil. Many toys have been reproduced. Be sure you understand the differences between old and new toys before you spend money on repairs. Libraries are filled with books on this subject.

See also the sections on dolls and music.

Sources

The American Marine Model Gallery, Inc., 12 Derby Square, Salem, MA 01970, 508-745-5777, Tues.-Sat. 10:00 a.m.-4:00 p.m.; fax: 508-745-5778. Antique marine models restored. Ship models serviced; custom models and custom cases. Mail order. Catalog $10.

American Toy Trucker Parts Department, Dennis and Marge Lowry, 1143 46th, Des Moines, IA 50311, 515-277-7589, answering machine, will answer all calls. Parts for toy trucks and race cars, approximately 1/16 scale. Wheels, rubber tires, parts for Tonka, Ertl, Smith Miller, MIC, Doepke, Thimble Drone, Ohlsson Rice, and All American racers. Mail order. Catalog $4.50.

Armor Products, P.O. Box 445, East Northport, NY 11731, 516-462-6228, 9:00 a.m.-5:00 p.m. Wooden wheels, axles, and turnings. Plastic eyes. Catalog.

Bear-"S"-Ence, Steve Schutt, 201 5th Avenue NE, Clarion, IA 50525. Teddy bears repaired and restored. Bear supplies, including glass eyes and mohair. Serving the Midwest.

Buddy K Toys, R.D. 9, Box 322, Bingen Road, Bethlehem, PA 18015, 215-838-6505, 8:30 a.m.-10:00 p.m.; if no answer, try 904-245-0204. Restoration and replacement parts, decals for pressed steel toys of the 1920s and 1930s. Catalog $3.

Buhrmaster's Decals, Stan & Jean Buhrmaster, 315 Iowa Street, Cedar Falls, IA 50613, 319-266-7852, Mon.-Fri. 5:00 p.m.-9:00 p.m. Decals for farm toys, Tonka toys, model toys, some construction toys, and gas pumps. Mail order.

Cabin Toys & Parts, Howard & Glenda Andrew, Route 1, Box 140, Cordova, MD 21625, 301-364-5490, Mon.-Sat. 8:00 a.m.-9:00 p.m. Parts for farm toys. Catalog $2.50.

Castle's Fair, Lawrence and Sara Castle, Marlow Peterson, P.O. Box 1857, Ogden, UT 84402, 801-393-8131, mornings; 801-544-7889, 5:00 p.m.-10:00 p.m. Marble polishing and heat treatment. Advice on type or value of marbles.

Chrome-Tech USA, Robert Shebilske, 2914 Rockwood Drive, Madison, WI 53713, 608-274-9811, after 7:00 p.m. Vacuum metalizing (chrome plating) metal or plastic model toy parts. Brochure with instructions for sending parts to be plated.

Continental Hobby, P.O. Box 193, Sheboygan, WI 53082, 414-693-3371, anytime; fax: 414-693-8211. Replacement parts; restoration and repair of trains, toys, and steam-related toys. Train catalogs: tinplate collector trains $2, HO trains $5, parts catalog $8. SASE for free paint chart. Mail order.

CTM Parts, Box 489, Rocanville, SK S0A 3L0, Canada, 306-645-4566. Replacement parts and decals for farm toys. Parts catalog $2.50, refundable with first order over $25.

Der Alt Mann of Auto's, Dwight E. Mauer, 4524 Luann Avenue, Toledo, OH 43623, 419-474-8750. Parts for model cars, wheels, rubber tires, lights, etc. Restoring, building, and painting of most die-cast, iron, and steel model vehicles. Send double stamped LSASE for information. Include phone number. Mail order.

Edinburgh Imports, Inc., Elke & Ron Block, P.O. Box 722, Woodland Hills, CA 91365-0722, 818-703-1122, outside California 800-EDINBRG, 8:30 a.m.-5:00 p.m.; fax: 818-703-6298. Teddy bear supplies, specializing in imported German fabrics, mohair, alpaca, wool, merino felt, and plush synthetics. Music boxes, imported glass and safety eyes, joint parts, stands. Retail, wholesale, and worldwide mail order. Send two first class stamps for brochure with prices. Showroom at 5111 Douglas Fir Road, Calabasas, CA 91302.

Egli Toy Salvage, R.R. 2, Box 115, Manson, IA 50563, 712-469-3949, 7:00 a.m.-11:00 p.m. Restoration of farm toys. New and used parts for farm and construction toys. Send double stamped LSASE for parts list. Mail order worldwide.

Euro-Chrome, Francois Spenard, 101 Ninth Avenue, LaSalle, QU H8P 2N7, Canada, 514-363-5857, 9:00 am.-9:00 p.m. Chrome and gold plating of model cars, trucks, and other toys. Chrome-plating of plastic, cast resin, or metal parts. Send SASE for brochure.

Flying Tails, John and June Reely, 1209 Indiana Avenue, South Pasadena, CA 91030, 213-256-8647, 8:00 a.m.-9:00 p.m. Processed horsehair and cow tails for rocking horses and other toys.

G. Schoepfer Inc., 138 West 31st Street, New York, NY 10001, 212-736-6934 or 212-736-6939, 9:30 a.m.-3:30 p.m.; fax: 212-736-6934. Glass and plastic eyes for dolls, mannequins, teddy bears, ceramic figures, and other projects. Mail order worldwide. Send SASE and specify project to get list.

Glass Shot Restoration, 216 Lincolnway East, New Oxford, PA 17350, 717-624-8231, 8:30 a.m.-9:30 p.m. Glass beading. Paint and rust removed from metal toys, tools, auto parts, and other metal items. Repair and painting of pedal tractors.

Grand Illusions, 26 Barton Street, East Hampton, CT 06424, 203-267-8682, anytime. Pre-1900 kaleidoscopes repaired. Mail order.

H & D Toy Co., Herman Reschke, 1016 Hickory Drive, Geneseo, IL 61254, 309-994-6688, 10:00 a.m.-8:00 p.m. Farm toys repaired and restored. Replacement parts and decals. Mail order parts. Parts catalog, send $1 for postage.

Merrily Supply, 8542 Ranchito Avenue, Panorama City, CA 91402, 818-894-0637, 10:30 a.m.-4:00 p.m. Supplies and tools for making and repairing dolls and teddy bears. Mail order only. Catalog $2.

New-Era Quality Toys, Marvin Silverstein and Avi Jerchower, P.O. Box 10, Lambertville, NJ 08530, 609-397-2113 or 609-397-1571, 9:00 a.m.-5:00 p.m. Restoration of pedal cars and other pressed-steel toys, Buddy-L, Keystone, etc. Custom-built trucks. Mail order.

Parts Shop, 9 Bunting Place, Elmira, ON N3B 3G7, Canada, 519-669-5079, Mon.-Sat. 8:00 a.m.-9:00 p.m. Ertl farm toys, replacement parts, and decals. Parts for Ertl and Eska pedal tractors.

Decals for pedal tractors, 8-in. gas pumps, reproduction signs. Supplying Canadian collectors. Mail order. SASE for parts/price list.

Pedal Car Graphics by Robert, 1207 Charter Oak Drive, Taylors, SC 29687, 803-244-4308, anytime. Decals for pedal cars. Catalog and color photos $2.

Phantom Antique Toy Restoration, Buddy George, 101 Bennett Street, Wrentham, MA 02093, 508-384-6376. Restoration and custom work done on pressed-steel toys. No mail order.

Scale Equipment Ltd., P.O. Box 10084, Bradenton, FL 34282. Model kits for scale automotive dioramas, including miniature workbenches, toolboxes, brooms, grease drums, tools. Mail order. Catalog.

Second Childhood, 283 Bleecker Street, New York, NY 10014, 212-989-6140, Mon.-Sat. 11:00 a.m.-6:00 p.m. Replacement bulbs and keys for antique toys. Mail order worldwide.

Smith-Miller Trucks & Parts, Steve Butler, 2912 Memory Lane, Silver Spring, MD 20904, 301-890-1738, 6:00 p.m.-10:00 p.m. Original, restored, and limited-edition Smith-Miller toy trucks and parts.

Thomas Toys, P.O. Box 405, Fenton, MI 48430, 313-629-8707 or 313-629-8744, 10:00 a.m.-8:00 p.m. Replacement parts for antique toys, including tires, wooden wheels, light bulbs, grilles, cast parts, and pressed-steel parts. Limited amount of restoration work. Send pieces UPS to 2017 Bly Drive. Mail order. Catalog $5.

Tin Toy Works, Joe Freeman, 1313 North 15th Street, Allentown, PA 18102, 215-434-0290 or 215-439-8268, 8:30 a.m.-5:00 p.m. Restoration tin parts and hardware for toys, missing parts manufactured, mechanisms repaired. Mail order worldwide.

"The Toy Doctor," R.R. 1, Box 202, Eades Road, Red Creek, NY 13143, 315-754-8846. Battery-operated toys repaired, specializing in robots, space toys. Will pay postage both ways if they can't repair the toy.

Klaus Banke, Schillerstrasse 33, D-4005, Meerbusch 3, West Germany, 40-2150-5950. Schuco parts. Mail order worldwide.

Tom Barry, 1456 Deer Park Road, Finksburg, MD 21048, 301-876-7555, answering machine 24 hours. Whitewall tire paint for model and toy cars. Can be used on rubber, does not crack. One ounce $2.98. Mail order.

Louis Bernier, 6443 Bl. Galeries D'Anjou, loc. #9, Anjou, QU H1M 1W1, Canada, 514-354-9121, 8:00 a.m.-midnight. Chrome, gold, and brass plating for model cars; wiring kits, cast reproduction parts, grilles, bumpers, wheels, hood ornaments, license plate frames. Mail order. Write for information.

Dana Edge, 512 SW 59th Street, #13, Oklahoma City, OK 73109, 405-634-6215. Restoration of wooden toys. Mail order.

Paul Fideler, Box 1591, Dept. KOV, Waltham, MA 02254. Parts for toy cars, decals, figures, tires, bulldozer and tank treads. Price list $2, refundable with order.

Jim Hall, 2179 West Sunset Drive, Palatine, IL 60067, 708-359-1977 until 8:00 p.m. Parts for model race cars. Model and original race cars and racing memorabilia. Mail order.

Russell Harrington, 1805 Wilson Point Road, Baltimore, MD 21220, 301-687-8596, 9:00 a.m.-8:00 p.m. Restoration of antique toys and banks.

Dean Hile, 2411 Sheridan Boulevard, Lincoln, NE 68502, 402-435-0406, 9:00 a.m.-9:00 p.m. Pedal cars, trucks, planes, license plates, hood ornaments, decals, new wheels, parts clinic. Will replace rubber on wheels of pedal cars, wagons, and buggies.

Stephen Leonard, P.O. Box 127, Albertson, NY 11507, 516-742-0979, 8:00 a.m.-5:00 p.m. Restoration of mechanical and tin windup toys, singing bird boxes, and whistling figures. Mail order worldwide.

Robert McCumber, 201 Carriage Drive, Glastonbury, CT 06033, 203-633-4984, may call at night. Repairs mechanical and still banks. Books on banks.

Gary Moran, 3 Finch Court, Commack, NY 11725, 516-864-9444, 10:00 a.m.-10:00 p.m. Repairs clockwork, battery-operated, friction, and sand toys.

Jim Newark, 1730 LaPorte, Whiting, IN 46394, 219-659-6576. Repair and restoration of antique toys, windups, battery-operated toys, pedal cars, and tin toys. Mail order. Write for information.

Tony Orlando, 6661 Norborne, Dearborn Heights, MI 48127, 313-561-5072. Rocking horses restored and cleaned, missing parts replaced. Horsehair tails, reproduction stirrups. Mail order.

Sy Schreckinger, P.O. Box 104, East Rockaway, NY 11518, 516-536-4154, 9:00 a.m.-10:00 p.m. Restoration and repair of toys and mechanical banks.

Bernard L. Scott, 117 Highview Drive, Cocoa, FL 32922, 407-632-0665, 8:00 a.m.-8:00 p.m. Restoration of farm toys. Will restore, modify, detail, custom build 1/16-scale die-cast model tractors. Sales literature for farm tractors 1970 or older bought and sold. Mail order.

David or Debbie Sharp, 6449 West 12th Street, Indianapolis, IN 46214, 317-243-3172. Tonka parts and decals. Send SASE for price list.

Jim Smith, P.O. Box 472113, Garland, TX 75047, 214-271-8917, 6:00 p.m.-10:00 p.m. Battery-operated, windup, and friction toys repaired. Mail order worldwide.

Paul N. Smith, 408 East Leeland Heights Boulevard, Lehigh Acres, FL 33936, 813-369-4663, 9:00 a.m.-5:00 p.m. Toys repaired.

Julian Thomas, P.O. Box 405, Fenton, MI 48430, 313-629-8707, 9:00 a.m.-9:00 p.m. Reproduction parts, tires for toys. Catalog $5.

Donald R. Walters, Route 1, Box 51 A, Curtiss, WI 54422, 715-654-5440, 8:00 a.m.-10:00 p.m. Toy refinishing, repair, repainting, customizing. Glass beading. Mail order.

Books

Collectable Machine-Made Marbles, Castle and Marlow Peterson (Utah Marble Connection, P.O. Box 1857, Ogden, UT 84402).

Greenberg's American Flyer Factory Manual, Richard D. Smith and I.D. Smith, 1988 (Greenberg Publishing Co., Sykesville, MD).

Greenberg's Guide to Lionel Postwar Parts, Alan T. Weaver, 1989 (Greenberg Publishing Co., Sykesville, MD).

Mechanical Toys, Athelstan and Kathleen Spilhaus, 1989 (Crown Publishers, NY).

Teddy Bear Catalog, Peggy and Alan Bialosky, 1980 (Workman Publishing Co., NY).

Videotape

Robert Dane: Making Marbles (Marble Glass Collectors' Society, P.O. Box 222, Trumbull, CT 06611).

Transportation

There are many collectors of old automobiles, automobile parts, instruction books, and memorabilia. Parts can be found through ads in automobile-related publications or your local newspaper. Word-of-mouth advertising through other collectors and dealers is also successful. Huge auto collectors' flea markets are held throughout the country. Almost every type of part--old or reproduction--can be found. Collectors often go to shows looking like walking billboards with lists of wants written in large letters on a shirt or sign. After a day of walking through miles of dealers' and collectors' booths and asking questions, you will probably get the answer about where to find your car part. Check at your library for more information about local clubs and events.

Railroads have a charm that never fades. Collectors are interested in toy railroads (see "Toys") as well as real ones. You can buy dining-car silverware or dishes or even whole train cars if you wish. Repairs are listed in the sections on toys, porcelain, and silverware.

In 1839, when roads were rough and the way long, a Scottish blacksmith named Kirkpatrick MacMillan invented the bicycle. It weighed 57 pounds and sported a carved horsehead at its front. The years have seen many improvements, including motors, steering, and rubber tires. Collectors of vintage motorcycles and bicycles often collect and ride the antique models. Parts can be found in commercial bicycle and motorcycle shops and at huge automobile flea markets. Although there are special clubs and publications for motorcycles, there is crossover with the car-collecting organizations. Check to see if your antique motorcycle would be welcome at local car events. If it is, you may find missing parts there. Look in *Kovels' Guide to Selling Your Antiques & Collectibles* for information on these publications and events.

The lure of the sea remains as romantic today as it has for centuries. Many collectors search for memorabilia about whaling, steamships, famous sinkings, sailboats, fishing, and other specialties. All these are included in maritime antiques. The Ivory section in this book includes information on scrimshaw.

Sources

Brass 'n Bounty, 68 Front Street, Marblehead, MA 01945, 617-631-3864, 9:00 a.m.-5:30 p.m. Marine antiques, telescopes, and navigation instruments repaired and polished. Mail order.

California Classic Boats, Al Schinnerer, 15632B Product Lane, Huntington Beach, CA 92649, 714-895-5303, 8:30 a.m.-5:00 p.m. Reproduction parts and instruments for antique and classic speedboats; custom reproduction work; automotive and marine instrument restoration and repair. Mail order sales worldwide. Catalog $5, refundable with purchase of $50 or more.

Classic Boat Connection, 1733 Gull Lane, Mound, MN 55364, 612-472-4814. Classic boats and refinishing supplies.

Classic Boating, P.O. Box 1634, Colton, CA 92324, 714-793-6091, 8:00 a.m.-5:00 p.m. Chris Craft decals, discounted paints and varnish, air horns, ensigns, pennants, caps, books, supplies, and engine manuals. Mail order.

Eagle Restoration, Sherman Langell, HCR 9547, Keaau, HI 96749-9317, 808-966-6148, 24 hours. Reproduction and custom step pads for antique and classic boats. Reproduction rubber parts for antique boats and cars. Remanufactured engine mounts for pre-1960 Chris Craft and Chrysler marine engines. Mail order.

Instrument Shop, Robert B. Prickett, 3816 Mockingbird Lane, Dallas, TX 75205, 214-528-8237, 9:00 a.m.-5:00 p.m. Specializing in repair and restoration of old Chris Craft (Stewart Warner) boat instruments. Mail order.

JGR Enterprises, Inc., P.O. Box 32, Route 522, Fort Littleton, PA 17223, 717-485-4344, 8:00 a.m.-5:00 p.m., 717-485-4693 after 5:00 p.m., 800-223-7112, 8:00 a.m.-4:30 p.m. Custom reproduction parts for antique, classic, and special-interest cars. Mail order.

Memphis Plating Works, 678-682 Madison Avenue, Memphis, TN 38103, 901-526-3051, Mon.-Fri. 8:00 a.m.-5:00 p.m., Sat. 8:00 a.m.-noon. Restores chrome on antique and show cars.

Speed & Sport Chrome Plating, Craig Bierman, 7477 SW Freeway, Houston, TX 77074, 713-981-1440, Mon.-Sat. 10:00 a.m.-6:00 p.m. Automobile parts chrome-plated.

Warehouse, 251 Orchard Street, Fairport Harbor, OH 44077, 216-352-7120, after 5:00 p.m. Motorcycle parts and accessories. Mail order.

Scott Anderson, P.O. Box 65596, West Des Moines, IA 50265, 515-223-5105, 8:30 a.m.-5:30 p.m.; fax: 515-223-5149. Gas pump parts, restoration. Mail order sales, service. Catalog $4.

Bill Hulbert, P.O. Box 151, Adams Center, NY 13606, 315-583-5765 after 5:00 p.m. Car and home radios repaired. Parts for 1929-1931 Chevrolet cars and trucks traded, bought, and sold. Mail order.

Joe Maier, 4380 Lagg Avenue, Fort Myers, FL 33901, 813-936-5490, after 6:00 p.m. Antique outboard motor decals, Bendix models SD and TD. Mail order.

Rex Walls, P.O. Box 1111, Harriman, TN 37748, 615-882-2561, 5:00 p.m.-10:00 p.m. Original equipment rubber mats for antique cars.

Videotape

Wood Boat Refinishing, Chamberlain Marine (115 Olive Street, Carterville, IL 62918).

Trunks

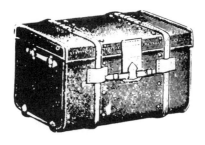

Old trunks should be restored to their original condition. If they are in very poor condition, they can be refinished in some decorative manner, but this will change the piece from an old trunk to a decorative accessory. One major problem with old trunks is that they may smell musty. To remove the odor, wash the interior of the trunk and let it dry in a sunny spot. If the odor persists, try storing some charcoal, crumpled newspaper, or other absorbent material in the trunk for a few days. There are many books about modern decorations for trunks, but very few on correct restoration. Parts, including hardware, leather handles, and trim, are available by mail. See also Hardware.

Sources

Antique Trunk Supply Co., 3706 West 169th Street, Cleveland, OH 44111, 216-941-8618, 9:00 a.m.-6:00 p.m. Trunk parts, catalog $1. Book on trunk repair, $4. Price and identification guide, $5.

Charlotte Ford Trunks, Box 536, Spearman, TX 79081, 806-659-3027, 9:00 a.m.-5:00 p.m. Trunk restoration and parts. Mail order.

House of Antique Trunks, 753B Northport Drive, P.O. Box 508K, West Sacramento, CA 95691, 916-372-8228, Tues.-Fri. 9:00 a.m.-4:00 p.m., Sat. 9:00 a.m.-2:00 p.m., 916-371-4979 other times. Antique trunk restoration, parts, and accessories. Iron, brass, tin, nickel-plated, and brass-plated hardware; straps, handles, doll trunk supplies, prints for lids, linings; rust remover, adhesives, and decorative supplies. Parts catalog $2.50, "Art of Trunk Restoration" $6.

Joyce's Choices, Route 1, Box 89F, White Point Road, Leonardtown, MD 20650, 301-475-7279, 9:00 a.m.-5:00 p.m. Trunk restoration, mail order parts for old trunks and doll trunks: locks, drawbolts, ornaments, straps, tools, etc. Catalog $2. Booklet, "Practical Trunk Restoration," $4.95.

Original Woodworks, 360 North Main, Stillwater, MN 55082, 612-430-3622. Trunk repair. Classes, tools, and supplies. Catalog $3.

Phyllis Kennedy Restoration Hardware, 9256 Holyoke Court, Indianapolis, IN 46268, 317-872-6366, 9:00 a.m.-6:00 p.m. Restoration hardware for antique trunks. Mail order. Catalog $2.

R. Shaw, 1142 Scotland, Cupertino, CA 95014, 408-255-9178, 8:00 a.m.-5:00 p.m. Trunk handles stitched and dyed to match original. Mail order.

Books and Leaflets

Art of Restoration of Antique Trunks & Parts Catalogue, Keen and Risley, editors (House of Antique Trunks, 753B Northport Drive, West Sacramento, CA 95691).

How to Repair-Decorate-Restore Antique Trunks, Martin and Maryann Labuda, 1968 (3706 West 169th Street, Cleveland, OH 44111).

Practical Trunk Restoration, Edward S. Tucker, Sr., and Joyce Y. Tucker (Joyce's Choices, Route 1, Box 89F, Leonardtown, MD 20650).

Trunk Talk, Volume V (Charlotte Ford Trunks, Box 536, Spearman, TX 79081).

Wicker, Rattan & Basketry

Wicker and rattan baskets, furniture, and other objects should be kept away from direct heat and sunny windows. Pieces should be washed occasionally or wiped with a damp sponge. Moisture will keep wicker from becoming dry and brittle. Repairs can be made. There are several books that include pictures and simple descriptions of how to fix a leg or mend a bit of snagged wicker.

See also Furniture.

Sources

Able to Cane, 67 Main Street, P.O. Box 429, Warren, ME 04864, 207-273-3747, 9:00 a.m.-5:00 p.m. Wicker repair. Chair seating and basket materials, tools, and advice on caning. Natural and fiber rush, splint, cane, and Shaker tape seating. Serving Northeastern U.S. Mail order nationwide. Catalog.

American Classics Antiques, 4944 Xerxes South, Minneapolis, MN 55410, 612-487-1349 or 612-926-2509, 10:30 a.m.-5:00 p.m., or 612-926-5634. Full-service antiques shop specializing in replacement of cane, splint, and rush seats and wicker repair.

Cane & Basket Supply Company, 1238 South Cochran Avenue, Los Angeles, CA 90019, 213-939-9644, Mon.-Fri. 8:30 a.m.-5:00 p.m.; fax: 213-939-7237. Chair caning and basketry supplies, tools, kits, and instruction booklets. Rattan, bamboo, willow, reeds, rush, splint, seagrass, pressed fiber replacement seats. Catalog.

Caning Shop, 926 Gilman Street, Berkeley, CA 94710, 415-527-5010, 800-544-3373, Tues.-Fri. 10:00 a.m.-6:00 p.m., Sat. 10:00 a.m.-2:00 p.m. Repairing woven furniture. Chair caning and basketry supplies and books. Cane webbing, splint, rattan, Hong Kong grass, Shaker tapes, pressed fiber seats, etc. Catalog $1, refundable with order.

Carolina Caning Supply, P.O. Box 2179, Smithfield, NC 27577, 919-934-0291, 9:00 a.m.-5:00 p.m. Cane for chair repair, woven cane cane for weaving, tools.

Connecticut Cane & Reed Co., P.O. Box 762, Manchester, CT 06040, 203-646-6586, Mon.-Fri. 9:00 a.m.-5:00 p.m., Sat. 10:00 a.m.-4:00 p.m. Mail order supplies for chair caning, reed, rush, splint, Shaker chair seat materials.

Deb's Cane-ery (Cane-ery Antique Mall), 2207 21st Avenue South, Nashville, TN 37212, 615-292-2451 or 615-269-4780, Mon.-Sat. 9:00 a.m.- 5:00 p.m. Chair caning and basket supplies; reproduction hardware. Wicker and caning repair. Caning classes. Mail order.

Frank's Cane & Rush Supply, 7244 Heil Avenue, Huntington Beach, CA 92647, 714-847-0707, Mon.-Fri. 8:00 a.m.-5:00 p.m.; fax: 714-843-5645. Chair caning and rattan products, reeds, basketry supplies, wood parts, brass hardware. Chair kits, seat weaving kits, woodworking books, and more. Catalog.

H.H. Perkins Co., P.O. Box AC, Dept. Y, Amity Station, 10 South Bradley Road, Woodbridge, CT 06525, 203-389-9501, 9:00 a.m.-5:00 p.m.; fax: 203-389-4011. Basket supplies, cane, splint, rush, Hong Kong grass, hoops, handles, stencils, finished baskets, craft supplies, books. Retail and wholesale. Mail order sales and service worldwide. Free catalog on request.

Jack's Upholstery & Caning Supplies, 52 Shell Court, Oswego, IL 60543, 312-554-1045, Mon.-Fri. 8:00 a.m.-5:00 p.m., Sat. 8:00 a.m.-noon. Upholstery and caning supplies for chairs. Mail order. Catalog $2, refundable with first purchase.

Newell Workshop, 19 Blaine Avenue, Hinsdale, IL 60521, 312-323-7367. Chair caning kit, seat weaving supplies for antique chairs, instruction books. Mail order only. Samples for matching sent by mail. Brochure.

Price House Antiques, 137 Cabot Street, Beverly, MA 01915, 508-927-5595, 10:00 a.m.-5:00 p.m. Wicker repair, chair caning, rush seats.

Restore-it Supply Co., P.O. Box 10600, White Bear Lake, MN 55110, 612-429-2222, Thurs.-Sat. noon-5:00 p.m. Restoration products for furniture, including cane and rush; tools and hard-to-find items. Serving surrounding five-state area. Catalog $3.

Robinson's Antiques, 170 Kent Street, Portland, MI 48875, 517-647-6155, 9:00 a.m.-9:00 p.m. Wicker repair. Mail order.

Susan K. Riley, Seat Weaver, 1 Ireland Street, West Chesterfield, MA 01084, 413-296-4061. Natural rush, splint, reed, and cane seats. Regluing and replacement parts.

Virgin Islands Reed & Cane, Dept. Y, P.O. Box 8478, Hot Springs Village, AR 71909, 800-852-0025, anytime. Basketweaving supplies, including reed, cane, hoops, handles, raffia, paper braid, and kits. Cane and reed for seat weaving. Mail order only. Catalog and over 30 samples $2.

Wicker Workshop, Larry Cryderman & Shoshana Enosh, 18744 Parthenia, Northridge, CA 91324, 818-886-4524, 8:30 a.m.-5:00 p.m., answering machine 24 hours. Restoration and repair of woven furniture, caning, rush seating, rawhide seating, splint seats, wicker, rattan. Demonstrations, seminars. Serving middle and southern California.

Dotty McDaniel, 1900 Stoney Ridge Road, Cumming, GA 30130, 404-887-8518. Wicker repair and caning, rush, split oak, Shaker tape, pressed and lace cane, binder cane, sea grass.

Books

Caner's Handbook, Bruce W. Miller and Jim Widess, 1983 (Van Nostrand Reinhold Co. NY).

Old New England Splint Baskets, John E. McGuire, 1985 (Schiffer Publishing Co., West Chester, PA).

Successful Restoration Shop, Thomas Duncan, 1985 (Sylvan Books, P.O. Box 481, Syracuse, IN 46567).

Techniques of Basketry, Virginia I. Harvey, 1974 (Van Nostrand Reinhold Co., NY).

Wicker Furniture, A Guide to Restoring & Collecting, Richard Saunders, 1990 (Crown Publishers, NY).

Wood Carving

Furniture restorers will repair some types of wood carvings but there are specialists who concentrate on only one type of carving.

Sources

Wedgwood Studio, 2522 North 52nd Street, Phoenix, AZ 85008, 602-840-0825, 9:00 a.m.-1:00 p.m. Restoration of wooden religious figures. Mail order. Serving Western U.S.

Bradford Blakely, 6228 SW 32nd Avenue, Portland, OR 97201, 503-245-4534. Restoration of small wood carvings, preferably under 3 inches. Missing inlays replaced.

Writing Instruments

Pens, automatic pencils, ink bottles, inkwells, and many other devices connected with writing are being collected. Early pens and the plastic-cased pens of the 1920s through the 1950s have suddenly become of interest to collectors. The only problems with old pens are stiff or leaky ink sacs or dirty pen points. These can be fixed carefully at home if the proper parts are purchased. There are also some specialists in pen repairs. See also Glass and Pottery & Porcelain.

Sources

Authorized Repair Service, 30 West 57th Street, New York, NY 10019, 212-586-0947, 9:00 a.m.-5:00 p.m.; fax: 212-586-1296. Antique fountain pens and writing instruments repaired, refurbished.

Fountain Pen Hospital, 10 Warren Street, New York, NY 10007, 212-964-0580, 8:00 a.m.-6:00 p.m.; fax: 212-227-5916. Fountain pen repair.

Pen Fancier's Club, 1169 Overcash Drive, Dunedin, FL 34698, 813-734-4742, 10:00 a.m.-10:00 p.m. Ink sacs for vintage pens. Pen repair manuals and books.

Pen Store Inc., 404 Zack Street, Tampa, FL 33602, 813-223-3865, Mon.-Fri. 9:00 a.m.-5:00 p.m. Mail order repair. Send pen for estimate.

Vintage Fountain Pens, P.O. Box 8212, Columbus, OH 43201, 614-267-8468 or 614-263-2084, anytime. Vintage fountain pen restoration and repair. Mail order.

Book

Fountain Pens, second edition, Cliff Lawrence (Pen Fancier's Club, 1169 Overcash Drive, Dunedin, FL 34698).

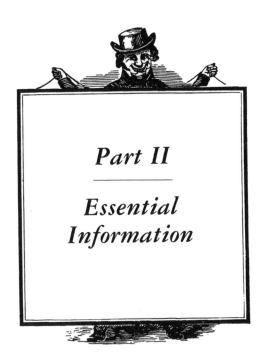

Part II

Essential Information

The best place to start looking for supplies is at your local hardware or art store. There are products that can be used to clean chandeliers still in place on the ceiling, tarnish-proof silver, replate silver, or remove candle wax from tabletops. Ask at the store. All types of metal polishes, battery-powered picture lights, felt pads to keep lamp bottoms from scratching the furniture, polishes to match any shade of wood, marble polish, dry cleaners to remove stains on cloth, linen wash that whitens old damask napkins, and even special cleaners to remove crayon or paint marks can be found.

Some supplies needed for the proper care of antiques are very difficult to locate, including such products as acid-free paper-backing materials, special soaps, special waxes, and the like. These are used primarily by the professional restorer or conservator, but collectors often need them as well. This is a list of these part and supply sources. Some of these companies sell only to wholesale accounts and will not sell to individuals, but will direct you to the store or dealer nearest you that carries the products. **Special items for use with one type of antique, such as clock parts or doll eyes, are listed in the appropriate sections.**

We have also included a few general books and pamphlets that are helpful to collectors. Again, look in specific sections for a book on a particular subject.

Sources

Abatron, Inc., 33 Center Drive, Gilberts, IL 60136, 312-426-2200, 8:00 a.m.-4:30 p.m.; fax: 312-426-5966. Wood restoration products. LiquidWood, a wood consolidant, reinforces, rebuilds, and waterproofs wood. WoodEpox, a high-strength adhesive paste. Booklet.

Albert Constantine & Son, Inc., 2050 Eastchester Road, Bronx, NY 10461, 212-792-1600, 8:00 a.m.-5:00 p.m., 800-223-8082 for ordering only; fax: 212-792-2110. Woodworking supplies, molding, dowels, veneers, marquetry kits, tools, clock parts, hardware, cane, reed, upholstery supplies, books. Catalog.

Allied Resin Corp., Weymouth Industrial Park, East Weymouth, MA 02189, 617-337-6070. Epoxies, resins, structural adhesives, tapes, auto body paste, solvents, and other supplies.

Arista Surgical Supply Co., Inc., 67 Lexington Avenue, New York, NY 10010, 212-679-3694, 8:30 a.m.-4:45 p.m.; fax: 212-696-9046. Supplies of all kinds.

Art Essentials of New York Ltd., **The Gold Leaf People**, 3 Cross Street, Suffern, NY 10901-4601, 914-368-1100, 800-283-5323, anytime, in Canada 416-787-7331. Genuine and imitation gold leaf sheets and rolls, brushes, tools, technical books, video, and supplies. Brochure and price lists.

Bailey & Walke Enterprises, P.O. Box 6037, Shreveport, LA 71136-6037, 318-865-3646, 8:00 a.m.-10:00 p.m.; fax: 318-861-2953. Tarnguard tarnish inhibitor cube. When placed in enclosed space, will protect silver, gold, brass, copper, and other metals from tarnish.

Bay City Paint Company, 2279 Market Street, San Francisco, CA 94114, 415-431-4914, Mon.-Fri. 9:00 a.m.-5:00 pm, Sat. 9:00 a.m.-noon. Specialty paints, brushes, products for wood graining and marbling, refinishing, restoration supplies, books on painted finishes. Free literature.

Bill Cole Enterprises, Inc., P.O. Box 60, Dept. RK, Randolph, MA 02368-0060, 617-986-2653, 8:30 a.m.-4:30 p.m.; fax: 617-986-2656. Archival supplies, including acid-free boxes and boards, heat-sealed Mylar sleeves, and Wei T'o, a nonaqueous deacidifier.

Broadnax Refinishing Products, Inc., P.O. Box 322, Danielsville, GA 30633, 404-795-2659, 8:00 a.m.-5:00 p.m.; 404-795-3410 after 7:00 p.m. Furniture care and refinishing products, including furniture refinisher, wood preservative, and furniture and household cleaner. Consulting. Send SASE with your question. Brochure. Newsletter.

Cereus Inc., 184 Warburton Avenue, Hastings-on-Hudson, NY 10706, 914-739-0754. Renaissance wax cleaner/polish for wood, marble, stone, metal, leather, furniture, artworks, etc.

Classic Accents, Inc., P.O. Box 1181, Southgate, MI 48195, 313-282-5525. Reproduction pushbutton light switches, solid brass cover plates, brass-finish picture lights and hooks, picture cords and tassels. Brochure.

Collector Items, P.O. Box 55511, Seattle, WA 98155, 206-365-1188, 24 hours a day, 7 days a week. Bubble wrap custom-made to size, protective doll covers, bubble-lined mailer bags, nylon bubble wrap for long-term protection of glass and china, polyethelene bubble wrap for mailing and shipping.

Competition Chemicals, Inc., P.O. Box 820, Iowa Falls, IA 50126, 515-648-5121, 8:00 a.m.-5:00 p.m. Simichrome polish.

Conservation Materials Ltd., P.O. Box 2884, 1165 Marietta Way, Sparks, NV 89431, 702-331-0582, 9:00 a.m.-5:00 p.m.; fax: 702-331-0588. Conservation and restoration supplies by mail order.

D.A. Culpepper Mother of Pearl Company, P.O. Box 445, Franklin, NC 28734, 704-524-6842, 9:00 a.m.-5:00 p.m., fax: 704-369-7809; Telex: 4937054 DAC UI. Mother-of-pearl for cutlery, jewelry, watches, inlay, etc. Abalone, bone, horn, coral, exotic skins, and soft stone. Brochure.

Daly's Wood Finishing Products, 3525 Stone Way North, Seattle, WA 98103, 206-633-4200, 800-735-7019, 8:00 a.m.-6:00 p.m.; fax: 206-632-2565. Refinishing products, stain matching, sealers, fillers, finish removers, LemOil. Retail and wholesale. Mail order.

Darworth Company, P.O. Box K, Tower Lane, Avon, CT 06001, 203-677-7721, 800-624-7767, 8:00 a.m.-6:00 p.m.; fax: 203-674-8659. Manufacturers of Fl:x Wood Patch, Fl:x Touch Up Stik, and Cuprinol, a water-repellent wood preservative. No mail order.

Demetrius Alfonso Art Restorations, Ltd., 39 West 38th Street, New York, NY 10018, 212-944-7969. Restoration of fine works of art.

Diversified Packaging Products, Inc., James S. McCrea, 1265 Pine Hill Drive, Annapolis, MD 21401, 301-974-4411. Packaging for shipping, foam wrap, bubble wrap, bags, boxes, mailing tubes, and tape. Catalog.

Easy Time Wood Refinishing Products Corp., 1208 Lisle Place, Lisle, IL 60532, 708-515-1160, 8:00 a.m.-4:00 p.m. Restoration products, wood refinishing products, tung oil, lemon oil, and metal polish. Electric heat gun. Send SASE for pamphlet. Mail order.

Epoxy Technology, Inc., 14 Fortune Drive, Billerica, MA 01821, 508-667-3805, 800-227-2201, Mon.-Fri. 8:30 a.m.-5 p.m.; fax: 508-663-9782. EPO-TEK epoxies for repair, restoration, protection, and preservation. Brochure.

Flitz International Ltd., 821 Mohr Avenue, Waterford, WI 53185, 414-534-5898, 800-558-8611, 8:00 a.m.-4:30 p.m.; fax: 414-534-2991. Distributor of Flitz Metal Polish and Fiber Glass Cleaner, which protects against rust, tarnish, and water stains, and Polier Hard Surface Protector for painted metal surfaces, lacquer, enamel, sealed wood, granite, marble, tile. Brochure, price list, samples available.

G. Schoepfer Inc., 138 West 31st Street, New York, NY 10001, 212-736-6934 or 212-736-6939, 9:30 a.m.-3:30 p.m.; fax: 212-736-6934. Glass and plastic eyes for dolls, mannequins, duck decoys, teddy bears, ceramic figures, taxidermy, sculptures, masks, other projects or restoration. Mail order worldwide. Send SASE and specify type of project to get list.

Gainsborough Products Co., Ltd., 3545 Mt. Diablo Blvd., Lafayette, CA 94549, 415-283-4187, 800-227-4187. Art restoration supplies, including chemicals for restoring oil paintings, frame glazes, canvas lining and facing, cleaning and varnish-removal kits, supply etchers engravers, and sandblasters. Brochure and price list.

Gaston Wood Finishes, Inc., P.O. Box 1246, 2626 North Walnut Street Bloomington, IN 47402, 812-339-9111, 8:30 a.m.-4:30 p.m. Wood finishing products, sandpaper, glues, sealers, hardware, clock movements, dials, numerals. Mail order, retail shop. Catalog $2.50.

George Basch Company, Inc., P.O. Box 188, Freeport, NY 11520 516-378-8100, 8:30 a.m.-3:30 p.m.; fax: 516-378-8140. Nevr-Dull cleaning polish for aluminum, brass, chromium, copper, gold, nickel, pewter, silver, and zinc. Specially treated cotton wadding cloth removes tarnish and dirt.

Gold Leaf & Metallic Powders, Inc., 2 Barclay Street, New York, NY 10007, 212-267-4900, 800-322-0323, 9:00 a.m.-5:00 p.m.; fax: 212-608-4245. Genuine and imitation gold leaf, bronze powders, tools, and accessories. Mail order.

H.F. Staples & Co., Inc., Webb Drive, Box 956, Merrimack, NH 03054, 603-889-8600, 9:00 a.m.-5:00 p.m.; fax: 603-883-9409. Wood repair products, Staples wax, carnauba paste waxes for floors and furniture, stove polish, antique paint remover, ladder mitts, and other products. Price list available.

Handcraft Designs, Inc., 63 East Broad Street, Hatfield, PA 19440, 215-855-3022; fax: 215-855-0184. Mini-Hold, a petroleum based wax, is a nonpermanent, nondamaging adhesive used to hold small items in place temporarily; not to be used on paper (oil in wax will stain).

Hollinger Corporation, P.O. Box 8360, Fredericksburg, VA 22404, 703-898-7300, 800-634-0491, 8:30 a.m.-5:00 p.m.; fax: 703-898-8073. Archival storage products, acid-free boxes and paper, photographic sleeves and envelopes, preservation and encapsulation supplies. Mail or phone orders worldwide. Catalog.

Homestead Paint & Finishes, 111 Mulpus Road, P.O. Box 1668, Lunenburg, MA 01462, 508-582-6426, Mon.-Fri. 8:00 a.m.-5:00 p.m., Sat. 8:00 a.m.-noon. Milk paint. Eight colors in powder form. Will answer questions about surface preparation, etc. Send SASE for brochure.

Hope Co., Inc., P.O. Box 749, Bridgeton, MO 63044, 314-739-7254, 8:00 a.m.-4:00 p.m., 800-325-4026 for orders only. Refinishing and home care products, available in stores or through mail order. Refinisher, tung oil, furniture wax remover, polishes, grill and stove black, refinishing gloves. Brochure and price list.

Howard Refinishing Products, 411 West Maple Avenue, Monrovia, CA 91016, 818-357-9545, 7:30 a.m.-4:30 p.m.; fax: 818-358-8510. Products for restoration and conservation of antiques, including wood finish restorer, wax furniture polish, orange oil, copper and brass polish, silver polish, jewelry cleaner, and all-purpose soap based cleaner for furniture and fabrics. Brochure and price list.

I.P.G.R. Inc., International Porcelain & Glass Repair, Inc., P.O. Box 205, Kulpsville, PA 19443, 215-256-9015, Tues.-Fri. 10:00 a.m.-5:00 p.m., Sat. 10:00 a.m.-2:00 p.m.; fax: 215-362-1842. Complete line of restoration supplies, including cleaners, removers, paints, brushes, glass restoration supplies, kits, books, and more. Mail order. Catalog $3 with coupon for $3 off first order.

J. Goddard & Sons, Ltd., P.O. Box 850, Manitowoc, WI 54221, 800-558-7621, 8:00 a.m.-5:00 p.m.; fax: 414-684-6573. Silver polishes, cleaners, polishing cloths; metal polishes and cleaners; furniture polishes and waxes. Mail order.

J.M. Gray, Inc., 509 West Fayette Street, Syracuse, NY 13204, 315-476-1003, 9:00 a.m.-5:00 p.m., 315-475-9498, evenings. Shipping containers for antiques, artwork. Northeastern U.S. Call first.

Janovic/Plaza, Inc., 30-35 Thomson Avenue, Long Island City, NY 11101, 718-786-4444, 7:30 a.m.-5:00 p.m.; fax: 718-361-7288. Specialty painting, decorating supplies, 250 different types of brushes. Mail order. Catalog $4.95, price applied to first purchase.

Kwick Kleen, P.O. Box 905, Vincennes, IN 47591, 800-457-9144; in Indiana call 800-742-9279, 8:00 a.m.-5:00 p.m.; fax: 812-882-4037. Manufacturers of industrial paint removers, paint removing equipment, and wood finishing products. Furniture stripping, refinishing school, mirror silvering school. Mail order.

Lee Valley Tools, Ltd., 1080 Morrison Drive, Ottawa, ON K2H 8K7, Canada, 613-596-0350, 9:00 a.m.-5:00 p.m.; fax: 613-596-6030. Woodworking tools, wood finishing supplies, refinishing and repair products, hardware. Mail order.

Leichtung, Inc., 4944 Commerce Parkway, Cleveland, OH 44128, 800-321-6840. Mail order supplies, tools, and books. Self-stick veneers, felt, wood bungs, buttons, and dowels,

Light Impressions, 439 Monroe Avenue, Rochester, NY 14607, 800-828-6216, 800-828-9629 in NY, 8:00 a.m.-7:00 p.m. Archival albums, paper and plastic pages, boxes, envelopes, tissues, papers, display cases. Home storage systems for photos, negatives, and slides. Free catalog.

Lin Terry, 59 East Madison Avenue, Dumont, NJ 07628, 201-385-4706, 8:30 a.m.-5:00 p.m. Enor Polypro plastic pages for binders.

Loctite Corporation, Laurie Kraus, 4450 Cranwood Court, Cleveland, OH 44128, 216-475-3600, 800-321-9188, 8:00 a.m.-5:00 p.m. Makers of Duro, Permatex, and Loctite products. Adhesives, repair products, rust and corrosion treatments, countertop repair kits, liquid steel, marble, tile, and fiberglass repair kits. Cleaning product that will remove chewing gum, grease, and oil from cars. Catalog. No mail order. Products may be found in stores in your area.

Marshall Imports, 816 North Seltzer Street, Crestline, OH 44827, 419-683-1666, 800-992-1503, 9:00 a.m.-5:00 p.m.; fax: 419-683-1258. Antiquax paste wax polish, chandelier cleaner, marble wax, furniture cleaner, silver polish, leather cream, and other products. Wholesale to the trade and by mail order to retail customers.

Masters Magic Products Inc., P.O. Box 31, Perry, TX 76677, 713-421-2179 or 817-896-2022, 800-548-6583 for orders, Mon.-Fri.

8:00 a.m.-5:00 p.m. Restoration supplies, veneers, strippers, wood stains, lacquers, and zap glues. Custom blending, strip tanks and systems. Free advice. Refinishing shop. Mail order. Catalog $2, refundable with order.

Micro Essential Laboratory, Inc., 4224 Avenue H, Brooklyn, NY 11210, 718-338-3618, 9:00 a.m.-4:00 p.m.; fax: 718-692-4491. Hydrion pencils measure pH reaction of any surface, including paper, metal, textiles, ceramics, finished surfaces, and film. Hydrion Humidicator Paper detects and estimates moisture. Other specialty test papers available. Mail order worldwide.

Mini-Magic, 3675 Reed Road, Columbus, OH 43220, 614-457-3687, 1:00 p.m.-5:00 p.m. Fabric conservation supplies and acid-free tissue and boxes. Fabrics, hat straw, ribbons, laces. Mail order only, worldwide. Catalog $5 by check or $3 cash.

Mylan Enterprises, Inc., P.O. Box 194, Dept. K, Morris Plains, NJ 07950. Wrapping pads and bubble pac. Mail order, prepaid by check or money order. Flyer with prices.

O'Sullivan Co., 156 South Minges Road, Battle Creek, MI 49017, 616-964-1226, 8:00 a.m.-10:00 p.m., answering machine other times. O'Sullivan's Wax Polish for furniture, wood paneling, floors, toleware, wrought iron, and leather. Mail order. Brochure.

Olde Virginia Restoration, P.O. Box 3305, Portsmouth, VA 23701, 804-488-7299, Mon.-Fri. 8:00 a.m.-noon. Supplies and kits for refinishing old porcelain, fiberglass, and acrylic bathtubs, basins, countertops, and major kitchen appliances. Tools and equipment. Mail order worldwide. Catalog.

Origina Luster, Box 2092, Dept. K, Wilkes-Barre, PA 18703. Origina Luster is a product that will cure "sick" glass. Glass repair kits and portable ultraviolet long-wave black lights are also available. Mail order only.

Packaging Store Inc., 5675 DTC Boulevard, Suite 280, Englewood, CO 80111, 303-741-6626, 800-525-6309, 8:00 a.m.-5:00 p.m.; fax: 303-741-6653. Shipper and packer specializing in large, awkward, fragile, and expensive items. Pack, crate, and ship anything from 1 to 1,000 pounds, antiques, art, furniture, electronics. Sell tape, boxes, packing materials. Brochure, list of store locations nationwide.

Pilot House, Box J, 184 Commercial Street, Malden, MA 02148, 617-322-0163, 800-225-4444, 800-732-3809 in Massachusetts, Mon.-Fri. 8:00 a.m.-4:00 p.m.; fax: 617-322-3911. Strippers, urethanes.

Pottery Barn, P.O. Box 7044, San Francisco, CA 94120-7044, 415-421-3400, weekdays 7:00 a.m.-7:00 p.m., weekends 8:00 a.m.-4:00 p.m. Candle wax remover, bobeches, chandelier rinse, faux stone adhesive paper, marbleizing kits, decorative accessories, cleaning products, and other items for the home. 24 stores. Catalog. Mail order.

Poxywood, Inc., P.O. Box 4241, Martinsville, VA 24115, 703-638-6284, 8:00 a.m.-5:00 p.m. Wood filler and wood putty. Poxywood is a putty wood paste available in pine, oak, maple, walnut, or universal color.

Custom wood carvings, exotic veneers.

PRG, 5619 Southampton Drive, Springfield, VA 22151, 703-323-1407, 9:00 a.m.-5:00 p.m. Conservation supplies, specialty instruments for measuring temperature and humidity, hard-to-find books on conservation. Brochure. Mail order only.

QRB Industries, 3139 U.S. 31 North, Niles, MI 49120, 616-683-7908, 9:00 a.m.-6:00 p.m. Furniture refinishing products, paint and varnish remover, stain, cassette tape "Refinishing with QRB." Mail order.

Ranzi Corporation, P.O. Box 620356, Woodside, CA 94062, 415-369-3711, 9:00 a.m.-6:00 p.m.; fax: 415-369-3713. Cleaning products, including metal cleaner, all-purpose cleaner/degreaser, restorative cleaning wax, tarnish-retarding sealer, stripper. Mail order sales only. Brochure.

Restorations, 563 North Pine Street, Nevada City, CA 95959, 916-477-5527, 8:00 a.m.-4:00 p.m. Mylar bags and restoration supplies, including ink touch-up kits, tape removal kits, stain removal kits, adhesives. Restoration services for artwork, baseball cards, books, cels, and magazines. Mail order.

Ron's Gallery Supply Co., 138 East 30th Street, New York, NY 10016, 800-735-7667, anytime, leave message. Museum board and conservation supplies, convex oval glass, UV absorbing glazing, picture moldings and frames.

Rug-Hold, Inc., 6608A Empire State Building, New York, NY 10118, 212-239-0135. Rug-Hold Multi-Grip, a reinforced vinyl pad that can be used between the rug and bare floor, keeps the rug from slipping or wrinkling and prevents mildew damage. Rug-Hold Rug-To-Rug, a polyester felt pad, can be used between a rug and carpet. Wholesale only. Contact the company for dealers in your area.

Ship's Treasures, P.O. Box 590-EM, Milton, MA 02186, 617-964-8010, anytime. Plastic bags, polyethylene and zipper bags, baseball card polyprotectors, easels, adjustable doll stands, plate hangers, scales, jewelry supplies.

Solar Screen, 53-11 105th Street, Corona, NY 11368, 718-592-8222, 9:00 a.m.-5:00 p.m., fax: 718-271-0891. Fluorescent bulb jackets, transparent window covering materials in sheets or roller shades, E-Z Bond clear UV glass film, and other products that protect displays from fading caused by the sun or fluorescent light. Mail order.

Sparkl-It Co., 12131 Magnolia Boulevard, North Hollywood, CA 91607, 818-762-0697 or 213-877-9519, outside California 800-245-4883, Mon.-Fri. 9:30 a.m.-5:00 p.m., Sat. 10:00 a.m.-2:00 p.m. Custom finishing products, art and craft supplies, pearl powders, bronze powders, glitters, acrylic lacquer, crushed glass, and other products.

Stroblite Co., Inc., 430 West 14th Street, Suite 500, New York, NY 10014, 212-929-3778, 9:00 a.m.-4:30 p.m. Ultraviolet black lights, to detect repairs, restorations, or tampering. Mail order. Brochure.

Talas, Division of Technical Library Service, Inc., 213 West 35th Street, New York, NY 10001, 212-735-7744, 9:00 a.m.-5:00 p.m. Archival storage products, including acid-free boxes, envelopes, and file folders, repair tapes and hinging tapes. Tools, supplies, equipment, books. Mail order worldwide. Catalog $5.

University Products, Inc., P.O. Box 101, South Canal Street, Holyoke, MA 01040, 800-336-4847, 800-628-1912 outside Massachusetts, 8:30 a.m.-5:00 p.m.; fax: 413-532-9281. Archival supplies and repair materials for paper, books, documents, negatives, photographs, prints, and slides. Acid-free board and papers, adhesives, albums, tapes, pens, labels, tools, microfilm and microfiche materials, deacidification materials. Bookbinding equipment and supplies. Specialized storage for stamps, comics, records, postcards, natural science collections, baseball cards, and other collectibles. Free catalog.

Wei T'o Associates, Inc., P.O. Drawer 40, 21750 Main Street, Unit 27, Matteson, IL 60443, 708-747-6660, Mon.-Fri. 8:30 a.m.-5:00 p.m. Deacidification sprays and solutions, application equipment, and related products. Wei T'o prevents yellowing and embrittlement and protects documents, books, and works of art. Consultant services. Available through distributors or mail order worldwide.

The Woodworkers' Store, 21801 Industrial Boulevard, Rogers, MN 55374-9514, customer service: 612-428-2899; credit card orders: 612-428-2199, Mon.-Fri. 8:00 a.m.-8:00 p.m. Woodworking supplies, hardware, and tools. Swiss musical movements, mechanisms for salt and pepper shakers and coffee mills, veneers, wood products, tools, books. Catalog.

S. Fodge, 10170 52nd Place South, Lake Worth, FL 33467, 407-968-1129, 800-525-8809, anytime. Nu Silver silver polish, replating by cold electrolysis. Mail order.

Floyd J. Rosini, Route 22 North, Millerton, NY 12546, 518-789-3582, 8:00 a.m.-4:30 p.m.; fax: 518-789-6386. Manufacturer and distributor of Rosini's Rejuvenator, Briwax, and Simichrome Polish. Mail order. Brochure.

John Sand, 1 North Federal Highway, Dania, FL 33004, 305-925-0856, 10:00 a.m.-4:30 p.m. Gold test kit. Mail order.

Books and Leaflets

Antiques: Professional Secrets for the Amateur, Michael Doussay, 1973 (Quadrangle/New York Times Book Co., NY).

Antiques and Art: Care & Restoration, Edward J. Stanek, 1978 (Wallace-Homestead Book Co., Radnor, PA).

Antiques Care & Repair Handbook, Robert Jackson and David Day, 1984 (Alfred A. Knopf, NY).

Fourth Old House Catalogue, Lawrence Grow, 1988 (Main Street Press, William Case House, Pittstown, NJ 08867).

Care of Antiques and Historical Collections, A. Bruce MacLeish, 1985 (AASLH, 172 Second Avenue North, Suite 102, Nashville, TN 37201).

Care of Historical Collections, Per E. Guldbeck, 1972 (AASLH, 172 Second Avenue North, Suite 102, Nashville, TN 37201).

Caring for Your Cherished Possessions, Mary Levenstein and Cordelia Biddle, 1989 (Crown Publishers, NY).

Design for Scientific Conservation of Antiquities, R.M. Organ, 1968 (Smithsonian Institution Press, Washington, DC).

Looking After Antiques, Anna Plowden & Frances Halshan, 1987 (Pan Books, London).

National Trust Manual of Housekeeping, Hermione Sandwith and Sheila Stainton, 1984 (Penguin Books, London).

Old House Journal Catalog, 1988 (Old-House Journal Corp., 69A Seventh Avenue, Brooklyn, NY 11217).

A Guide to Resource Organizations, leaflet (AASLH, 172 Second Avenue North, Suite 102, Nashville, TN 37201).

Conservators & Restorers

Listed here are some restorers and conservators who work on a variety of objects. Others are listed in the appropriate sections of this book. This is only a partial listing of the conservators in America. For a more complete list, contact the American Institute for Conservation of Historic and Artistic Works, Suite 340, 1400 16th Street NW, Washington, DC 20036, or phone 202-232-6636. They publish a directory of conservators ($40 postpaid) and have a referral service. You can call or write and tell them what you need and they will send you a list of conservators in your geographical area who specialize in your problem.

The following is only a reference, not a recommendation of quality, because we have not seen the work done by the conservators listed here.

Be sure to check further if you decide to hire someone to restore a valuable work of art.

Dover Publications has a list of books of reprints of old patterns suitable for antique restoration work, such as stencils, tin painting, and clock faces.

Sources

A. Ludwig Klein & Son, Inc., P.O. Box, 145, Dept. 13, Harleysville, PA 19438, 215-256-9004, Tues.-Fri. 10.00 a.m.-5:00 p.m., Sat. 10:00 a.m.-2:00 p.m.; fax: 215-362-1842. Repair and restoration of porcelain, glass, jade, ivory, dolls, and other objects of art. Mail photo of object and blank audio cassette tape; Klein will send instructions on how to do repair yourself.

American Institute for Conservation of Historic and Artistic Works, 1400 16th Street, NW, Suite 340, Washington, DC 20036, 202-232-6636. Write or call for information.

Archival Conservation Center, Inc., 8225 Daly Road, Cincinnati, OH 45231, 513-521-9858, 8:30 a.m.-3:30 p.m. Repair and restoration of books, Bibles, newspapers, historical maps, prints, parchment documents, works of art on paper, Chinese scrolls, and Japanese screens. Removal of water stains, foxing, and creases. Prints cleaned. Removal of prints glued to acidic cardboards. Bookbinding, deacidification, fumigation, disaster assistance, and freeze-drying of water-damaged books and documents.

Archival Restoration Associates, Inc., P.O. Box 1395, North Wales, PA 19454, 215-699-0165, 24 hours, 7 days a week. Restoration and preservation of items on paper and parchment, oil paintings, watercolors, photographs, and textiles. Repair and restoration of fine bindings. Paper can be treated to prevent deterioration. Items should be sent registered, return receipt, and insured as works of art. Archival consulting services available.

Attic Unlimited, 1523 West Struck Avenue, Orange, CA 92666, 714-997-1322, Tues., Fri., Sat. 10.00 a.m.-4:00 p.m. Restoration of objects of art, including furniture, glass, oil paintings, picture frames, and pottery and porcelain. Serving the southern California area; other areas by mail.

Barron's Art Restorations, Ed Chambers, 4944 Newport Avenue, Suite E, San Diego, CA 92107, 619-224-7788, 8:00 a.m.-4:00 p.m. Restoration of alabaster, bronze, chandeliers, doll's heads, furniture, glass, paintings, porcelain, gold leafing, and all art restoration.

Broken Art Restoration, Michelle and Bill Marhoefer, 1841 West Chicago Avenue, Chicago, IL 60622, 312-226-8200. Restoration of ivory, ceramics, pottery and porcelain, wood, metal, and stone art objects. Invisible repair. Missing parts replaced. Brochure.

CHILIAD, Susan L. Wilson, Principal, 6 Ottawa Street, Toronto, ON M4T 2B6, Canada, 416-928-0659, evenings. Collection assessment and planning for preventive conservation. Furniture restoration and conservation. Ontario and northeastern U.S.

The Clayton Store, Sue Connell, Star Route, Southfield, MA 01259, 413-229-2621, 9:00 a.m.-5:00 p.m. Restoration of painted and decorated furniture, baskets, tins, and hatboxes. "Smalls" repaired: chalkware, whirligigs, fireboards, folk carvings, quillwork. Fancy paint of all kinds on walls, woodwork, and floors restored and reproduced. Faux marbre, trompe l'oeil, graining, custom stencil design, murals. Will travel.

David Jasper's Glass Clinic, R.R. 3, Box 330X-13, Sioux Falls, SD 57106, 605-361-7524, 9:00 a.m.-4:00 p.m. Restoration of glass, pottery, porcelain, dolls, ivory, oil paintings, picture frames, and other objects of art. Missing parts replaced, stoppers removed or fitted, marbles polished, lamps repaired or converted.

Glass Restoration, 308 East 78th Street, New York, NY 10021, 212-517-3287, Mon.-Fri. 9:30 a.m.-5:00 p.m. Jade, quartz, ivory, and glass restored.

Harry A. Eberhardt & Son, Inc., 2010 Walnut Street, Philadelphia, PA 19103, 215-568-4144, Mon.-Fri. 9:00 a.m.-5:00 p.m. Repairs and restoration of china, porcelain, glass, cloisonné, ivory, jade, and other objects of art. Replacement parts, including antique cut-glass prisms, bobeches, and arms; porcelain handles, knobs, heads, and hands. Mail order.

Hess Restorations, 200 Park Avenue South, New York, NY 10003, 212-741-0410, 212-260-2255 or 212-979-1443, 10:30 a.m.-4:00 p.m. Restoration of antiques, such as porcelain, ceramics, wood, ivory, or jade. Parts and supplies. Blue glass liners for salts. Mail order.

Intermuseum Laboratory, Allen Art Building, Oberlin, OH 44074, 216-775-7331, 8:30 a.m.-5:00 p.m. An alliance of museums established for the conservation and study of works of art. Gallery inspections and advice on treatment. Minor treatment is done on site, other work at laboratory.

John Scott Conservators, Inc., 521 West 26 Street, New York, NY 10001, 212-714-0620, 9:00 a.m.-4:30 p.m. Conservation of sculpture and art objects, all materials, sizes, and finishes, including outdoor, architectural, and monumental installations. Consulting and treatment services. No mail order service.

Just Enterprises, 2790 Sherwin Avenue, Unit 10, Ventura, CA 93003, 805-644-5837, Mon.-Fri. 8:30 a.m.-5:30 p.m., answering machine other times. Repair and restoration of almost every type of collectible, including alabaster, carousels, china, clocks, cloisonné, enamel, figurines, furniture, glass, ivory, jade, jewelry, lamps, marble, metal, onyx, paintings, porcelain, sculpture, silver, telephones, tools, toys, trunks, and wood. Send photo, description of item, and description of damage, plus SASE for estimate. Second studio at 679 Santa Ysabel Avenue, Los Osos, CA 93402, 805-528-5445. Mail order.

Kalesse, Fine Arts Building, 1017 SW Morrison Street, 507-C, Portland, OR 97205. Restoration of pottery, porcelain, jade, ivory, glass, crystal, cloisonné, marble, folk art, enamels, and related objets d'art. Mail order service worldwide.

McKenzie's Art Restoration Studio, Keeta McKenzie, 2907 East Monte Vista Drive, Tucson, AZ 85716, 602-323-1466, Tues.-Sat. 9:00 a.m.-noon and 1:00 p.m.-5:00 p.m. Repair of bisque, china, porcelain, pottery, earthenware figurines, bisque and china doll heads, oil paintings, and frames. Mail order service worldwide.

National Institute for the Conservation of Cultural Property, Arts and Industries Building - 2225, Smithsonian Institution, Washington, DC 20560, 202-357-2295. Write or call for information.

Old World Restorations, Douglas Eisele, 347 Stanley Avenue, Cincinnati, OH 45226, 513-321-1911 or 513-321-1914, Mon.-Fri. 9:00 a.m.-5:00 p.m. Restoration and conservation of art objects, including chandeliers, clocks, cloisonné, enamels, glass, gold leaf, ivory, metals, murals, music boxes, paintings, papier-mâché, photographs, picture frames, porcelain, stained glass, stone, and on-site architectural restoration. Brochure. Mail order or bring to antiques show exhibit (call or write for schedule).

Restoration & Design Studio, Paul Karner, 249 East 77th Street, New York, NY 10021, 212-517-9742, Mon.-Fri. 10:00 a.m.-5:00 p.m., Wed. 1:00 p.m.-5:00 p.m. Restoration and repair, missing parts reproduced, silver and gold replated, pewter and other metals restored, flatware blades replaced, lamps repaired, ivory and small wooden articles repaired. No furniture repair.

Rosine Green Associates, Inc., 45 Bartlett Crescent, Brookline, MA 02146, 617-277-8368, Mon.-Fri. 9:00 a.m.-5:00 p.m., Sat. 10:00 a.m.-noon. Restoration of art objects, including cloisonné, enamel, tortoiseshell, mother-of-pearl, tole, papier-mâché, silver, other metals, boxes, caddies, frames, furniture, pottery, and glass. Custom-design pedestals and display cases.

Sotheby's Restoration, John Stair, 440 East 91 Street, New York, NY 10128, 212-860-5446. Restoration of decorative arts.

Spnea Conservation Center, Lyman Estate, 185 Lyman Street, Waltham, MA 02154, 617-891-1985, Mon.-Fri. 9:00 a.m.-5:00 p.m. Conservation of furniture, upholstery, and wooden decorative arts. Repair and replacement of veneer, marquetry, carved and turned elements. Collection surveys, lectures, and seminars.

Strong Museum, Richard W. Sherin, Director of Conservation Division, One Manhattan Square, Rochester, NY 14607, 716-263-2700, Ext. 281, Mon.-Wed. 9:00 a.m.-5:00 p.m.; fax: 716-263-2493. Consultation on conservation of furniture, decorative arts, dolls and toys.

Trefler and Sons, Leon Trefler, 177 Charlemont Street, Newton Highlands, MA 02161, 617-965-3388 or 617-965-7489, Mon.-Fri. 9:00 a.m.- 5:00 p.m., Sat. 10:00 a.m.-2:00 p.m.; fax: 617-965-7489. Restoration of porcelain, crystal, marble, ivory, books, paintings, prints, paper, frames, metals, and furniture. Mail order worldwide.

Washington Conservation Studio, 4230 Howard Avenue, Kensington, MD 20895, 301-564-1036, 9:00 a.m.-5:00 p.m. Conservation of fine arts, antique and modern paintings, frames, and related art objects.

Wiebold, Inc., 413 Terrace Place, Terrace Park (Cincinnati), OH 45174, 513-831-2541, Mon.-Fri. 9:00 a.m.-5:30 p.m. Antique and art restoration, including paintings, frames, ceramics, metals, crystal, ivory, miniature frames and lenses, jade, wood carvings, sculpture, chandeliers, silver and other metals. Leaflet, "The Care and Treatment of Paintings." Brochure.

Williamstown Regional Art Conservation Laboratory, Inc., 225 South Street, Williamstown, MA 01267, 413-458-5741, 8:30 a.m.-5:00 p.m. Conservation of paintings, paper, furniture, objects, and works of art. Group tours, lectures, courses. Serving the New England-New York-Pennsylvania area. Brochure.

John Edward Cunningham, 1516 Dustin Drive, #1, Normal, IL 61761, 309-454-8256, anytime. Restoration of art and antiques, specializing in mother-of-pearl inlays and gold leaf. Missing parts made. Mail order.

Nelson Dale, Restoration Services, 621 Main Street, #3, Waltham, MA 02154, 617-647-7865, 8:00 a.m.-5:00 p.m. Restoration of glass, pottery, porcelain, ivory, lacquer, statuary, and wooden objects. Missing parts duplicated. Mail order.

Carl "Frank" Funes, 57 Maplewood Avenue, Hempstead, NY 11550, 516-481-0147, 9:30 a.m.-5:00 p.m., 516-483-6712 after 5:00 p.m. Repair and restoration of arms, armor, cast iron, ivories, marble, paintings, carvings, sculpture, pewter, silver, wood items, artifacts, objects of vertu, etc. Serving New York State, New Jersey, and Connecticut. Mail order service.

Richard George, 45-04 97th Place, Corona, NY 11368, 212-271-2506 or 212-271-2507, 9:00 a.m.-4:00 p.m. Restoration of furniture, coromandel screens, ivory, antique marble and faux finishes.

Eric Gordon, 2101 Lake Montebello Terrace, Baltimore, MD 21218, 301-366-2835, anytime. Conservation of fine art, including paintings, murals, and painted surfaces. Serving the mid-Atlantic states.

Andrew Hurst, 2423 Amber Street, Knoxville, TN 37917, 615-974-6924 or 615-523-3498, 8:30 a.m.-8:00 p.m. Repair and restoration of oil paintings, picture frames, porcelain, and furniture. Special crating of art and antiques. No mail order. Serving eastern Tennessee.

Jeanette Parkman, 900 North Federal Highway, Suite 106, Pompano Beach, FL 33062, 305-782-2277, 10:00 a.m.-2:30 p.m. Restores art objects, including china, ivory, silver, and crystal. Castings of broken metal objects and figurines. Appraises damaged art objects.

Victor von Reventlow, 13 Bergen Street, Brooklyn, NY 11201, 718-858-0721. Conservation and restoration of decorative arts; treatments, collection condition surveys, consultation. Specializing in furniture and traditional wooden panel paintings.

Regina Wenzek, 2966 Briggs Avenue, Bronx, NY 10458, 212-733-5040,

9:00 a.m.-5:00 p.m. Specializing in restoration of porcelain, Oriental lacquer, painted furniture, and gold leaf. By appointment only.

Ideas for Displaying Your Collection

There are some special problems in displaying antiques properly. Rough porcelain or glass bases should not scratch furniture tops, picture hooks should be strong enough, and collectibles should be displayed to their greatest advantage.

Many display items can be purchased at local giftware, hardware, and art supply stores, but we have listed items that are not always found with ease. Other supplies can be found in the section Conservation, Restoration, & Preservation Supplies.

Sources

Aluma-Case Company, 11205 River Road, Grand Rapids, OH 43522, 419-832-6655. Display cases and shelving available in aluminum and hardwood. Custom variations available. Free brochure.

Bard's Products, Inc., 1427 Armour Boulevard, Mundelein, IL 60060, 800-323-5499. Plate racks, hangers, stands, display cases, cabinets, ornament stands, shadow boxes, picture frames, domes, and shelves.

Brass Anvil, Inc., Jim Horack, 186 North DuPont Highway, Bldg. 30, Airport Industrial Center, New Castle, DE 19720, 302-322-7679, 9:00 a.m.-5:30 p.m.; 302-733-0617, evenings. Custom display cases.

Carv/Craft, 417 Valley Road, Madison, WI 53714, 608-222-1100,

8:00 a.m.-9:00 p.m. Cast-iron carousel animal stands. Brochure.

Classic Accents, Inc., P.O. Box 1181, Southgate, MI 48195, 313-282-5525. Brass finish picture lights and hooks, picture cords and tassels. Brochure.

Display Case Co., Box 880, Exmore, VA 23350, 804-442-2299. Lucite display cases, doll stands, lucite easels. Custom-made cases.

Elco Manufacturing, 313 West 37th Street, New York, NY 10018, 212-695-4567, 9:00 a.m.-4:30 p.m.; fax: 212-643-0583. Leather albums for matchcovers, postcards, sports cards, household inventory, financial records, etc. Brochure.

Enchanted Doll House, P.O. Box 3001, Manchester Center, VT 05255, 802-362-3030 for orders, 802-362-3037 for customer service. Doll and teddy bear accessories, stands, display cases, glass domes, plastic covers. Acid-free paper to wrap dolls, silver, jewelry, bridal gowns, textiles, and works of art on paper. Brochure.

Exposures, 9180 Le Saint Drive, Fairfield, OH 45014, 800-222-4947. Picture frames, albums, archival-quality album pages, special lights to illuminate paintings, custom framing. Catalog.

Hobbymaster, 221 Yoho Drive, Anoka, MN 55303. Albums for matchcovers. Mail order.

Liros Gallery , P.O. Box 946, Blue Hill, ME 04614, 207-374-5370, 9:00 a.m.-5:00 p.m. Portrait lights.

Rogay, Inc., 4937 Wyaconda Road, Rockville, MD 20852, 301-770-1700, 7:30 a.m.-4:00 p.m.; fax: 301-468-1032. Display cases and cabinets made to order.

Ron's Gallery Supply Co., P.O. Box 1791, New York, NY 10016, 800-735-7667, anytime, leave message. Museum board and conservation supplies, convex oval glass, UV absorbing glazing, picture moldings and frames. Picture-hanging systems, cordless picture lights, print display racks, tools, supplies.

Ship's Treasures, P.O. Box 590-EM, Milton, MA 02186, 617-964-8010, anytime. Easels, adjustable doll stands, plate hangers.

Vitrines by Bernardo, 1611 Chicago Avenue, Evanston, IL 60201, 708-864-6400 or 708-570-7850, 8:00 a.m.-5:00 p.m. Lucite display case for figurines, dolls, sculptures, and other collectibles. Custom sizes available. Mail order.

Wrecking Bar, 292 Moreland Avenue, NE, Atlanta, GA 30307, 404-525-0468, Mon.-Sat. 9:00 a.m.-5:00 p.m. Architectural components for displaying art. Custom-designed pedestals.

Vincent Azcarate, 2472 Nightingale Drive, San Jose, CA 95125, 408-267-8966, 9:00 a.m.-5:00 p.m. Princess doll stands. Illustrated flyer. Mail order.

Book

Living With Art, Holly Solomon and Alexandria Anderson, 1988 (Rizzoli International Publications, NY).

Part III

Loving Care
for
Your Collection

A good housekeeper usually washes the dishes, makes the bed, sweeps the floor, and dusts each day. That rule only applies if the housekeeper is not a collector. There are special housekeeping rules for collections and antiques. Placement of the antiques is one of the most important. As far as possible--and we know you have to live in the house in comfort, so the furnishings may not have the perfect environment--most collectibles should not be placed in strong sunlight, extremes of heat or cold (attics or unheated porches), areas with very high or low humidity (basements and attics), or too close to working fireplaces. Even the smoke from cigarettes can eventually damage some items.

Don't be too clean. Furniture should be lightly dusted and polish should be used when needed. Wax and dust can eventually build into a dark layer that must be carefully removed with cleaner or the appropriate soap-and-water treatment.

If you ever find sawdust or rodent or insect droppings in your house, call an expert to help you look for the cause. Old furniture can harbor eggs from wood-eating insects and worms that might infect other furniture in the house.

If you have cats or dogs (or even a pet cheetah) who gnaw on wood, find a way to keep them away from the legs of old tables and chairs. There are several products on the market that discourage animals. Hot pepper sauce rubbed on the wood might help.

Most dishes and glassware can go in the dishwasher, but hot water and strong detergent can fade some, remove the overglaze gold decoration, or craze the glaze on old pottery or damaged pieces.

Silver and pewter should be kept clean. Any commercial polish is good, but you can also protect the shine with an anti-tarnish polish that will save you from frequent cleanings. Never ever use harsh abrasives such as scouring powder or steel wool.

Fabrics are the only collectibles that should be cleaned often. Dirt can do more damage than cleaning. Washable fabrics should be laundered with the proper soap or special detergent.

To store fabrics, roll them, do not fold. Old quilts, coverlets, curtains, and pillows can be used, but always remember that the threads are fragile and easy to damage. Rugs should be swept or vacuumed and occasionally cleaned. Always protect fabrics from extremes of heat and light. Store woolens and other insect-attracting fabrics with cedarwood or moth balls.

Books should be dusted regularly. If the climate is damp, be sure to protect against insects. All paper collectibles attract small insects and fungus that will cause damage. Be sure paper items are kept in an environment that is not too humid, too hot, or too bright. Handle paper (except books) as seldom as possible and never fold or tape it. Even the new removable self-stick notes like "Post-Its" leave some bits of glue on a page that will eventually discolor. This problem becomes serious if you leave one of these markers on glossy-finished paper, like that used in fancy auction catalogs. Never use cellophane tape or regular household glues on paper collectibles.

Be sure to have fire alarms and fire extinguishers handy. Check them at regular intervals. A burglar alarm is a good investment. If your collection is of value, carry special insurance. A fire, hurricane, or earthquake can destroy everything.

The sections that follow contain more detailed information about home care of furniture, silver and other metals, paper, and textiles.

Care of Furniture

The grimy, dirty, scratched, and even slightly marred old chest you just found has waited for a new finish for more than 50 years. The waiting has been important. If the old patina (appearance of aging) were not desirable, total stripping and refinishing would be the solution to all refinishing problems. The old color and patina are the most important features on an antique piece of furniture. Always try to restore the finish that remains. Remove the finish or sandpaper and restain the piece only as a last resort. Restoring a finish is easier than total refinishing and the results are more worthwhile from the view of the collector and the decorator.

REFINISHING

Do not try to refinish antiques to look like new pieces. If you prefer the high-gloss, unscarred look, buy new furniture or paint old but not antique pieces. A few minor imperfections can be cured without refinishing. Small scratches can be covered using a commercial stain polish and scratch remover. Shoe polish often works just as well.

REPAIRING

All noticeable repairs should be made before you begin stripping the paint or other finish. Clean off all old glue, glue all wobbly legs, remove dents, and fill holes. Reglue and clamp all of the stretchers, spindles, dovetail joints, and other spots that may be loose. Replace all missing pieces with new ones. For more detailed information, see one of the books listed in the furniture section.

Stick shellac can be heated and pressed into large holes. After the first refinishing coat is on, you can patch with any good plastic-wood filler. Wax-type scratch removers are used on a completed finish. Dents sometimes can be removed by pressing over them with a damp wool strip and a hot iron. The warm, moist air frequently will cause the wood to swell.

If the surface was painted, *do not* remove the old paint unless the piece is so hopeless you could not give it house room. Frequently, most of the value of an old painted piece is removed with the paint. Even faded old designs are more desirable than repainted new ones. If you prefer a freshly painted chair, buy a reproduction.

STRIPPING

There are many excellent methods of stripping old paint, varnish, or shellac from a piece of furniture that is to be refinished. Several rules must apply to all methods of stripping. Most of the paint removers are quite strong, so wear gloves and old clothes. Do the work in a well-ventilated room or garage. Protect the floor by covering it with papers. Have all the needed chemicals, removers, rags, burlap, newspapers, tools, steel wool, sandpaper, brushes, scrapers, small sticks, and toothbrushes available and keep them handy. It is frustrating to have to stop in the middle and search for things. Keep a large wastebasket handy. *Do not smoke*, as many of the removers are flammable. Do not eat near the work.

A screwdriver, pliers, and hammer will be of help. All hardware should be removed before you start. Be sure to save all of the screws, nuts, and bolts to replace the pieces later. A box to hold small items is helpful. Remove all doors that can be easily removed from their hinges. Refinish all of the drawers separately.

COMMERCIAL STRIPPERS

Put the piece to be stripped in a well-ventilated room on several layers of newspaper. It must be a cool day. The remover will dry too quickly on a very hot day. Remove all the hardware. If you are stripping a chair, keep an empty tuna-fish can handy. The chair leg can be set in the can and the remover that drips down can be rebrushed on the chair leg. Read all of the directions on the can of remover. Pour some of the remover into an old can and flow it on the wood with an old brush. Use short strokes in one direction, with the wood grain. Work on only a small section of the piece at a time. Let the remover stand 10 to 20 minutes until the finish softens. *Do not stir or rebrush the remover once it is on.* This just speeds the evaporation and slows down the work of the remover. Scrape the finish off with a very dull knife, scraper, and steel wool.

Carvings can best be cleaned with remover and steel wool pads, a stiff brush, or a toothbrush. The scraping tool should be dull with rounded edges. It must not make scratches. When working on a large tabletop, you may find it handy to scrape the sludge directly into an old coffee can.

If the finish is not completely removed, repeat the process. After all of the old finish is removed, wash the piece with water, lacquer thinner, or turpentine, whichever the directions suggest. Then wipe the piece, let it dry, and rub very lightly with 0000 steel wool and very fine sandpaper. When you think you have steel-wooled or sanded enough, do it again.

The used rags are highly flammable. If you are going to reuse them, they should be washed or placed in a safe, well-ventilated place. Wash your hands after all of this and use a hand cream. These chemicals are strong.

FINISHES

If the table or chair to be refinished is stripped to its naked glory and several types of wood appear, we suggest you find an artistic friend who can match color, paint it, or decide to live with the several shades in the finished piece. We have no objections to a variation in shades and believe it adds interest. However, some purists feel that it shows that the refinishing was the work of an amateur. Anyone with a good eye for color can rub stain into the offending wood until a good match is obtained.

If you wish to stain the wood, buy any commercial penetrating oil stain or stain sealer and follow the directions on the can. Colored stains also can be used.

Some woods need a sealer coat to ensure that the color will be uniformly absorbed. Test a small area where it won't show and if the color of the wood is blotchy, seal the wood first. Use a diluted coat of whatever clear finish you plan to use, either varnish or shellac. Mix the varnish with an equal amount of turpentine or mix the shellac with eight times as much denatured alcohol. Brush the sealer on the wood, let dry 15 minutes, wipe off with a dry cloth, and let it dry thoroughly for about 24 hours. Rub with 0000 steel wool, dust with a cloth, and then apply the stain.

Shellac is easy to use and easy to polish, but it does chip and is not good for tabletops where wet glasses may leave a ring. Do not use old shellac. Use white shellac on any wood, orange shellac on dark wood. Before starting to shellac, be sure the room is free of dust. Buy as much denatured alcohol as you do shellac. Thin the shellac with an equal amount of alcohol or until the shellac flows from the brush like water.

The process of putting shellac on wood is simple if you remember two things: Never work in a damp room or the finished piece will turn white; and never try to rebrush the shellac after it has been applied. Place the piece to be shellacked so that the surface is horizontal. It may mean a few more hours, but the result and lack of errors are well worth the trouble.

When you do the top of a chest, let it dry for at least four hours. Rub the piece with 0000 steel wool or very fine sandpaper. Coat it again with shellac, let dry, and again rub with 0000 steel wool and wipe clean with a rag to remove any particles. Four coats give the best finish, but two coats will be satisfactory for most pieces. If the wood is very porous, more coats may be needed. After the final coat has been applied, steel-wool or sand again and wax the entire piece of furniture.

The directions for using varnish are very similar to those for shellac. Varnish is much harder and more durable, giving a better finish for tabletops. Applying varnish is slow and a bit tricky. Always apply varnish to furniture in a room with a temperature about 70 degrees. If it is too cold or too hot, the finish might be streaky and bumpy. *Do not use spar varnish.*

Apply the varnish with the grain, flowing it on by brush in a light coat. Do not overlap the brushstrokes. Let the varnish dry 24 hours or, better yet, a week. Rub down with 6-0 waterproof garnet paper used wet or with wet 500-A sandpaper. Wash with a wet chamois, then wax if you wish. Rottenstone and oil can be used for the final polish.

Lacquer is applied in much the same manner as shellac. It is tricky to use and most beginners do not succeed. Prepare the furniture as before by sanding and coloring. Buy a good-quality lacquer and use it full strength, brushing it on quickly. Let it dry and sand with no. 360 sandpaper and turpentine. Another method is to thin the lacquer with lacquer thinner in equal parts. Brush it on, then wipe off the excess with a dry cloth. After an hour, rub with 0000 steel wool, dust, and brush on a coat of full-strength lacquer.

The finished piece may be waxed. Lacquer is for strength, not shine, and if gloss is the desired finish, use shellac.

The most famous and difficult, but probably the finest, finish for a choice antique is the method known as French polishing. Be sure the piece has been sanded and is clean and dry.

Cut a piece of cheesecloth about two by five inches. Fold in the loose ends and make a pad about half that size. For large areas, cut a piece of cheesecloth a yard square and fold in the loose ends. Hold the pad with your index finger folded behind it for pressure. Grasp the pad with the thumb and other fingers. It is possible to buy a commercial product called French polish that will give good results. The other method is to dip the pad into boiled linseed oil, wring it dry, then dip it into shellac and rub in small circles. Add more oil, more shellac, and do more circular rubbing until a finish has been built up. This takes time and skill. It is best to experiment on a piece of unimportant wood, because too much shellac, too long a wait, too much oil, or not enough pressure will cause trouble.

If you really feel brave enough to try this finish on a large piece, read any of the many books about refinishing that devote several chapters to this technique. The finished piece will be smooth, glossy, and well worth the trouble.

WAXING AND POLISHING

The finished piece, now sanded and dry, probably needs a coat of wax or polish for added gloss and protection. Just wax on wood isn't always good enough because it will wear off quickly. However, maple, cherry, or other close-grained hardwoods sometimes seem satisfactory with a wax finish.

Use a carnauba-base paste furniture wax. Apply with a soft, lint-free cloth, pretending that you are shining shoes. Apply a thin coat of wax, and rub. Remember, the more you rub, the better the shine.

It is often best to simply wipe furniture with a clean dry cloth to remove marks and smudges. Too much wax and weekly spray-dusting with the newer products will frequently tend to build up a layer of dirt and oil that can hide the beauty of the wood. Paste wax is best. Apply as we have mentioned, using a pad with a thin layer of wax and rubbing to a polish. Liquid wax is a paste wax dissolved in a solvent. Shake the bottle, and apply with a damp, soft cloth. Polish with another damp, soft cloth.

Keep furniture out of direct sun if possible. Keep moisture near old wood (plants help). Never use a self-polishing floor wax on furniture; it destroys the finish.

Care of Paper

Centuries have passed since Ts'ai Lun, a Chinese eunuch, accidentally mixed some woven scraps with water, then poured them on a bamboo screen where they dried into paper. Over time the quality of paper has degenerated because of the use of chemical additives such as alum.

To avoid any problems, handle paper antiques with special care:

1. Use clean hands to handle books and pictures.
2. Use two hands to lift matted or unmatted pictures to prevent bending, creasing, or tearing.
3. Unmatted pictures should never be stacked directly on top of each other. They should be separated by a smooth, nonacid cover tissue.
4. Valuable pictures should be matted rather than left loose. They may be kept in acid-free folders or envelopes.
5. Be careful not to drag anything across the surface of a picture.
6. Handle pictures glued on old cardboard or wood carefully.
7. Always open a mat by the outer edge, not by the window on the inner edge.

8. Pictures in mats or folders should be stored in drawers or a solander box (a special box built to hold books). Airtight metal boxes are not recommended, as they condense moisture and will quickly transmit heat in case of fire.

9. To carry, mail, or ship loose pictures, pack them between two heavy pieces of cardboard. Rolling a good picture could cause it to crack.

STORAGE AND DISPLAY ENVIRONMENT

The best environment for your treasured prints, newspapers, and documents consists of the following features:

Humidity should be around 55 percent: not less than 45 percent or more than 60. Excessive moisture encourages mold.

Beware especially of dampness on outside walls in stone houses and in basements and cellars. Houses that are closed up for any extended time can become very humid.

Use an air conditioner to keep humidity under the dangerous 70-percent level. Silica gel can be used as a dehumidifying agent in airtight containers. Small sachets or dishes of thymol crystals can be put around as a preventative.

Mold growth often shows up as dull rusty patches that discolor the sheet of paper. "Foxing" is caused by the chemical action of mold on the colorless iron salts present in the paper. It feeds on sizing and paper fibers and thereby weakens the sheet.

Protection from light. Sunlight and ultraviolet light tend to cause brittleness, fading, and rapid oxidation. Fluorescent lights can also accelerate the destruction of paper. Allow only enough light for good viewing. To avoid excess light, never place pictures on a wall directly opposite a sunny window.

Translucent curtains and louvered blinds will provide protection. Plastic sleeves on the fixture will protect against ultraviolet light from fluorescent lights. Plexiglas sheets will filter ultraviolet light and may be substituted for glass in a picture frame.

Heat is another destructive agent. Never hang pictures or put books over a radiator, heat register, or air duct. And be doubly wary of that spot above the fireplace. Not only is the heat from the fireplace destructive, but the soot and gummy residues produced by the fire stick to anything.

Air pollution also threatens paper. It causes discoloration and eventual disintegration of paper fibers. The sulfur dioxide in the air is absorbed by the paper and converted into sulfuric acid. This may cause severe brown stains on pictures lacking a backing, and can cause leather book bindings to turn to powder.

To prevent this kind of damage, an air conditioner and air filter can be installed. Rag-board mat in front and back of the picture provides some protection.

Insects are another danger to paper valuables. Paper should be kept off the floor and out of the damp, warm, dark places preferred by insects. Paper should be kept out of basements or attics. Insect spray, sodium fluoride, or moth crystals are recommended as protection. Clean and inspect the dark spaces behind and beneath books to avoid this problem. Beware of silverfish (silvery, pearl-gray insects). They will cut through a large picture to get at the flour paste and glue sizing, and they move so quickly they can cause considerable damage before they are noticed. Cockroaches can cause damage to parchment, leather, paper, and glues. Termites and wood worms also do damage.

FRAMING AND MATTING

Proper framing and matting provide the best protection for pictures.

Never use glue. The chemicals can be destructive. Pressure-sensitive tapes cause permanent stains. Staples and pins cause rust stains and tears. Acidic pastes cause deterioration, and rubber cements cause permanent stains. Gummed brown wrapping tape is also damaging.

Never use wood-pulp matting board. Its highly acidic composition disintegrates, leaving stains on the picture and weakening the paper.

"Museum board" is composed of a high-grade cellulose from cotton fibers. It is the only safe matting material. It comes only in white or off-white. The 1/16-inch thickness provides an adequate depth to allow for minor buckling as well as sufficient breathing space between the glass and the picture. Be sure to provide this space, since moisture condenses and may cause mold growth.

There is also the possibility of the picture adhering to the glass. Even if a mat is not desirable, a narrow strip of mat board should be cut and hidden beneath the inner edge of the frame. If for some reason (for example, an artist's signature) a wood-pulp mat must be saved, it can be placed on top of an all-rag board.

Never spray cleaner on the surface of the glass or covering of a picture. Liquid may run down inside the frame and stain the mat. Always apply the cleaner with a cloth.

Pictures and paintings should be hung to allow air to circulate behind the frame. Use "hangers" or small pads on the lower corners of the frame back. Be sure the picture wire is strong and secure.

SPECIFIC PROBLEMS THAT MAY HAVE ALREADY OCCURRED

Candle wax. Scrape with an artist's spatula; carefully remove the rest with mineral spirits or paint thinner.

Buckling. Excessive buckling suggests too much pressure on the edges of the picture by either the mat or the frame. This can be corrected by a framer. Localized puckering may be caused by the presence of old tape, patches, or glue on the back of the picture. In that case the picture should be taken to a restorer. Never paste down a picture to remove a few waves of slight buckling. Stains and weakening of the paper will eventually result.

Water-soaked documents. If you have a number of documents that are soaked, place them in the freezer. This will stop any further water damage. They can be defrosted and ironed at a later time.

Care of Textiles

Textiles are among the most perishable antiques. Old clothing, draperies, linens, samplers, and tapestries have usually seen a lot of wear. They may be disintegrating from careless handling, vigorous washing, or use of the wrong cleaning solvent. Textiles are subject to the fading and weakening effects of natural or artificial light, direct or reflected, and to the corrosive effects of city air. They may be destroyed by moths, insects, fungus, or mold. Temperature and humidity variations, stains, and tears also cause damage.

First decide what type of fiber was used in the fabric. In general, natural fibers are from animal sources (wool and silk) or vegetable sources (cotton and linen). Animal fibers will shrink and lose their luster when washed in hot water or chlorine bleach. They are more sensitive to rubbing and in great danger from insects and fungi.

There is a simple test to determine animal from vegetable fibers: Take a few threads from the article and burn them in a dish. Animal fibers burn slowly, producing a bead and an odor of burning feathers. Vegetable fibers burn more quickly, producing a soft ash and an odor of burning paper. Synthetics melt like cotton candy.

REPAIR

First take care of any rips or holes in the fabric, however small, before they become larger. Cigarette burns can be stitched around the hole, then cross-stitched, as in darning. Large rips should be caught up immediately with thread and then mended by a professional. Never use tape as it is difficult to remove.

Patching old fabrics with contemporary ones will probably be conspicuous, unless reproductions of period patterns are used. Even these need to be washed, bleached, and sunned first to take out the "newness." Appropriate patching material may often be found at rummage sales and thrift stores.

CLEANING

Cleaning should begin with the removal of loose dirt. Use a hand vacuum on low suction through a piece of nylon screen to protect delicate fabrics or embroidery.

Old textiles can be safely washed if they are strong enough to be creased without breaking the fibers. This generally means they should be washed in water only if they are in very good condition. If possible, spot washing is preferable to washing the entire piece. Before trying to wash an article, test each color for fastness by placing the fabric between two pieces of clean white blotting paper and using an eyedropper to apply a few drops of water to each color. If a color does not appear on the paper, it's safe to proceed. Embroidery or hand painting may also run if washed. Always check the linings.

Some general rules for washing:

1. If you must use a washing machine, be sure to use the gentle cycle and cold water. Always put the fabric in a net bag in the machine.

2. Never use commercial detergents. Bleaches and additives may damage fabrics. Ivory Flakes, Lux, or special museum-preferred soaps can be used on cotton or linen; Woolite is all right for colorfast woolens. Special silk-washing liquids can be used.

3. Use only soft water; add softener to hard water.

4. Use only cold or lukewarm water. Hot water hardens wool and shrinks wool and linen.

5. Use distilled water for rinsing in order to avoid rust flecks from iron traces in tap water.

6. Don't rub old fabrics during washing. Dirt, if not removed by soaking, can be dislodged by gentle agitation. Water may be forced through sturdy pieces, such as quilts, by the careful use of a plunger.

7. Avoid using chlorine bleaches; they will eventually weaken the fabric. Don't use an alkaline bleach on wool or silk. If an alkaline bleach is used, add vinegar to the rinse water to neutralize it.

Generally, the effect of washing is to expand fibers; that of drying, to contract them. The ability of fibers to bear up under this strain should be taken into account. Quilted pieces have the added stress of the swelling of filler material.

Washing protects the fabric from moths and other insects. Eggs can thrive in the smallest amount of dirt. Fabrics should not be put away dirty. Damage from insects and mold may well exceed any harm that could come to the fabric during careful washing.

Some special cases: If a material has a special finish to give it a glaze or a sheen, such as watered silk or moire, the finish is probably water soluble and will be ruined by washing. Canvas has often been treated with sizing; if washed, it may go limp and could possibly shrink.

Fabrics are much heavier when wet, so their weight must be supported during washing. Support the fabric with a nylon net; otherwise, the added weight may cause the fabric to tear or weaken. Quilts, in particular, should be washed between two pieces of net stitched together.

An hour's soaking in cold water should remove most dirt. The water should be changed several times, or whenever it looks dirty. If a small piece of fabric is strong enough to be agitated, it can be washed in a two-gallon jar with a large opening. Rock the jar gently back and forth. To change the water or to rinse, finger-drain while running in clear water.

If, after an hour, the fabric still appears dirty or greasy, it can be washed with a mild soap in a diluted solution.

Rinse the fabric thoroughly. Any residue not rinsed out may cause a brown stain during ironing. Quilts must be rinsed several times to remove all residue. Put the fabric on a large towel. Roll it up in the towel and let it sit until damp dry. Spread it out onto another towel or blotting paper to remove the remaining moisture. Pin the piece into shape, using stainless steel pins to avoid rust spots. Smooth out all folds and wrinkles and shape lace and ruffles by hand. Folds and creases cause undue stress in the fabric.

Let the fabric dry naturally under average temperature and humidity conditions. In general, don't hang fabrics, as this will cause unnecessary strain. Don't use direct heat or hot-air blowers. Don't expose old fabrics to direct sunlight. White cottons and linens may be prevented from yellowing by brief exposure to the sun, but be careful, as a long exposure could weaken them.

Iron fabrics carefully and slowly. Always make sure to control the heat. When ironing embroidery, use a well-padded ironing board and cover the fabric with sheeting. Never iron quilts.

Lace can be dry-cleaned by sprinkling powdered French chalk (powdered soapstone) over the lace, then brushing it off with a camel's-hair paintbrush. If it must be washed in water, first try soaking it in distilled water. If necessary, wash it in warm water with a few drops of detergent and rinse in warm water. Lay the lace on white blotting paper and pin into shape to dry.

If your textile can't be washed but is in obvious need of cleaning, then try dry cleaning. Stain removal is a highly sophisticated science and the use of the wrong solvent, or too much of the right one, can be disastrous. The National Institute of Dry Cleaning, 909 Burlington Avenue, Silver Spring, MD 20950, has names of local dry cleaners experienced in this work.

Even if done by professionals, dry cleaning of old textiles should be attempted only after testing has shown that the solvent won't damage the fabric or the dyes and that the fabric is strong enough to handle the process. Solvents tend to have less effect on the material than water, but they can have greater effect on the dyes. Each color should be tested individually with minute amounts of solvent and blotting paper. Don't forget the lining. Often, several different solvents will have to be tried before the correct one is found.

STAIN REMOVAL

There are many different types of stains, each with its appropriate
solvent. Charts are provided in many books found in your local library.
It may be necessary to test several different solvents on longstanding
stains, using a tiny amount and carefully observing the effect. Once the
right solvent is found, use as small an amount as possible. A little bit
on a Q-tip may be enough. Apply the solvent and lift the stain off--don't
rub it in. For larger stains, stretch the fabric, stain down, over a
white blotter. Use an eyedropper to drop the solvent in a ring around the
stain. This will allow the solvent to work inward toward the stain,
rather than spreading it. Fresh stains should be taken care of as quickly
as possible, preferably before the stain has a chance to dry.

Before treating old stains with a solvent, it's useful to soak the
fabric overnight in cold water. When grease spots are fresh, they can
often be removed with soap, warm water, and persistence. Older grease
spots can be dusted with talc or Fuller's earth and left to set for 24
hours.

STORAGE

Old fabrics should be stored in the dark, under controlled temperature
and humidity conditions. Small closet humidifiers or dehumidifiers are
good for this purpose. Stored textiles need air. Storage in zippered
bags, trunks, or other tightly sealed containers may trap moisture and
invite mold. Don't put fabrics away dirty; dirt provides a breeding
ground for moths, silverfish, beetles, or other insects. Rolling fabrics around a tube is preferable to folding them; folds and creases
cause strain. If a cardboard tube is used, cover it with acid-free
tissue. If folding is the only alternative, pad the folds with tissue.
Periodically unfold the fabric and refold along different lines. To
prevent yellowing, wrap whites in blue sulfite-free tissue, available
from most dry cleaners. Don't allow cottons and linens to come into
direct contact with wood, which is acidic. It's better to use old towels
or undyed sheeting to wrap textiles than to use paper or tissue that
isn't acid-free. Do not hang stored clothing on wooden hangers. The wood
can discolor the fabric.

Stored textiles should be rolled or folded, wrapped, and packed loosely
to allow for air circulation.

Index